BRITISH SLAVERY
AND ITS ABOLITION

1823–1838

BY

WILLIAM LAW MATHIESON

HON. LL.D. ABERDEEN

LONGMANS, GREEN AND CO. LTD.

39 PATERNOSTER ROW, LONDON, E.C. 4

NEW YORK, TORONTO

BOMBAY, CALCUTTA AND MADRAS

1926

In tracing the movement which always aimed at abolition, but the immediate object of which was at first amelioration, I have relied mainly on the despatches and reports which were printed from year to year as Parliamentary Papers. These are cited in the notes as P.P., with the date and number of the volume. A slight extension of the work has been deemed advisable in order to bring to a conclusion the controversy between the Jamaica Assembly and Parliament. In these last few pages the reader will see something of the effects of emancipation ; but I hope to deal with that subject in another book.

The inquiry is confined to the West Indian group of colonies, including British Guiana and British Honduras. There were two other slave-holding colonies, Mauritius and the Cape of Good Hope ; but to have dealt with these—remote in situation and the latter also in character—would, I think, have impaired the unity and coherence of the work.

Acknowledgment is due to Mr. Travers Buxton, Secretary of the Anti-Slavery and Aborigines Protection Society, for the loan of an important volume.

To the Carnegie Trustees for the Scottish Universities, who have assisted me in publishing, I tender my cordial thanks.

EDINBURGH,
September 1926.

CONTENTS

INTRODUCTION

CHAPTER I

SLAVERY

CHAPTER II

AMELIORATION, 1823–1826

CONTENTS

CHAPTER III

ABOLITION, 1826–1833

CHAPTER IV

The Apprenticeship, 1833–1838

BRITISH SLAVERY AND ITS ABOLITION

1823–1838

INTRODUCTION

SLAVE labour in the West Indies was employed mainly in the production of sugar ; and, before we examine the condition of the British slaves, it will be well to review the development of an industry in which about two-thirds of them were engaged.

The colonial system which was established or consolidated by the English Navigation Act of 1660 was based on the principle that dependencies must contribute to the cost of their defence, partly by employing only British ships and seamen, and partly by confining their commerce to British ports.   The latter method could be applied only with obvious limitations to most of the North American colonies, which, with a European population and a temperate climate, were capable of being rivals as well as customers ; and it was only in the West Indies that the parent State could venture to go the whole length of its double monopoly, engrossing commodities which she did not herself produce and exchanging for them the products of her own furnaces and looms.   Slavery, recruited from Africa and devoted exclusively to the cultivation of tropical plants, was lauded by a writer of 1745 as " the great pillar and support of the British plantation trade," because it enriched the mother country without exposing it to the drain of emigration or the stress of competition, and was the means of maintaining a large portion of the mercantile marine.[1] In the seventeenth century Sir Josiah Child had computed that every Englishman who went to the West Indian colonies employed on an average eight or ten negroes and that the feeding, clothing, and equipping of this group employed four men at home, whereas, if ten Englishmen emigrated to New England, their addition to exports and imports would not employ one man.[2] By far the greatest export of these colonies was sugar, the value exported in 1787 being over £2,600,000, whilst that of cotton, which came next on the list, was only about £327,000.[3] The planter had not only to send all his sugar to Great Britain, but, in consequence of a prohibitory duty on refined sugar, had to send it raw ; and this was a great hardship, because the buildings and apparatus required for the making of raw sugar would, with a trifling addition, have sufficed for the process of refining ; and sugar, when shipped raw, had to be drained on the voyage at a loss which was estimated at one-seventh or one-eighth of the cargo.[4] Indigo and cocoa had once been cultivated with great success in Jamaica ; but, not being in accord with our commercial policy, they were ruthlessly discouraged ; and coffee languished under a similar proscription till 1783.[5]

An equivalent was indeed allowed for these restraints,

[1] Cunningham, *Growth of English Industry and Commerce*, ii. 476.
[2] *The Importance of the Sugar Colonies to Great Britain*, 1731, p. 30.
[3] Macpherson, *Annals of Commerce*, 1805, iv. 160.
[4] " This glaring absurdity is cherished by the British Government because it increases the tonnage required for the West India trade and gives the mother country a small branch of manufacture at the expense of the colonies. As well might the planters be forced to send so much rubbish in proportion to each hogshead of sugar or to pay the passage of one empty cask for every seven full casks which they ship ; for this would be increasing the shipping interest. As well might they be compelled to send over raw canes from which British workmen could manufacture sugar ; for this would both wonderfully promote the shipping interest and add a large branch to our home manufactures."—*Edinburgh Review* (1809), xiii. 404.
[5] Bryan Edwards, *History of the British West Indies*, 5th ed., 1819, ii. 333, 339, 549, 571, 574.

protection under this system being the reward of subjection; but it was more specious than solid. British
plantation sugar had a monopoly of the home market;
and this would have been a valuable concession if the
demand had been equal to the supply. The consumption
of sugar, expanding with the use of tea—which rose from
800,000 lbs. in 1730 to 4,400,000 lbs. in 1774—enormously
increased throughout the eighteenth century; but it
failed to keep pace with the extension of British rule in
the West Indies. If Barbados, Jamaica, and the other
islands we held before the peace of 1763 had not been
added to then and later, the consumption and the supply
would have balanced at 140,000 tons in 1823 [1]; but in
point of fact there was always a surplus for exportation;
and, as foreigners would not have come to us for sugar
if they could have got it cheaper elsewhere, the planter
had no real protection—his profit being determined in the
open and not in the exclusive market.

The financial condition of the colonies linked them
even more closely than their commerce to the mother
country. Sugar-planting was an attractive but extremely hazardous speculation; and it was said that of
those who engaged in the " West Indian lottery " not
one in fifty drew a prize. Hurricanes, floods, droughts,
conflagrations, insects, and epidemics upset the best laid
plans [2]; and the quality of sugar varied greatly, not only

---

[1] So said Huskisson—Hansard (1823), ix. 466.

[2] The following quaint and vivid description of the precariousness of
sugar-planting was penned as early as 1690 : " The plants in the ground
are often subject to be devoured, wounded, and torn by ants or under-
mined and destroyed at the roots by mug-worms. Too much rain or
too much drought in either season is a certain diminution of the crop,
if not a total destruction of the plants, nay, if the rains come too late,
which often happens, a whole year's planting is lost. When all these
mischiefs are escaped and the canes of a considerable height, then are
they liable to be twisted, broke, and totally spoiled by the furious hurricanes that once in three or four years, like a fit of an ague, shake the
whole islands, not only do the crops an injury, but sometimes tumble
down and level their mills, work-houses and strongest buildings ; but,
escaping all these, as the canes ripen they grow more and more com-
bustible and are thereby subject to the malice and drunken rages of
angry and desperate run-away negroes, as well as many other accidents

with the fertility of the soil, which was said to range in value from £5 to £150, but with the degree of care and skill in its manufacture. We are told indeed that under bad management " the fairest fruits of a cane-field " might be " rendered a mass of thick, slimy, dark, sour, cloddy, unprofitable, unmarketable substance." [1] A good many of the proprietors had inherited their estates, and some of these were men of great wealth, such as Lords Darlington, Romney, Harewood, and Holland ; but most of the plantations were owned by those who had purchased or formed them. In either case the average outlay was estimated at about £30,000 ; and a new plantation, or one which had been allowed to fall into decay, did not become remunerative in less than seven years.[2] A large proportion of the capital was usually advanced by the merchant who was to dispose of the sugar, to purchase supplies and manage the freight and insurance, and the great fortunes amassed in the West Indian trade were the fruits of this practice, which yielded a profit, including both interest and commission, of 12 to 20 per cent.[3] " Almost all our sugar colonies," wrote a planter in 1733, " are over head and ears in debt and the merest slaves imaginable to their creditors."[4] It frequently happened that, when a stage of cultivation had been reached which promised large returns, the merchant, on the pretext of

of fire ; the fury whereof when once got into a field of canes is extremely quick, terrible, and scarcely to be resisted before it has destroyed the whole parcel ; but when they are brought to full perfection for cutting, and the planter's expectation as ripe as they, if unseasonable rains happen, or that no winds blow, then do they all rot and perish in the ground ; the slaves and servants all stand idle, looking down upon their master's decaying fortune, and at last are only employed in clearing the ground again from that useless rubbish in which all the year's hope is perished."—" Historical Account of the West Indies, 1690," in *Harleian Miscellany*, 1746, ii.

[1] Roughley, *The Jamaica Planter's Guide*, 1823, p. 86.

[2] Long, *History of Jamaica*, 1774, i. 392.

[3] *East and West India Sugar*, 1823, pp. 41, 42.

[4] *An Enquiry into the Methods proposed to retrieve the Sugar Trade*, p. 12.

some emergency, called up his loan and, by forcing the property into the market when still undeveloped, secured it for himself at a low price ; or the planter was unskilful or unfortunate, and the creditor had to take over an unprofitable estate.[1] " In no part of the earth," said a writer of 1830, " is the transition from opulence to indigence and ruin a twentieth part so common as it confessedly is among the proprietors of the sugar colonies." [2] It appears from a report of the Assembly that in 1791 there were 769 sugar plantations in Jamaica. Of these 47 had been recently established, but of the remainder only 451 were retained by those, or their descendants, who had held them in 1772. During the same period of twenty years 177 estates had been sold in payment of debts, 92 were still in the hands of creditors, and 55 had been abandoned. A speaker in the House of Commons in 1824 said that the state of the West Indian colonies was " more deplorable than that of the most wretched and inhospitable parts of the world. Everywhere else, even in Lapland, prosperity was the rule and distress the exception." [3]

The greatest difficulty experienced by the planters was that of foreign competition, and not till nearly the end of the eighteenth century, and then only by a stroke of good fortune, was it temporarily overcome. The Spaniards, who had discovered and appropriated the West Indies, were of little account in this industry, and our only serious rivals were the French. Martinique and Guadeloupe, their oldest islands, came into their possession in 1635, some ten years after Sir Thomas Warner had occupied Barbados ;[4] they acquired Grenada about

[1] Edwards, ii. 296–306.

[2] Stephen, *The Slavery of the British West India Colonies Delineated*, ii. 69.

[3] Gardner, *History of Jamaica*, ed. 1909, p. 320 ; Hansard (1824), xi. 732.

[4] Barbados was considered in those days our oldest West Indian colony ; but the small island of St. Christopher had been occupied a year or so earlier.

the time of Cromwell's conquest of Jamaica in 1655 ; and their settlement in western Santo Domingo was recognised by Spain at the Peace of Ryswick in 1697. From this period, or a little later, their output of sugar rapidly increased ; and there were reasons why this development should be resented as well as envied in Britain. The syrup drained from raw sugar and known as molasses had once been almost useless to the French planter ; for the rum that might have been made of it was excluded from France as prejudicial to the consumption of brandy. He now exported his molasses to New England, " selling for something what was formerly worth nothing " ; [1] and this " something " was the lumber, provisions, and horses which ought to have been reserved for our own sugar islands and which, it was said, he could not have obtained elsewhere. " Good wholesome rum " was of course to be had only from the British planter. French rum was bad ; American rum, made from French molasses and popularly known as " Kill-Devil," was worse ; and to prohibit both would " save the lives of many hundreds of poor wretches." [2] Attention was drawn to the matter in a sheaf of pamphlets published in London, but some of them written in the West Indies. To debar our rivals from the American market would be " to touch their vitals, or at the least to take off their chariot wheels and make them drive heavily " ; and such was their present rate of progress that they were " cutting us out from all foreign markets." [3]

Parliament was easily induced to restrict the foreign trade of New England ; but neither the Molasses Act of 1733 nor the acquisition by Great Britain of new islands in 1763 had any effect in crippling the sugar trade of France. It expanded on all sides, but nowhere so rapidly

[1] *Considerations on the Dispute between the British Southern and Northern Plantations*, 1731, p. 8.

[2] *The Importance of the Sugar Colonies to Great Britain*, 1731, p. 20.

[3] *An Enquiry into the Methods proposed to retrieve the Sugar Trade*, 1733, p. 28 ; *The Importance, etc.*, p. 11.

as in St. Domingue,[1] which became " the garden of the West Indies," and the richest sugar colony in the world. In the short space of ten years, 1782–1792, the number of slaves employed on its plantations was believed to have almost doubled.[2] Historians dwell with enthusiasm on its vast warehouses and crowded harbours ; and a British army doctor who visited the colony in 1797 thus describes its appearance at the time of the French Revolution : " The plains were loaded with sugar, rows of limes and citrons forming the fences of the canes ; the sides of the hills were clothed with coffee ;[3] canals and other well constructed aqueducts brought bounteous streams to the estates ; excellent roads led to the towns and dwellings ; plantations of provisions, of cotton and indigo ; elegant houses and substantial sugar-works ; orange groves and orchards of other delicious fruits ; neatly enclosed gardens, ornamental hedges and improved grounds appeared on every quarter to grace the magnificent scenery."[4] In 1787 the total value of West Indian produce exported to Europe was £14,000,000 ; and of this sum the French islands contributed a half and the British islands only from a quarter to a third.[5]

It has often been remarked that cultivation by slaves is wasteful, because, owing to their lack of intelligence, and interest and the difficulty of teaching them anything new, it must dispense with a rotation of crops, and consequently exhausts the soil. The smaller British islands having reached this stage, their planters had no new land to exploit. In Jamaica the best, or at least the most accessible, lands were fully occupied ; and, as compared

[1] I follow Sir Harry Johnston in retaining the French spelling as the only means of distinguishing this part of the island (the modern Haiti) from the Spanish colony of Santo Domingo.

[2] *Edinburgh Review* (1807), xi. 157.

[3] In 1770 the quantity of coffee exported was 5,000,000 lbs. In 1789 it had increased to 76,000,000 lbs.—Edwards, ii. 354.

[4] Pinckard, *Notes on the West Indies*, 1816, ii. 495.

[5] *Oil without Vinegar, or British, American and West India Interests considered*, 1807, p. 39.

equalled that of St. Domingue before the French Revolution.[1] Moreover, the Americans were importing the colonial produce of our enemies, France, Spain, and Holland, and re-exporting it under cover of their neutral flag to Europe, where it undersold the produce of our colonies on account of its immunity from war obstacles and risks. Their own shipping would have been quite inadequate for this purpose ; but all French and Dutch and nearly all Spanish merchantmen, not required as coasters or privateers, had been sold for the duration of the war to American owners.[2]

At the close of the eighteenth century the cultivation of sugar throughout the West Indies had been pushed to an extent which far exceeded the level of consumption in Europe ; and about the middle of 1799 the market collapsed, the maximum price for 1800–1801 being no more than 50s. and the minimum as low as 28s. In Hamburg, which was the principal mart for British sugar, no fewer than eighty-three houses failed in four months ; and their correspondents in this country were so hard hit that Parliament voted a loan of half a million to the West Indian merchants of Liverpool.[3]

The prosperity so long hoped for by the planters had gone almost as suddenly as it came. For several years before 1800 they had been making an average profit of 10 per cent. Now many of them were working at a loss. In 1804 a committee of the Jamaica Assembly reported in reference to the distress then prevalent in the island that " a faithful detail would have the character of a frightful caricature." Three years later, they declared that about a fourth of the sugar estates had been either

[1] *Edinburgh Review* (1807), xi. 158, 159.

[2] The rise of the United States had upset the British rule that a State which monopolised its colonial trade must not open it to neutrals in time of war. By their fiction of the " broken voyage " the Americans could claim to be exporting their own merchandise. See Stephen, *War in Disguise, or The Frauds of the Neutral Flags*, 1805.

[3] Tooke, *History of Prices*, i. 235.

abandoned or compulsorily sold ; and in 1813 a prominent West Indian remarked that during the previous twenty years there were few sugar estates which had not changed hands.[1]

Lower duties, a bounty on exportation, and a blockade of hostile colonies were the remedies most favoured by the planters ; but friends and critics were at one in exhorting them to restrict their cultivation of sugar and, by breeding cattle and growing more food, to withdraw as much as possible from a falling market. The same advice had been tendered to them during one of their periodical crises in 1748 ; and the objections then made to it had lost none of their force : that seven-eighths of the planters were not only in debt but dependent on credit ; that the merchants, if not reimbursed by the usual consignments of sugar, would sell them up or at least cut off supplies ; that any scheme of restriction could be enforced only by general agreement, and that this was impossible, most of the islands being far apart, and some not even in communication with each other, except through Great Britain.[2] All the witnesses examined by a Committee of the House of Commons in 1807 agreed that the scrapping of sugar-works and the necessity, where the negroes did not grow their own food, of supporting them during the process of transition, were insuperable obstacles to the diversion of cane-lands, which were not suited to other tropical products, and, if turned into pasture, would yield only a small supply of " very bad grass " ; and one witness declared that the planters would probably be ruined if they continued the production of sugar and inevitably if they gave it up.[3]

The cloud of " perennial ruin " which encompassed

---

[1] *East and West India Sugar*, 1823, pp. 19, 121, 123 ; Hansard (1824), xi. 732.

[2] *Reasons Grounded on Facts as to Sugar*, 1748, p. 7.

[3] *Report of Commons' Committee*, especially p. 41.

the British sugar industry was intensified by the slave trade, the destructive character of which had become apparent to some even of the planters. The purchase of slaves was a highly speculative business, and the risks were greater in the West Indian than in the African market; for, whilst the importer lost on an average about 17 per cent. of his stock before sale, the planter had to reckon with a loss of 33 per cent. in the process of what was called " seasoning." The negroes had never been accustomed to such regular and protracted toil as was exacted on sugar plantations; and their ability to stand the training was usually impaired by mental depression and the effects of their hardships before embarkation and during the voyage. Most of them suffered from some form of venereal disease which, owing to the means adopted for a temporary cure, often proved fatal. Even the jobber, who purchased with a view to forming a picked gang for hiring out to planters, and who, it seems, was frequently a medical man, lost many of his hands. When a slave-ship came into port, its occupants were " made up " for sale, which meant that their skins were rubbed with oil and their sores, cuts, and bruises closed with " mercurial ointments and repellent drugs "; and these precautions must have proved ample when, as often happened, they were disposed of by " scramble." According to this method, the slaves were lined up for inspection—males on the main-deck, females on the quarter-deck; and, the vessel having previously been darkened by awnings, a gun was fired to intimate that the market was open. A crowd of people then rushed frantically on board, and each buyer, having seized upon the objects of his choice, encircled them with cords or handkerchiefs bearing his name. This violent onslaught in a confined space proved so terrifying to its victims that they had been known to jump overboard; and it became more usual to land the slaves and expose them in a yard. The " refuse," consisting of the old and unfit, were put up to auction or allowed to die in the streets. Sometimes, of course, the planter was fortunate enough to get good value for his money ; but in that case he was confronted with a new series of risks. Negroes torn from the African jungle were a less tractable and more superstitious race than those known as creoles, who had been born in the West Indies. The mutinies and revolts, not infrequent in our colonies, invariably originated in this class, which was also peculiarly susceptible to the influence of " obeah-men " or sorcerers. " Vast numbers," it was said, " languish and die when they believe themselves bewitched." If the victim did not succumb to terror, the sorcerer, in order to save his reputation, frequently resorted to poison ; [1] and a Jamaica planter declared that the practice of obeah had deprived him of about a hundred slaves in fifteen years.

Under such conditions it may be supposed that the planters promoted to the utmost the natural increase of their slaves and availed themselves as little as possible of African recruits ; but breeding could not be attractive where estates so frequently changed hands ; and those who adopted this policy found it very difficult to carry out. Of the negroes imported two-thirds were always males ; and the women, being mostly prostitutes, were little disposed to rear or indeed—if they could prevent it—to have children. The ignorance of negro midwives often proved fatal to both mother and child ; and the loss of infants, especially within two weeks after birth, was " great beyond what can be imagined." Thus the average planter was never long out of the slave-market, particularly as he was encouraged to purchase on a credit of twelve or eighteen months ; and the " scramble " bore witness to the urgency of his needs. Long declared in 1774 that the buying of slaves was " the most chargeable

---

[1] Stewart, *View of Past and Present State of Jamaica*, 1823, p. 277. As late as 1891 severe laws were passed against obeah-workers.— Livingstone, *Black Jamaica*, 1899, p. 198.

article " on estates, and that the debts incurred to make " these inconsiderate purchases " were mainly responsible for financial distress ; and he even suggested that the landing of negroes, except for re-exportation, should be stopped by a prohibitive duty for four or five years. The same proposal was made in 1790 by Beckford, also a planter, who said he was convinced that, " of the astonishing numbers of judgments " obtained by creditors in Jamaica, at least six out of seven originated in " a hasty and improvident purchase of slaves." Finally, the slave trade was the main cause of that over-production which was at all times the undoing of the planter ; and, as the British traffic was not by any means confined to our own colonies,[1] it injured him in yet another way by stimulating the competition of foreign-grown sugar.[2]

Without the slave trade, there could, of course, have been no negro slavery in the West Indies ; but the English slave trade was older than English slavery, and with such zeal was it prosecuted that before long we were not only supplying the foreign market but glutting our own. This aspect of the case was forcibly presented by the Council and Assembly of Antigua in a protest to Parliament against " the malignant feelings " which had been excited against the slave-owners by demagogues and interested persons " in coalition with the canting pretenders of the day to religion." They pointed out that, when Queen Elizabeth permitted her subjects to engage in the slave trade, and " personally took a share in it," no English transatlantic settlement had yet been

---

[1] Of 74,000 slaves brought into the British West Indies in 1791, 34,000 were re-exported.—*Parl. Hist.* (1792), xxix. 1203.

[2] *Abstract of Evidence against the Slave Trade before the Select Committee of the Commons*, 1791, pp. 49–52 ; *Concise Statement as to the Question of Abolition*, 1807, pp. 11, 61 ; Macpherson, *Annals*, iv. 146–149 ; Long, i. 401, ii. 433–437 ; Edwards, ii. 150 ; Beckford, *Descriptive Account of Jamaica*, 1790, ii. 340, 344, 345 ; Stephen, ii. 55, 68 ; *Negro Slavery in the United States and West Indies*, 1823, p. 60 ; Williamson, *Medical and Miscellaneous Observations relative to the West Indies*, 1817, ii. 130.

formed ; and they showed that the colonial legislatures had more than once tried to check excessive and indiscriminate importation.   South Carolina did so in 1760 ; but the Act was annulled, the Governor reprimanded, and his indiscretion exposed in a circular despatch.   In 1765 a Bill to limit the bringing in of Africans was read twice in the Assembly of Jamaica and was dropped only when the Governor intimated that he would be unable to give it his assent.   In 1774 two Bills for this purpose were actually passed.   Bristol and Liverpool petitioned against them ;   and Lord Dartmouth, the President of the Board of Trade, declared in answer to a remonstrance from the agent for Jamaica, " We cannot allow the colonies to check or discourage in any degree a traffic so beneficial to the nation." [1]   Dartmouth, it may be added, was a prominent Evangelical, nicknamed " The Psalm-Singer," and extolled by the poet Cowper as " one who wears a coronet and prays."

Mischievous, however, as was the operation of the slave trade, there was an argument for its continuance more plausible than any that could be urged against it ; for there had always been more deaths than births amongst the negroes, and, but for importation, the planters would have been unable to keep up, much less to increase, their supply of labour.   Wilberforce, who in 1787 opened his campaign for abolition, had of course to meet this objection ; and he met it by asserting that the vacuum filled by the slave trade was of its own making ; that the negroes were ill-treated and over-worked just because they could so easily be replaced ; that, if this resource were cut off, they would rise in the social as well as in the numerical scale ; and he looked forward to a time, however distant, when the abolition of the slave trade would be followed by the abolition of slavery.[2]

[1] Hansard (1824), xv. 223–226.

[2] " It is singular how often the Slave Trade is confounded with slavery," wrote the biographer of Buxton in 1848.   The confusion still

It was no part of his policy to complicate the former question by anticipating the latter; but tactics more comprehensive, though at the same time more dilatory and cautious, were advocated by a statesman in sympathy with his views. Burke, who supported the movement till it was vitiated in his eyes by the influence of the French Revolution, would have preferred not to dissociate the two questions, and thought that a policy, not indeed of abolition but of restriction, should be applied to both. He held what proved to be the mistaken idea that the British trade could not be wholly suppressed so long as slavery existed, and consequently that its real source was "not in the place it was begun at but at the place of its final destination"; and, as the negroes were obviously not ripe for emancipation, he was "fully convinced that the cause of humanity would be far more benefited by the continuance of the trade and servitude, regulated and reformed, than by the total destruction of both or either." It appeared that he had gone into the question long before it attracted public attention; and, when immediate abolition was defeated in 1792, he published a scheme which he had drawn up nearly twelve years earlier. Slave traders were to be licensed; the dimensions of their ships and the proportion of negroes to tonnage were to be registered; and the seeds of industry and civilisation were to be sown in Africa. Churches, schools, and hospitals were to be built; European artisans were to take apprentices from the natives; and no negro was to be purchased who was seriously ill or over thirty-five years of age or able to read. In the West Indies the Attorney-General of each colony was to be appointed Protector of the Negroes; he was to be assisted by local inspectors; and a record of his proceedings was to be transmitted by the Governor

prevails; but what is more singular is that, while slavery still existed, Byron in *Don Juan* (1822) should twice refer to Wilberforce as having " set free the negroes."

to the Secretary of State. Districts were to be formed, each with a church and school. Negroes were to be secured in the possession of their property and as fully protected as whites in life and limb ; they were not to work on Saturday afternoon or Sunday ; flogging, if it exceeded thirteen stripes, was to be inflicted only by order of a magistrate ; marriage for those in good health, and church-going, were to be compulsory ; no negro, if he was married or had lived for twelve months on a plantation, was to be sold apart from the estate ; married couples of a certain age and service were to have first one day, and then two days, in the week to themselves ; every slave of thirty years and over, who had three lawful children and whose character was attested by a clergyman or other religious teacher, was to be entitled to purchase his freedom and that of his wife and family at rates fixed by two Justices of the Peace ; and the Protector was to be empowered to redeem any negro whom he considered to be of more than ordinary intelligence and technical skill, and to sell to another master any negro whom he knew to be ill-used.[1]

Burke published this scheme in the form of a letter to Henry Dundas, no doubt because Dundas had expressed views which were substantially in agreement with his own, the chief difference being that Burke had supported immediate abolition, when it was the *only* proposal, whilst Dundas had opposed it. Both held that the root of the trade was not in Africa but in the West Indies ; that it could be stopped more completely, and even more speedily, under a system of regulation than by prohibition ; that the concurrence of merchants and planters was essential ; and that this would be obtained if free labour increased in proportion as slave labour diminished. When Burke's pamphlet appeared, the House of Commons, going with Dundas and against

---

[1] *Works*, 1812, vol. ix. It will be seen later that Burke took some of his ideas from the Spanish system.

that " the West Indies never could have been nor ever can be cultivated to effect without the right, of which we trust no power shall endeavour to deprive us, of obtaining labourers from Africa."

The agitation against the slave trade was of too popular a character to make headway during the war of the French Revolution, when many people regarded it with Burke as " a shred of the accursed web of Jacobinism." The peace of 1802 lasted only about a year ; but the Napoleonic War was national rather than anti-democratic in spirit ; and in 1807 the struggle which had been so long maintained against a powerful vested interest was crowned with success. A few days before the Abolition Bill became law, Earl Percy proposed as a separate measure that a date should be fixed for giving freedom to the children of enslaved negroes. He was supported only by Sheridan ; and Wilberforce said that he was glad the motion had been made, as it enabled him to show that he not only did not favour emancipation but was ready to oppose it when advocated by others.[1]

The first Power to prohibit the slave trade was Denmark, which provided in 1792 that it should cease at the end of 1802. The British and American Abolition Acts were practically simultaneous, both being passed in March 1807 and coming into force on the first of January 1808. The penalties under the British Act were severe—£100 for every slave carried and the confiscation of both ship and cargo ; and liberal rewards were offered to informers and captors.[2] But slaves could now be bought cheap in Africa owing to reduced demand and sold dear in the West Indies owing to diminished supply ; and the smuggler made a large

[1] Hansard (1807), ix. 142.
[2] A bounty of £40 for every adult male captured, £30 for every woman, and £10 for every child. Half the fine of £100 was awarded to the informer who obtained a conviction.

profit if he succeeded in only one venture out of three. More than half the trade had been in British hands; and throughout great part of north-west Africa it ceased when our agents gave up business at the end of 1807; but it was soon revived, partly by the Portuguese under their own flag, but mainly by Americans in ships which they had sold nominally to Spain. In the autumn of 1809 these vessels " swarmed " on the coast; and their depredations were unchecked till a small British squadron arrived early next year and, exercising a right of seizure which was subsequently upheld in the courts, liberated 2800 slaves. Most of the American supply was intended for Cuba, but part of it found its way into the British West Indies. The Danish island of Santa Cruz, then in our hands, and the Swedish island of St. Bartholomew were the great distributing centres; and batches of sixty or seventy slaves were frequently landed in the creeks of Demerara from boats which had been despatched by the planters to ships lying as far off as the mouth of the Orinoco. British ships and British subjects were sometimes detected in this traffic under Spanish names,[1] and it was prosecuted even from home ports. Ships left Liverpool which, after they had got to sea, were fitted with the platforms and bulkheads essential to a human cargo; and in 1810 the destination of a large vessel then being equipped in the Thames was made manifest by the opportune discovery of 55 dozen padlocks, 93 pairs of handcuffs, 197 iron shackles, 13 cwts. of iron chains, and " one box of religious implements." It was estimated that the net profit on this venture, had it succeeded, would have been £60,000. Pecuniary penalties were obviously inadequate to extirpate a branch of commerce in which such prizes could

---

[1] Thus the supercargo Don Jorge Madre Silva turned out to be George Woodbine, who had sailed from the Thames in a vessel then called the *Queen Charlotte*, but afterwards the *Gallicia.—Edinburgh Review* (1811), xviii. 308.

INTRODUCTION

be won. In 1811 slave trading was made felony, punishable with transportation, for British subjects anywhere and—within the British dominions—for foreigners; and in 1824 it was made piracy, or, in other words, capital.[1]

Denmark and Great Britain were still the only European Powers which had abolished the slave trade, and even in the United States it had not been made criminal. Lord Castlereagh, the Foreign Secretary, appears to have done his best to extend this reform; but, having opposed to the last the abolition of our own slave trade, he naturally incurred suspicion. Sweden consented to abolition in 1813, Holland in 1814; but the French attitude was warmly denounced in this country, where nearly a thousand petitions had been presented to Parliament in favour of a general condemnation at the Peace. The slave trade of France had been in abeyance for twenty years, having ceased when she lost or was cut off from her colonies in 1793. Yet the restored Bourbon Government concluded a treaty with Great Britain in May 1814 by which they agreed to abolish the trade in five years, but stipulated that meanwhile it should be tolerated or, in other words, revived; and in August the slave merchants were invited to resume their operations with the old privilege of exporting duty-free to Africa goods, stores, arms, and ammunition. That Britain should have been made a party to this arrangement was keenly resented; and Castlereagh was much blamed for not having provided against such a contingency when the French colonies were restored.[2]

In November 1814 the Congress of Vienna recorded its condemnation of the slave trade,[3] and the intentions

---

[1] *Fourth and Sixth Reports*, 1810 *and* 1812, *of the African Institution*; Hansard (1810), xvii. 662, 668–673; (1811) xix. 233–237; (1824) x. 1424.

[2] Hansard (1814), xxviii. 268, 384.

[3] The efforts of Great Britain in this matter have been justly

of France were soon nullified; for Napoleon on his return from Elba in the following March sought to propitiate British opinion by prohibiting the traffic; and Louis XVIII, when he was again restored, did not venture to reverse this decision. Not till 1818, however, did the French legislature take action, and the only offender who was then made liable to a slight penalty was the slave-ship's captain. In 1820, when the Spanish trade had been closed, Portugal was the only recalcitrant Power; and even Portugal had agreed not to operate north of the Equator. But it soon appeared that prohibition and authorisation as understood by the Spaniards and the French were pretty much the same thing. Spain, having lost her continental colonies, sought to secure the dependence of the islands, and especially of Cuba, by flooding them with negroes. The Captain-General of Cuba denied all knowledge of the slave trade; but as compensation for an uneasy con-science he and three other officials were allowed to divide between them a tax amounting to £3 10s. 10d., which was levied on every negro imported; and just under the windows of his official residence there were two *barracoons* or depots for the detention and sale of negroes which could accommodate respectively 1500 and 1000 and were reported to be almost always full. In 1825 the coming and going of slave-ships at Havana were almost of weekly occurrence; and five or six of them were some-times despatched "absolutely under the convoy of a Spanish frigate." At this period as many as 2642 negroes were brought to Cuba in two months. In the thirty years which succeeded our abolition of the slave trade in 1807, Great Britain was supposed to have spent nearly £10,000,000 in trying to put down the traffic;

---

applauded, but they were not wholly disinterested. Our West Indians, having been compelled to give up their own slave trade, were naturally anxious to stop that of foreign colonies. Their change of attitude after 1807 was, indeed, remarkable. See Hansard (1810), xvii. 676.

and about the end of that period the Cuban importation amounted to over 20,000 a year.[1]

The most shameless, if not the worst, offenders were, however, the French, whose operations were the despair of British diplomacy, being conducted almost within sight of our shores. " In the very ports of France herself," wrote Canning to our ambassador at Paris, " these undertakings form the entire and almost public concern of companies of her merchants." Baron de Staël commented on the " bare-faced impudence " of Nantes, where slave-dealing was the common topic at the Exchange. To this port alone belonged eighty slave-ships, which were believed to have made a profit, since 1815, of 90,000,000 francs. These vessels plied between Senegal and Guadeloupe, and their business was conducted under peculiarly horrible conditions. They were schooners or brigs of about 130 tons, built for speed and usually armed. They had " false decks "—that is, a platform three feet high was superimposed on the deck—and in this space the victims were " crowded together in one mass of living corruption." If too many had been shipped, those of least value were thrown overboard. In an intercepted letter the human cargo is referred to as " ebony," and we read that 328 " logs "— damaged ones excepted—have been sold for 225 dollars apiece at Guadeloupe, where the Commandant is " devoted to us." [2]

Unfortunately there was one of our colonies in which the French found ample material for recrimination when they sought to silence our complaints. The island of Mauritius had surrendered to a British expedition in

[1] Turnbull, *Cuba*, 1840, pp. 59, 155, 156 ; Madden, *The Island of Cuba*, 1849, p. 44.

[2] *Nineteenth and Twentieth Reports* (1825 and 1826) *of the African Institution*. The French had a bad record as regular traders before the abolition. The mortality on their ships at sea was nearly 10 per cent., whilst Dolben's Act of 1788 reduced the mortality on British ships from 4⅛ to little more than 3 per cent.—*Parl. Hist.* (1792), xxix. 1126.

1810 and was ceded by France at the Peace of 1814. The Governor, Sir Robert Farquhar, reported to the Colonial Office in 1811 that negro labour was deficient and yearly decreasing, and that the colonists " are likely to be rendered desperate if the supply of slaves be refused them." It soon appeared that they had not waited to be refused. The slaves, who numbered 60,000 in 1809, had increased to 87,000 in 1815 ; and, whereas in 1814 only three million pounds of sugar had been exported, the quantity shipped in 1822 was about twenty-three millions. General Hall, who was acting Governor in 1818, declared that the slave trade had " obtained a degree of effrontery " which was a disgrace to the administration, that even the tribunals were " deeply interested " in it, and that informers were threatened with death. The regular trade had been horrible enough ; but we have seen that the irregular and consequently unregulated trade was much worse ; and the loading of a Mauritius slave-ship was conducted by an official, armed with a heavy club, who was significantly and quite appropriately known as " the packer." [1]

There was no such scandal in the British West Indies ; but, when Frenchmen and Spaniards were surreptitiously regaling themselves at the table of a revived slave trade, it was inevitable that our colonists should be suspected of picking up the crumbs ; and this in fact was just about the extent of their participation. There certainly were facilities for evasion ; for Jamaica was only a night's sail from the southern coast of Cuba, which abounded in secluded harbours and creeks ; and, British manufactures being much cheaper and more plentiful than Spanish, there was a large contraband trade between the two islands. It was so popular in Jamaica that the authorities did not venture to interfere ;

[1] Hansard (1826), xv. 1017, 1035 ; xvii. 838 ; *Anti-Slavery Reporter*, ii. 734.

and there was nothing to prevent a smuggler bringing back a few slaves, whom he could easily disguise as members of his crew. The likelihood of such dealings was pointed out by a naval officer in a letter to Wilberforce,[1] who, however, was not convinced ; for, in introducing a Bill in 1815 to prevent illicit importation, he instanced Jamaica as an exception to his statement that the practice prevailed " to a great extent " in the British West Indies. His remedy was to establish by Act of Parliament in every colony a register of slaves on the model of one which had already been instituted in the Crown colony of Trinidad.[2] In that island there was a registrar whose duty it was to procure every three years a census of slaves ; and duplicates both of the original record and of the triennial returns had to be deposited with the Governor for transmission to England. The session was too far advanced to permit of the passing of Wilberforce's Bill, especially as it was strongly opposed. The West Indians complained that it assumed a participation in the foreign slave trade which had yet to be proved, that it violated the right of the colonies to manage their internal affairs, and, owing to its expense, would be equivalent to the imposition of a tax ; and Castlereagh had the House with him when he urged that, if the colonial legislatures could be persuaded to pass such a measure of their own accord, it would be far better than forcing upon them an Act of Parliament which they would probably try to evade.

[1] Stephen, *Defence of the Registration Bill*, pp. 160–165.

[2] There were four Crown colonies in the New World : Trinidad, St. Lucia, Demerara, and Berbice; but the latter two were united in 1831 as British Guiana. All the other colonie sexcept Honduras had received charters of self-government, establishing in each a Council and a House of Assembly, and were consequently known as the chartered or legislative colonies : Jamaica, Barbados, Grenada, St. Vincent, Tobago, Dominica, Antigua, St. Christopher or St. Kitts, Montserrat, Nevis, Tortola or the Virgin Islands, the Bahamas, and the Bermudas. Honduras was administered by a Superintendent, holding office under the Governor of Jamaica in his military capacity as Captain-General. See *Journals of the Commons*, June 12, 1827.

An injunction was thus laid on the colonies with which during the next three years they all in some measure complied. Tobago distinguished itself by adopting the Trinidad system of registration, and a similar Act was passed, though only for four years, in Grenada ; but nowhere else was the sale of unregistered slaves made illegal. Jamaica did not establish a separate registrarship, leaving its Secretary to act in that capacity for 350,000 slaves ; and, though the office was created in all the other colonies, some of them did not provide for the transmission of duplicates. This defect was remedied by Parliament in 1819, when an Act was passed appointing a registrar in London and invalidating the sale or mortgage in this country of any slave who had not been entered in his books. No attempt was made to improve the colonial registers ; but the British prohibition of the slave trade was so severe and so vigilantly enforced that it is questionable whether any further security was required.[1]

In 1815 an address to the Crown, similar to that of 1796, was voted by both Houses in which it was declared that the Assemblies should be recommended "in the strongest manner" to promote the moral and religious improvement as well as the comfort and happiness of the slaves. According to Canning, this was the meaning of the address : " You are safe for the present from the interference of the British Parliament in the belief that, left to yourselves, you will do what is required of you." [2]

A slight retrospect will suffice to show that *hope* would have been a more suitable word in this connexion than "belief." The planters lived in constant fear of revolt ; and any proposal from outside to alleviate the condition of the slaves, no matter how harmless in itself,

[1] Hansard (1815), xxxi. 772–785 ; 59 Geo. III. c. 120 ; *Review of Colonial Slave Registration Acts*, 1820. Gardner, a most judicious and well-informed writer, shows that in Jamaica there had been no illicit importation.—*History*, p. 253.

[2] Hansard (1816), xxxiv. 1220.

was regarded as breaking the spell of subjection. When Dolben's Bill of 1788 to prevent the overcrowding of slave-ships was before the House of Lords, the Duke of Chandos declared that the negroes, " who read the English newspapers as constantly as the ships from England came in," would conclude that their emancipation was at hand." He said he had many letters from Jamaica testifying to the general alarm ; and " the universal massacre of the whites might be the consequence." If there was one restriction of the slave trade which the planters might have been expected to welcome, it was the proposal to prohibit British merchants from supplying foreign colonies. Yet, when Wilberforce brought in a Bill for this purpose in 1794, Jenkinson, afterwards Lord Liverpool, pronounced it " highly dangerous " ; and only one of the West Indian members had the sense to be astonished " that any British colonists should be anxious to raise up rivals to supplant themselves." Jamaica petitioned against the abolition of this suicidal traffic in 1806 ; and we can imagine what " a fatal paroxysm of insurrection and revolutionary horror " was anticipated and predicted when the British slave trade was abolished in 1807. Similar apprehensions were aroused by Wilberforce's Registry Bill of 1815, and unfortunately next year they were to some extent realised in Barbados, where a rumour had spread among the slaves that their masters had received and were withholding a decree of emancipation. Sixty estates are said to have been more or less damaged. The loss of life was confined, with one exception, to the negroes, several hundreds of whom were killed ; but the colonists could now point to a verification of their fears, and did not hesitate to assert that Parliament and the press ought to abstain from meddling further with slavery, lest their intentions should be misrepresented in the West Indies. Bryan Edwards rebuked his fellow planters for the " glaring absurdity " of this plea. " If, in deference to this new tropical principle, nothing is to be uttered or written but that of which the sense is incapable of being perverted by designing men, the pen and the tongue may slumber in a long repose." But the colonists did not observe the caution which they enjoined upon others. That there was a party in Parliament bent on freeing the slaves was constantly asserted in the Jamaica newspapers ; and the debates said to be so inflammatory were there republished, and their consequences depicted with so lively an imagination as almost in some cases to suggest to the negroes a plan of insurrection.[1]

No definite proposals had yet been brought forward for the amelioration of slavery ; but the planters ought even now to have realised that they must either amend their system of labour or submit to have it reformed, if not abolished, by Parliament. They continued, however, to trifle with the question, and might have enjoyed a still longer period of immunity if their interests had not come into conflict with those of the East India Company.

We have seen that the colonial system was a doubtful boon to the West Indians ; but its restrictions had now been greatly relaxed. In 1808, as a temporary measure, which was afterwards made permanent, they were allowed to export their sugar, coffee, and cocoa to any port in Europe south of Cape Finisterre. In 1813, when the commerce of Hindustan, hitherto monopolised by the East India Company, was thrown open, their sugar was protected by an additional import duty of 10s. imposed on the sugar of Bengal ; and in 1822 they were allowed to trade with all European ports and with foreign countries and colonies in the New World.[2] Ever since the destruction of St. Domingue in 1791 the East Indians

---

[1] *Review of Arguments against Parliamentary Interference on behalf of the Negro Slaves*, 1823, pp. 4, 7, 8, 11, 12 ; Edwards, v. 102–107 ; Hansard (1816), xxxiv. 1158.

[2] 48 Geo. III. c. 69 ; 52 Geo. III. c. 98 ; 3 Geo. IV. c. 45.

had been endeavouring with little success to increase their output of sugar ; and they had protested against the 10s. duty when it was introduced in 1813. They now demanded its repeal on the ground that the restrictions which were its alleged justification had in great measure been removed ; and they were confident that their rivals, if reduced to compete with them on equal terms, would be driven from the field.[1] The difference between East and West Indian sugar in the London market, free of duty, was admittedly 5s. a hundredweight ; and, in addition to this burden, the public was taxed to provide a bounty of 3s. on exportation. Ricardo maintained that the planter was in the same position as the British agriculturist, except that the sugar duties did not protect the former as the corn laws protected the latter ; for sugar, unlike corn, being exported, the price was fixed in the open market ; and the effect of protection in this case was merely to guarantee a large but unremunerative sale. The state of the West Indians being rather worse than usual—it was said indeed " to surpass all description "—they were not disposed to quarrel with this argument ; but they pleaded vested interests and urged that Parliament, if it had acted precipitately in the past, ought at least to repent at leisure. A prominent politician whose colonial experience had been gained in Canada said that, if we were at the outset of legislation, he might admit the impolicy of peopling the West Indies with slaves in order to produce articles which we could obtain more cheaply from other countries in exchange for our manufactures ; but a system so long established could not be overturned without ruining those who had staked their capital on its permanence ; and this plea was endorsed by

---

[1] " The griping horrors of East India sugar " were admitted by an opponent of the duty, who, however, was confident that its quality could easily be improved.—*Suggestions on the Abolition of Slavery. By a Member of the University of Cambridge*, 1831, p. 10.

Brougham, who said that, if the duty in question was repealed, " we should very speedily see the whole of the West Indian Archipelago laid waste."

On the other hand, Huskisson, who replied for the Government as President of the Board of Trade, thought that the capacity of India as a sugar-producer was much overrated. He said that Indian sugar was cheap only because the small quantity at present imported came, free of freight, as ballast ; that Bengal imported more sugar from China and Java than it sent to Europe ; and that before the French Revolution St. Domingue had supplied with sugar even those countries which had factories in India. But, whilst belittling the proposed change, he refused to countenance the motion for a Committee, because, if appointed, it would concern itself less with the 10s. duty than with "the fearful and delicate question of negro slavery." This indeed might fairly have been inferred from the debate. Slavery was not abolished, or rather did not cease to be legal, in British India till 1843, and was not made criminal till 1863 ; but it was a social rather than an industrial institution, it was prohibited to Europeans, and had long been discouraged by the Company ; [1] and the East Indians sought to excite popular feeling in their favour by representing the controversy as one between free-grown and slave-grown sugar. They said that India was now taking from us the cotton fabrics which she had recently manu-factured for herself ; and that the weavers of Lancashire and Scotland would be greatly benefited if she should be encouraged to grow sugar as a means of obtaining more of their wares. But Huskisson pointed out that the cotton we manufactured was grown—" every ounce of it "—by slaves in the United States and Brazil, and

---

[1] Peggs, *India's Cries to British Humanity*, 3rd edition, 1832, pp. 312, 329, 331, 339, 378 ; *Nineteenth Century*, February 1925. In St. Helena, where the East India Company did hold slaves, it had begun the process of emancipation. In 1818 all children born after Christmas Day of that year were declared free.

that it was mainly our demand for cotton that kept up the Brazilian slave trade. The East Indians had, however, other grounds for the altruism they professed. They talked of extending Huskisson's own principle of free trade, though all they asked for was to be allowed to participate in the colonial monopoly ; they said that the longer freight from the East as compared with the West Indies would be a boon to shipping ; and, commiserating the depressed condition of the working classes, they claimed the satisfaction of enabling them to purchase sugar and of thus " mixing one drop of sweet in the bitter cup which they were bound to drink." [1]

It will be seen later that the movement of which emancipation was the ultimate goal originated in this fiscal controversy between the East and West Indians ; but we are committed to a study of British slavery as well as of the movement for its abolition, and must now address ourselves to this part of our task.

[1] Hansard (1822), vii. 675, 681, 685, 691, 698. Some of the points are taken from later debates.

CHAPTER I

SLAVERY

As slavery consists in placing one person at the disposal of another who may or may not abuse his power, its essential feature is not the misery of its victims but their degradation ; and our first object must be to consider as the measure of this debasement the laws and customs under which the slave lived. Wilberforce complained that people wished only to be assured that the slaves were well treated, a question equally appropriate to cattle, and were too often blind or indifferent to their social condition ;[1] and a recent American writer has said, " If you deny the rights of man to the negro slaves, you cut the heart out of the anti-slavery argument."[2] Slavery in itself admits of no justification ; and, if we wish to estimate fairly any one of its types, we must consider it, not in isolation, still less on a background of freedom, but in conjunction with others. In the West Indies, if we leave out of account the small Swedish island of St. Bartholomew, there were four systems of slavery besides our own—Spanish, French, Dutch, and Danish. Examples of all these systems, except the last, had come permanently under British rule ; but the Spanish system was universally admitted to be much the least onerous ; and it will be well to examine this system, and then, with this model before us, to consider the condition of the slaves in our own and other colonies.

[1] Hansard (1816), xxxiv. 1154.
[2] Professor Bassett, *John Hopkins University Studies in History and Political Science*, series xvii.

Spanish slavery in the West Indies was a century older and lasted considerably longer than that of any other European Power. It began and it ended as probably the worst in the world; but there was an intermediate period, happily of great length, during which its reputation for mildness was fully deserved. We often forget that there was a trade in negroes between Africa and Europe before the discovery of the New World. It had been established by the Portuguese, whose king about 1480 assumed the title of " Lord of Guiney " ; and there was a slave market not only at Lisbon, where as late as 1539 about 10,000 negroes are said to have been sold annually, but also at Seville.[1] The Spaniards began their career as slave-owners at the expense of the aborigines of Santo Domingo, then called Hispaniola, where Columbus had planted his first colony in 1492. Their action, being neither welcome nor expected at Madrid, was first annulled and then permitted under rigorous limitations ; but, as a modern historian has said, it is impossible to license crime by halves ; [2] and a population of about 800,000 was worked to death, chiefly as gold-diggers, in less than twenty years. The Dominican missionaries, who have been called the abolitionists of their day, protested vehemently against the immolation of this feeble race ; but they had less compassion for the more robust negroes who as labourers were considered four times as effective, and a few of whom had been brought to Hispaniola even during the lifetime of Columbus. Cardinal Ximenes is said to have reprobated the iniquity of enslaving one race for the sake of liberating another ; but Charles V, with the approval of Las Casas, the famous Churchman, who had been appointed Protector General of the Indians, inaugurated the regular slave trade in 1516 by authorising a contract with some Genoese merchants for the annual importation of 4000 blacks.

[1] Madden, *The Island of Cuba*, 1849, p. 19.
[2] Prescott, *History of Mexico*, 1843, i. 198, 342.

It is probable that the negroes were at first treated little better than the Indians, for Las Casas lived to repent bitterly of his error ; but Crown and Church, assisted no doubt by the slackening of colonial enterprise, succeeded before long in greatly ameliorating their lot. Spaniards could buy negroes when offered for sale in foreign markets ; but, unlike the subjects of all other European Powers, they were forbidden to go to Africa for the purpose of enslaving them. Masters were required to prepare their slaves for baptism, which was to be administered within a year after their importation, and to send them to mass on Sundays and festivals ; and they were compelled by law to afford them every facility for marriage. The slave's choice of a wife was not confined to his own plantation. If he wished to marry a woman on some distant estate, his master must buy the wife for him at a fair valuation, or the wife's master must buy *him*. No married couple could be separated by sale, even where they lived on adjoining estates and belonged to different masters ; and the breaking up of families by sale for debt, whether voluntary or judicial, was of course unknown. In no European colony was the slave legally entitled to hold property ; but under Spanish rule the growth of many humane customs had reduced the disability to a mere form. Houses, land, and even slaves, could be held by slaves.

But the outstanding and distinctive feature of Spanish slavery was the facilities allowed for the purchase of freedom. The slaves were in two classes—those who could be sold by the owner for any sum he might be able to obtain, and those known as *coartados* because their price had been limited or *cut*. There was no restriction on the voluntary manumission of slaves, which indeed was inculcated as a pious duty, except that, if old or infirm, they must be provided for by their masters ; but the slave could obtain his liberty or make himself *coartado* by purchase ; and in both cases the transaction could, if

they regarded as a necessary evil. In the Cuban market freedom was the only commodity which could be bought untaxed ; every negro against whom no one had proved a claim of servitude was deemed free ; and freed negroes had, with some trifling exceptions, all the privileges of whites. Unquestionably there were abuses in practice, for administrative corruption was rampant in all the Spanish colonies ; but we have it on the high authority of a British international judge at Havana that to ameliorate the lot of the slave and to smooth his path to freedom was " held paramount to all other considerations," and that this was the branch of the law which was " best and most impartially administered." [1]

British slavery will be fully discussed later ; but it may be well at this stage to consider how it stood in reference to the points which have been indicated in the preceding sketch. In our colonies the presumption in all doubtful cases was against freedom. No negro who could not repel the imputation of servitude was allowed to be at large. He was apprehended and advertised and, if nobody claimed him, was sold for the public benefit as a runaway slave. If the immigrant had been manumitted and could produce his papers, he was safe, for the law was justly, though strictly, administered ; but great was his danger if he had been born of free parents in another

[1] For the Spanish manumission law, see the original materials collected and summarised in the *Anti-Slavery Reporter*, ii. 253, and especially the statement drawn up for the information of Canning in 1824 by Mr. Kilbee, the British Chief Commissioner at Havana. It is singular that the writer makes no allusion to the disastrous effect of the illicit slave trade ; but it is impossible to agree with Dr. Madden (*Island of Cuba*, p. 143)—who acknowledges the fullness and accuracy of the statement—that the slave code was never generally effective, because in those evil days its operation was confined to the towns. As it was based more on custom than on positive law, it must have been the outcome of practice ; and the best testimony to the practice of the Spaniards is that only in their colonies was there a large free coloured population. See also General Flinter's *Account of the Present State of Puerto Rico*, 1834. The Spanish Cedula of 1789 is printed in the Fifth Report of the African Institution, and is summarised by Sir Harry H. Johnston in *The Negro in the New World*, 1910, p. 43.

colony. Not only was the existence of slavery assumed,
but the liberation of its victims was discouraged. In
Demerara no slave could be set free without consent of
the Governor and Council. In most of the colonies
heavy taxes had been imposed on manumission. In
some, including Demerara, they were still levied, whilst
in others the owner was required to give security that the
object of his benevolence should not become chargeable
to the parish. The alleged reason for this restriction—
that owners might release their slaves, when old or infirm,
in order to avoid the cost of maintaining them—was
obviously a pretence ; for no discrimination was made
of age or health ; testamentary manumissions were not
excepted ; and it was notorious that the great majority
of paupers in our islands were whites.[1] The legislature
of Barbados must have wished to keep down the growth
of a free coloured class when in 1801 it taxed the manumission of females much more heavily than that of males.
Next year manumission was taxed for the first time in
St. Christopher. The Act declared it to be " a great
inconvenience that the number of free negroes and of free
persons of colour [2] was augmented by the enfranchisement of slaves," and it contained the extraordinary provision that any slave who had been released from service
by his master, but not formally enfranchised, should be
" publicly sold at vendue." [3] The result of all this was

[1] H. N. Coleridge, nephew of the poet, described the lower class
whites of Barbados as " without exception the most degraded, worthless, hopeless race I have ever met with in my life." Some of the
women washed and mended for the slaves, but many whole families
were dependent on their charity.—*Six Months in the West Indies in* 1825,
p. 294.

[2] This restriction of the term " colour " to the browns as distinguished from the blacks was common, but then, as now, all browns were
called mulattos. Strictly speaking, a mulatto was the offspring of a
black woman, a quadroon of a mulatto woman, and a mestize or mustee
of a quadroon woman—all by whites. The children of the last were
white by law.—Edwards, ii. 18.

[3] *Anti-Slavery Reporter*, i. 285 ; *Negro Slavery*, No. xv ; Stephen,
British West Indian Slavery, i. 368, 396–402, 412. This is a valuable

that the British free coloured population was not only extremely small but, as we shall see, subjected to almost every imaginable social, civil and even professional disqualification. In Cuba alone in 1827 there were some 20,000 more free persons of colour than in the whole British West Indies ; [1] and not till 1796 in Jamaica were such persons allowed, as a special concession, to give evidence against whites in cases of assault.

In regard to property, the British slave was in the same position as the Spanish, his capacity to hold it being actually, though not legally, recognised. He had no right of redemption ; but freedom could of course be bought either for him or by him provided the owner was willing to sell. A white man who wished to ransom his negro mistress or her children had frequently to pay an extravagant sum ; and the same extortion was too often practised on the hard-working slave. The market value of a slave in Jamaica in 1824 was £45 sterling, and under the Spanish system of appraisement he could not have been called upon to pay more ; but we find male slaves paying for themselves £100 to £200.[2]

One cannot read the Spanish regulations without seeing that their main object was to promote the moral and social welfare of the slave, and that they were designed only incidentally and as a matter of course to secure him from ill-treatment. In our colonies only the second of these purposes was attempted, and we shall find that its accomplishment was rendered hopeless by the entire neglect of the first. British slaves had no legal status which they could assert either personally or through a guardian. "In the contemplation of law," wrote Wilberforce, " they are not persons but mere chattels ; " [3] and it is hardly an exception to this statement that in all

and exhaustive work, but the author's bias against the slave-owners amounts to an obsession.

[1] Flinter, p. 225.
[2] *Reporter*, i. 279–282.
[3] *Appeal on behalf of the Negro Slaves*, 1823, p. 11.

the colonies, but quite recently in some, the murder of a slave had been made a capital crime ; for in England people could still be put to death for maliciously killing or maiming cattle. Slaves could be sold collectively or individually in payment of their master's debts ; and, though allowed to give evidence for and against each other, their testimony was not admitted against free persons, whether white or coloured. The reason for this restriction was said to be their incapacity to understand the obligation of an oath, and this again was due to the deficiency of religious teaching. The Church of England in the West Indies concerned itself almost exclusively with the whites. " It was no more calculated for the negro," said Canning, " than for the brute animal that shares his toils ; " [1] and indeed its limited function was very imperfectly performed ; for the first Bishop of Jamaica reported in 1825 that " the parishes in the interior are absolutely without the semblance of the forms of religious worship." [2] There was no church in Dominica, St. Vincent, Berbice, and Trinidad, and only one in Demerara ; [3] and the task of converting the negroes was prosecuted by a few missionaries, mostly Moravian and Methodist. It might have been supposed that the planters, especially after the abolition of the slave trade, would have favoured the diffusion of Christianity as the best means of promoting marriage ; but they were too dependent on credit to amend the law which allowed the families of their slaves to be sold and dispersed for debt. British slaves could not be legally married, and they knew that the religious unions pressed upon them by the missionaries might at any moment be dissolved. Jamaica

[1] Hansard (1824), x. 1098.
[2] *Reporter*, i. 193. Some of the West Indian clergy were by no means a credit to their profession. Early in the nineteenth century a Mr. Audain of Dominica was conspicuous as a boxer, duellist, smuggler, and buccaneer. In Jamaica in 1832 we read of another clerical duellist who took the lead in pulling down a Baptist chapel ; and we shall see something later of the notorious R. W. Bridges.
[3] Stephen, i. 210–212.

had one clergyman who really devoted himself to the negroes, and amongst them in his parish during the five years 1821–1825 there were 1085 marriages ; but in nine of the other parishes the number of marriages during this period ranged from one to five ; and Jamaica was " the very temple of Hymen " as compared with the other colonies, in the majority of which no marriage of slaves had ever taken place.[1]

It was due mainly, but not wholly,[2] to the good management of the Spaniards that for over two hundred years their slaves had never, or almost never, rebelled. Santo Domingo was quite unaffected by the great negro rising which destroyed the French part of the island in 1791 ; and during the revolt of the colonies in Central and South America the slaves on both sides are said to have been equally faithful to their masters. In our islands risings were only too frequent ; but it would be unjust to ascribe them altogether, or even mainly, to illtreatment. The British colonies, owing to their unlimited command of the slave trade, had more than the usual proportion of Africans to creoles ; and our planters, at least in Jamaica, had an unfortunate preference for the Gold Coast negroes, known as Koromantis, who, though their powerful physique made them valuable as labourers, were so fierce and intractable that the French and Spaniards would not knowingly admit them. In Jamaica, after a serious outbreak in 1760 had been followed by further trouble in 1765, it was proposed to put a prohibitive duty on the importation of these negroes ;[3] and shortly afterwards thirty-three of them mutinied and in an hour had killed or wounded nineteen whites. The desire of his fellow-planters to obtain members of " this detestable race " was unaccountable to

[1] *Reporter*, i. 268 ; *Christian Observer*, 1826, p. 405. Marriage was, and still is, exceptional even amongst the Spanish negroes ; but in 1827 there were 1381 slave marriages in Cuba.

[2] Another cause, as we shall see, was the preponderance of whites.

[3] See p. 15.

Long. " Nature does not instruct the farmer to yoke tigers in his team or to plough with hyenas." [1]

Adam Smith has said that slavery is always more tolerable under arbitrary than under constitutional rule ; for in a free state not only do the slave-owners make or help to make the laws, but, being unaccustomed to the interference of the Government, they are more likely to resent it when exerted in restraint of their authority. We shall find, however, that even absolute monarchy might be no protection to slaves ; and we must take into account economic as well as political and religious conditions if we wish to understand how it was that they fared so much better under the Spanish than under the British Crown.

Early in the seventeenth century, when Englishmen were attempting to establish themselves within the Spanish preserve of the New World, they shared the belief of their enemy that the West Indies could be peopled as well as exploited by Europeans. Both movements promised well for a time in Barbados, an island no bigger than the Isle of Wight, which was occupied by a few settlers in 1627. It produced for some years only indifferent cotton—which was made into hammocks— ginger and indigo and some very bad tobacco ; but the level expanse of its fertile soil was turned to much better account in 1641 when the culture of the sugar-cane was introduced from Brazil ; and it soon developed a great trade, partly legitimate in shipping provided by the Dutch, and partly illicit with the Spanish colonies. An influx of wealthy Royalist refugees both during and after the civil war in England contributed to its progress ; and the Navigation Act of 1651, which gave British shipbuilders a monopoly of the colonial trade, was aimed at Barbados as well as at Holland. The Act was renewed on purely national grounds after the Restoration ; but " the mother of all the sugar colonies " continued to flourish, and Charles II is said to have conferred baronet-

[1] *History of Jamaica*, ii. 443, 470, 471, 475.

cies on thirteen of its planters whose incomes ranged
from £1000 to £10,000 a year. Fortunes made in sugar
attracted many new settlers ; but it soon appeared that
the development of this industry, however it might enrich
the whites, would diminish their number and greatly
increase that of the blacks. The cultivation and manufacture of canes could be conducted economically only on
a large scale ; for it was estimated that to make ten hogsheads of sugar cost almost as much as to make a hundred.
The small proprietors who had supported themselves by
growing cotton on ten-acre lots were unable to adapt
themselves to the new conditions. Their lands were
bought up by the more enterprising of their number or
by new capitalists and massed into large estates ; and
this process was accelerated as the cost of producing sugar
increased with the exhaustion of the soil. Not only were
there fewer planters, but many of them, being rich enough
to dispense with personal superintendence, became
non-resident. Barbados, which called itself " Little
England," and was the ripest and most settled of our West
Indian colonies, had always much the largest proportion
of whites. That they were ever as many as 50,000 is no
doubt a gross exaggeration ; but, according to returns
supposed to be rather deficient than excessive, their
number declined from 21,000 in 1676 to 12,000 in 1712.[1]

The same process went on in the other British islands,
and notably in Jamaica. The number of Europeans in
this island continued to increase till peace was made
with the Maroons[2] in 1738, for the requirement that
proprietors should maintain a certain proportion of
white servants was " then very religiously complied

[1] Macpherson, *Annals*, ii. 275, 417 ; iii. 700 ; Merivale, *Coloniza-
tion and Colonies*, 1841, i. 74, 76 ; Long, *Jamaica*, 1774, i. 409 ;
Burke, *European Settlements in America*, ed. 1808, ii. 107. It is
evident that Burke wrote a great deal of this work, despite his statement to Boswell that he merely revised it.

[2] These " wild negroes " consisted of the descendants of the Spanish
slaves who had taken to the mountains at the English conquest of the
island, and also of runaways. There was another Maroon war in 1796.

with." Thenceforth it could be disregarded at no greater risk than that of an inadequate fine ; but this was not the only cause of depopulation ; for estates were said in 1774 to " have grown progressively from small beginnings to their present magnitude and swallowed up by degrees all the little settlements around, which, from their contiguity and being ready cleared for canes or pasturage, the lordly planter has found convenient to be purchased and added to his territory." In one parish of Jamaica 106,000 acres were in the possession of only 120 persons.[1]

We have seen that the importation of negroes into the West Indies was defended as creating a market for our manufactures without diminishing the number of our workers at home or exposing them to transatlantic competition ; but it was viewed very differently by Burke, who declared that our sugar colonies would soon comprise only a few planters and merchants and " a numerous and disaffected herd of African slaves," and that by settling a number of our poor and unemployed in these islands we might secure their safety at a much cheaper rate than by providing them with troops. Had this suggestion been carried out, it might not have succeeded much better than one which was adopted a few years later by the French Government. Soon after the Peace of 1763 they sought to compensate their country for the loss of Canada by planting a ready-made colony in the swamps of Guiana. Fourteen thousand lives and a vast sum of public money are said to have been lost in this expedition, which, in addition to whole families of peasants and artisans, included adventurers from every class and a whole staff of officials. In order to beguile the tedium of their exile, the emigrants had even been provided with a company of comedians and musicians.[2]

<hr />

[1] Long, i. 386.
[2] Malouet, *Mémoires sur l'Administration des Colonies*, 1802, iii. 5 ; Burke, ii. 143.

Returning now to the Spanish colonies, we are confronted with a process almost the reverse of that which has just been reviewed—an increase of the white population much greater than that of the black ; and this need not surprise us when we consider that for nearly three centuries these islands were not even at the stage of development which had been reached in Barbados before the number of its whites was diminished by the formation of large sugar estates. Barbados had had at least a dozen years of unrestricted commerce, and always enjoyed that boon within the British Empire ; but so heavy was the hand of Spain on her colonies that they were not allowed to trade even with each other. Santo Domingo declined with the exhaustion of its gold mines, which for some years yielded a revenue of £90,000. Writing of this island about 1770, a French statesman said that, though the Spaniards retained the larger and better part, their state was rather worse than it had been at the death of Columbus. Despite the manifest richness of their soil, it was used mainly for pasture ; coffee, sugar, and tobacco were grown only for domestic consumption ; two or three vessels sufficed for their trade with Spain ; and their towns and villages were peopled with monks, soldiers, and " citadins nonchalans, qui dorment ou se reposent le jour et la nuit." [1] Porto Rico was a penal settlement. The more energetic of its settlers were smugglers, and the rest lived, or were supposed to live, a pastoral life, " rocking themselves to and fro in their hammocks without making any efforts, bodily or mental." [2] Trinidad was described in a law of one of our own colonies as " a spot which holds out a retreat for fraudulent debtors and stealers of slaves, and where no redress or justice can be had," [3] and, when it became a British possession in 1802, was spoken of generally as " uncultivated." In Cuba, the largest and all but the

[1] Malouet, iv. 112.   [2] Flinter, p. 2.
[3] Robinson, *Memoirs of General Picton*, i. 57.

richest of the Antilles, tobacco and sugar were indeed grown to some purpose ; but here too in 1730 there were " infinite numbers of cattle," and the colonists were mostly small proprietors, living familiarly with their slaves, if they had any, and even working with them in the field. The Spanish settlements long retained their evil reputation as mining camps ;[1] but under the more stable conditions of later days their character improved ; for the Spaniards, having a tinge of Africa in their skin,[2] and not being fastidious as to colour, married and multiplied in the West Indies, whereas the British did not marry and always looked forward to the competency which would enable them to go home. It has been said that the colonies of Spain were commonwealths at a time when ours were mere factories.[3] There was an archbishop of Santo Domingo. The city was compared by a too partial inhabitant to Barcelona, and was so substantially built that no more than a third of it could be burned by Drake in 1586.[4] Havana was the most populous town in the West Indies ; and there were thirty grandees of Spain amongst the resident proprietors of Cuba.

It can hardly be doubted that in this backward but not unwholesome society the slaves were admitted in great measure to the benefits of their code ; for fear and industrial pressure, the two great motives for their oppression in other colonies, could here have little scope. They were numerous enough for the small demand, but far too few to be formidable, being vastly outnumbered by the total free population, and even to a considerable extent by the whites alone. In Cuba in 1817 there were

---

[1] Cervantes described them as " the refuge of the profligates of Spain ; sanctuaries for homicide ; skulking places for gamblers and sharpers ; receptacles of women of free manners ; places of delusion to many, of amelioration to few."—Quoted in Madden's *Cuba*, p. 1.

[2] " Les Epagnols sont, ou à peu près, de l'espèce des nègres."— Malouet, iv. 347.

[3] Merivale, i. 39.　　　　[4] Edwards, ii. 44.

240,000 whites and not quite 200,000 slaves. In Porto Rico in 1820 there were 102,000 whites and 21,000 slaves. In these two islands the Europeans were at least six times more numerous than in all the rest of the West Indies ; and, when Froude landed at Havana in 1887, he was surprised to find that boatmen, porters, cab-drivers, and carters—all negroes in our islands—were whites.[1]

But the cause which had so long prevented the colonies of Spain from competing with other tropical dependencies in the markets of the world was at last removed ; and the effect of this development on the slaves was foreshadowed in 1803 by Brougham, who recalled that the Spaniards, when scouring the lands and seas of the New World in quest of treasure, were no better than other mercenary adventurers in their treatment of their captives, and that their reputation for humanity had been acquired only when their eagerness in the pursuit of wealth had given place to " an indifference about gain." [2] By a series of edicts extending from 1765 to 1809 the restrictions on commerce were gradually withdrawn. In 1789 the importation of negroes was allowed in foreign, and in 1792 even in Spanish, vessels ; [3] and a competition then began with the British islands in which Cuba had two great advantages—a vast reserve of unexhausted soil and a persistence in the slave trade for thirteen years legally, and for thrice as many illegally, after it had been closed to our planters in 1807.[4]

We have seen that Spain's abolition of the slave trade in 1820 was merely nominal, and in fact down to about 1840 her share in it actually increased. All the provisions devised for the relief and protection of the slaves

---

[1] *The English in the West Indies*, 1888, p. 303.

[2] *Colonial Policy*, i. 75.

[3] Heeren, *Political System of Europe and its Colonies*, 1834, ii. 122 ; Madden, *Cuba*, p. 29.

[4] We have seen that the slave trade was, on the whole, a disastrous speculation for individuals ; but it certainly gave a collective advantage to one body of planters as against another, inasmuch as it secured an adequate supply of labour.

must have been withheld from those who were illegally imported. No attempt indeed was made to distinguish between the two classes of field-slaves; and extracts have been published from a manual issued for the guidance of magistrates in the interior which virtually annulled the whole code. There was a sort of international Admiralty Court at Havana, known as the Mixed Commission, whose function it was to determine the legality of captures by British cruisers. When a slave-ship was condemned, its negroes up to 1835 were handed over to the Captain-General of Cuba on the understanding that they should be taught some handicraft trade; but the Captain-General made his own profit out of the transaction by selling them for seven years to the planters, and very few of them survived the term of their indenture. In other words, these *Emancipados* were worked to death in seven years, whereas the life of a slave on the Cuban sugar plantations was reckoned as ten years. One writer assures us that this was the average mortality admitted to him by many of the *mayorals* or overseers; and we are told by another that, going "unknown and unexpected" to the sugar estates, he became familiar with atrocities, not exceptional but common, which had been hidden from him when he was the guest of their proprietors. "So terrible were these atrocities, so murderous the system of slavery, so transcendent the evils I witnessed over all I had ever seen or heard of the rigour of slavery elsewhere, that at first I could hardly believe the evidence of my senses." This language will not seem too strong in view of the well-established fact that during the four or five months of harvest the slaves usually worked twenty hours out of the twenty-four.[1]

France established herself in the West Indies just at the time when her monarchy was being made absolute by Richelieu; and it might have been supposed that under a despotic and Catholic government her system of

[1] Madden, *Cuba*, pp. 25, 39; Turnbull, *Cuba*, p. 150.

slavery would develop in the same way as that of Spain. Louis XIV may have had some such idea when in 1685 he promulgated his famous but useless *Code Noir*. Slaves cannot be secured from ill-usage by merely admonishing their owners ; and this edict annihilated their personality without in some measure restoring it to them through the medium of a protector. They were declared " incapable of possessing anything except to the use of their master," and all dispositions in their favour, whether by gift, will, or inheritance, were declared void. They could be brought into court only as culprits or witnesses ; and their evidence was received under this extraordinary limitation, that it " shall be considered as no more than a bare narrative, from which it shall not be lawful to draw any presumption or conjecture or the least circumstance corroborative of proof." They were also declared to be included in the personal estate of their master, and liable to be disposed of in the same manner as other movables, but with two exceptions which were not admitted in our colonies—that from fourteen years of age to sixty they should not be sold for debt apart from the plantation, and that a family belonging to the same owner should not be sold separately. A master might punish his slaves at discretion, but not to the extent of killing, torture, or mutilation ; and without his consent they were not allowed to marry. Nor were they to be constrained to marry.[1] On the other hand, by way of ameliorating their lot, they were to be baptised and educated in the Catholic faith ; on Sundays and Church festivals they were to have twenty-four hours' rest ; certain allowances of food and clothing were to be distributed by the master, who could not release himself from this obligation by allowing them to raise their own food ;[2] if ill-used, they might complain

[1] A most superfluous prohibition, unless it was intended to restrain the zeal of the priests.

[2] Nevertheless, this was the plan actually adopted. Malouet (ii. 20) appears to be mistaken in citing Martinique as an exception.

to a magistrate ; and manumission was so far encouraged
that it could be granted by a minor without consulting
his relatives or guardians.

There was no executive principle in this code, and,
as a means of coercing the slave-owners, it was never
operative—at least in the West Indies.   French slavery
has been described as " a system of servitude unsur-
passed for severity, cruelty, nay ferocity." [1]   This is
almost certainly an exaggeration even if the statement
be confined, as perhaps the writer intended, to St.
Domingue ; but one can easily believe that this colony
did not so quickly outstrip all its rivals without anticipating some of the subsequent horrors of Cuba. Malouet,
Minister for the Colonies, and himself a planter, has
vividly described the feverish activity, the constant
coming and going, the indifference to all but immediate
gain, which prevailed in St. Domingue some fifteen years
before the culmination of its prosperity in 1790.   Every-
body was eager to become rich.   Those who succeeded
went home ; those who failed exhausted themselves
and died.   " Tous veulent le quitter ; chacun se hâte,
se dépêche ; ils ont l'air de marchands dans une foire."
People who did not spare themselves were not likely to
spare their slaves.   A French officer who visited the
colony in 1751 said that some of the planters mercilessly
overworked their negroes and treated them " when old
and infirm, worse than their dogs and horses " ; and we
learn from an official source that slaves received at the
prisons to be worked in chains had to be medically
examined because their owners, in order to avoid the
expense of their illness, sometimes sent them " sous le
faux prétexte de correction." [2]   Such miscreants were to
be found more or less in every slave colony, and too often,
as in this case, they could not be called to account.

---

[1] Sir Spenser St. John, *Hayti*, p. 31.
[2] Stephen, i. 354, note.   The practice was described as prejudicial,
not to the slave, but to the King.

Malouet maintained that French slavery, though not so mild as Spanish, was far milder than British, and that almost all the rich planters treated their slaves better than was supposed in Europe. But ill-treatment could neither be prevented nor punished ; and the slave of a needy or unprincipled owner was in this condition : " Un coin de terre, travaillée par le nègre aux heures qui devroient être pour lui celles du repos, pourvoit à sa subsistance; le reste de son temps, ses bras, sa sueur, appartiennent au maître, qui peut forcer les châtimens sans que la loi, impuissante, le recherche et le punisse : de-là désespoir, la vengeance, les empoisonnemens, les incendies."

So completely unfettered indeed were the slave-owners that Malouet considered there were two independent jurisdictions in the colony—the public and the private ; and, the *Code Noir* and all subsequent regulations being wholly ineffective, he proposed that the planters of each parish should elect three of their number to consider all matters relating to the management of the negroes and to hear their complaints. This trifling and illusory reform was to be tried in some of our own colonies ; and the timidity of its author was shown in his opposition to another scheme then contemplated by the Government. The religious instruction of the negroes had been entirely neglected, at all events since the suppression of the Jesuits in 1764 ; and, by way of restoring the discipline of the clergy, it was proposed to institute a bishopric of St. Domingue. Malouet succeeded, according to his own account, in defeating this project, which he regarded with the utmost alarm, believing that the spell of subjection would be broken if the slaves obtained a protector reverenced by all classes and able to speak with authority to their masters. " Ils le prendroient pour un Dieu, and le prélat seroit le seul maître des habitans et des habitations." [1]

French slavery was no doubt at its worst in St.

---

[1] Malouet, iii. 115 ; iv. 116, 346 ; v. 78.

Domingue ; and it is difficult to say whether the system as a whole was or was not exceptionally severe. The colonists of Guadeloupe and Martinique were in some respects like the Spaniards. They lived familiarly with their slaves ; they really expatriated themselves ; their towns were equipped with churches, theatres, coffee-houses, clubs, promenades, baths ; and it was said of them in 1826 that "they marry, educate and build for the West Indies and the West Indies alone." On the other hand, unlike the Spaniards, they shrank with horror from the slightest tinge of African blood ; [1] and *bête* and *nègre* were with them synonyms. In our colonies the fourth in descent from a negro ancestor was both legally and socially a white ; but in theirs the stigma was indelible, at least so long as it could be traced. We have seen that under the *Code Noir* the evidence of slaves was not absolutely excluded ; the prohibition to break up their families by sale or to detach them from the plantation, though never enforced, had possibly some effect ; and the French slave-owner seems to have been less niggardly than the British in his gifts of freedom. Malouet had a motive for understating the facts when he said that those who yearly obtained their liberty were not one in a thousand and were nearly all townspeople. The French coloured population was much larger than ours ; and St. Lucia, when placed on the list of our colonies, had all but the highest percentage of manumissions. The French had the sense and humanity to import a larger proportion of females than the British ; but they were equally indifferent to the marriage of their slaves ; and the mortality amongst the latter was higher both at sea and

[1] " In St. Lucia persons of colour were not by law at liberty to wear the same dress as a white man. There was a positive law, strictly adhered to, by which, however wealthy, they were not to be called in any legal document 'Mr.' or 'Madam,' but were designated ' le nominé, la nominée,' that man and that woman."—Jeremie, *Four Essays on Colonial Slavery*, 1831, p. 30. This able writer was a lawyer of Guernsey who, in 1823, was appointed Chief Justice of St. Lucia. At the present day the French attitude to colour is a complete contrast.

on the plantations. After 1818 the illicit slave trade must have greatly depressed their condition ; and one is not surprised to find that no record, religious or civil, was then kept of their births and deaths.[1]

The Danes were not of much account as slave-owners in the West Indies, their rule being confined to Santa Cruz and the small islands of St. Thomas and St. John. The slaves of St. Thomas must have been well off early in the eighteenth century, if it be true that no sugar was then made at night ; but St. John in 1733 was actually captured by the negroes, and could be recovered only with the help of the French. The Danish planters were entirely favourable to the religious instruction of their slaves ; and, though they retained *in terrorem* a rather savage code, their reputation for humanity stood high. It was said of them about 1787 that they could sleep in security with doors and windows open and travel anywhere without even a penknife to protect them. When Great Britain had abolished slavery, her islands became cities of refuge to the oppressed negro. From St. John to Tortola is scarcely a mile, yet very few of the Danish slaves attempted to escape, whereas thousands of the French slaves tried to reach British soil from Guadeloupe and Martinique, though the distance is from fifteen to twenty miles, and nearly two-thirds are said to have perished in the attempt.[2]

The few small islands possessed by the Dutch flourished mainly as centres of contraband trade ; but in Guiana they had a large and extraordinarily fertile domain which was almost a replica of their own country in Europe,

---

[1] Pinckard, ii. 327–332 ; Macpherson, *Annals*, iv. 226 ; Flinter, pp. 218, 219, 224 ; Malouet, v. 126 ; Coleridge, p. 143. Jeremie, referring to the illusory nature of French safeguards, said that the British plan of leaving the slave "without any protection, even nominal, was infinitely less disgraceful to the national character than such rank legislative hypocrisy."—*Essays*, p. 22.

[2] Taylor, *Leaflets from the Danish West Indies*, 1888, pp. 10, 101, 204 ; Turnbull, *Cuba*, p. 565 ; Lloyd, *Letters from the West Indies*, pp. 120–136 ; Sturge and Harvey, *The West Indies in* 1837, p. 115.

being flat, intersected by rivers and canals, and protected from the sea by dykes. Here they grew sugar, cotton, and tobacco, and practised slavery after a fashion which had gained for them an unenviable reputation. The Dutch slave laws, in so far at least as they provided for some sort of Protector, were better than the British, but equally ineffective. As outrages occurred under every system of slavery and are not unknown even in free and civilised communities, it took a good many of them to prove general and habitual cruelty; but the requisite number does appear to have been supplied by the Dutch. Like the British in Jamaica, they had to deal with a considerable body of Maroons which the brutality practised on their plantations continually increased; and throughout the eighteenth century we find them competing in the barbarities of savage warfare with these bush negroes and attempting with equal ferocity to keep down their exasperated or mutinous slaves. It is difficult to imagine more diabolical punishments and executions than those described—and many of them witnessed and sketched—by Captain Stedman, a humane Scottish officer in the Dutch army, who in 1773 volunteered for service in Guiana; and other writers confirm the lamentable account he gives of the ordinary industrial regime. On one occasion he interceded for a girl of eighteen, suspended naked by her wrists from a tree, who had received two hundred lashes; and the overseer doubled the punishment, saying that he always did so when anybody interfered. Immediately afterwards he was informed that a male slave had been flogged to death. " My ears were stunned," he writes, " with the clang of the whip and the dismal yells of the wretched negroes on whom it was exercised from morning to night." The same remark and in almost the same words was made by Dr. Pinckard during the British occupation of Demerara in 1796. The wanton killing of slaves was said to be quite common, the evidence of their fellows not being available against whites;[1] slaves unfit for work were frequently despatched under cover of accident or by semi-starvation; and a French traveller wrote thus : " Il n'y a point de bête de somme dont la condition soit aussi triste que celle des ces esclaves. Ils étaient obligés de travailler sans relâche et on les traitait sans miséricorde."

Self-interest being more potent than coercion, slave-labour was found to be least inefficient when employed on piece-work, or, as it was then called, task-work. Brougham remarks that the Dutch were the only planters who had fully adopted this system, but that their avarice and brutality neutralised its effects. The tasks imposed and the penalties for non-completion were " infinitely too severe." Stedman tells us of a vigorous young negro who, being anxious to provide for his wife and children, usually contrived to finish his task by four in the afternoon. The overseer soon deprived him of this motive, telling him " for his encouragement " that, if he could dig five hundred feet by four o'clock, he would certainly be able to dig six hundred before sunset.[2]

We have now to develop the slight sketch already given of British slavery; and it will be best to begin by considering the character of those who were responsible for its management. Proprietors who had inherited their estates and lived on them made much the best slave-owners; and there were still resident in Jamaica some descendants of the original planters. These men were often connected by kinship as well as sympathy, their

[1] Admissible apparently in law, but not in practice.

[2] Stedman, *Narrative of an Expedition against the Revolted Negroes of Surinam*, 1806, i. 96, 339; ii. 304; Pinckard, i. 348; ii. 328; Brougham, *Colonial Policy*, ii. 517. If the reader cannot lay hands on Stedman's book he will find most of the gruesome facts and illustrations in Sir H. H. Johnston's *The Negro in the New World*. There were slaves even amongst the Dutch so well treated that they would not accept their freedom, but the majority of owners were cruel, and especially the women.—Stedman, ii. 60, 213, 301, 305. Brougham described the Dutch as " of all nations in the world the most inhuman masters."—*Colonial Policy*, i. 75.

families in the dearth of suitable matches having frequently intermarried ; their spirit was territorial rather
than commercial or speculative ; and the negroes who
had been born on their estates took a pride in the bond
which associated their ancestry with that of their master.
Long calls them humane and indulgent and says that if
any cruelty could be laid to their charge—which he had
never known and had seldom heard of—it was always
the work of some British " barbarian " whom they had
taken into their service. Various causes had operated to
alienate the estates or to expatriate the members of this
native aristocracy.[1] Personal extravagance, profuse hospitality, or the desire to engross land often proved ruinous
to the family of a proprietor, which at his death was
" turned adrift to make room for some worthless upstart."
Children had once been taught by tutors on the estates,
where they became accustomed to the occupations and
pastimes of the island and were early initiated into the
mysteries of planting ; but it had long been the custom
for every man of means to send his children " of whatever
complexion " to be educated in Britain. Some returned
only to dissipate their property, having gained no " other
acquisition than the art of swearing, drinking, dressing,
gaming and wenching ; " some regretted their exile from
more cultivated society ; and the majority as soon as
they became their own masters settled permanently in
Europe. About the middle of the eighteenth century,
when the Crown had disallowed an Act imposing a
differential tax on absentees, the Jamaica Assembly
declared " that it has of late years been so much the

---

[1] A fine example of a creole proprietor was Chief Justice Fearon, a
highly cultivated man who had never left the island. There were two
stately buildings within his grounds—his house and his library. Five
baronets of the Modyford family are buried in the parish of St. Catherine.
—Gardner, *History of Jamaica*, pp. 166, 169. In Antigua in 1825 the
President of the Council was a descendant of Sir Thomas Warner, the
founder of British rule in the West Indies ; and the original grant
of Charles I was framed and hung in his dining-room.—Coleridge,
Six Months in the West Indies, p. 249.

custom for the proprietors of estates in the island to emigrate from thence to Europe that it is left almost destitute of proper persons to supply the exigence of the various duties, civil and military, which are merely honorary and ought to be executed by men of liberal education, fortune and experience." In 1835 about seventy per cent. of all the proprietors in Jamaica were believed to be non-resident,[1] and the proportion must have been greater amongst the sugar-planters, who were much the wealthiest class.

Jamaica, unlike the other old colonies, had plenty of new land available for the speculator ; and the great mass of its European population consisted of those " exotic whites " who had come out, not to settle, but to make money and go home. Marriage, if no longer held in " the utmost derision," was still considered an encumbrance ; and gaps could thus be filled only by immigration. Malouet said of St. Domingue that the colonists could not find time to attend to the comfort and embellishment of their houses ; and a Jamaica planter was often content to dispense the most splendid hospitality in " a hovel not superior to an English barn." In St. Domingue successful artisans soon exchanged their workshops for plantations, and in Jamaica they usually became " adventurers in the soil." There were a great many Jews, and Scotsmen abounded. They stood the climate better than Englishmen and held together in the same clannish spirit which had made them at one time so unpopular in London. Nearly every third person was said to be either a Scotsman or of Scottish descent.[2] " To say the truth, they are so

---

[1] *Jamaica as it was, as it is, and as it may be*, 1835, p. 101.

[2] Long had " heard a computation of no féwer than one hundred of the name of Campbell " ; and there seems to have been no lack of Gordons. See Bulloch, *The Making of the West Indies : the Gordons as Colonists.* Some survivors of the Darien expedition had settled in the parish of Portland.—Long, ii. 203. The Scottish Church, though it " could hold only secondary rank in Jamaica," was established by a vote of £3500 about 1815.—Bridges, *Annals of Jamaica*, 1828, ii. 335. Six parishes of Demerara were under ministers of the Church of Scot-

clever and prudent in general as, by an obliging behaviour, good sense and zealous services, to gain esteem and make their way through every obstacle." Relations with coloured women were all but universal;[1] even the married planter had often a mixed family of whites and browns; and unfortunately for the slaves, who suffered most from its effects, there was a good deal of hard drinking. This was mainly an " exotic " vice, the creole whites being temperate and some of them drinking nothing but water; and Long refers to " an enormous multitude " who served no other purpose than " the depopulation of their country, the impoverishment of their families, and the abridgment of their own contemptible lives." The drinking of laudanum appears to have lost " the firm hold which so horrid a fashion " had obtained in his day, and the tone of social life had somewhat improved with the closer intercourse with England which followed the peace of 1815. That so few survived middle life is said to have been due to recklessness in business as well as in pleasure; for the British colonist, despising the umbrella carried by other Europeans and even " the load of handkerchiefs " twisted round their heads by the negroes, was to be seen, even at high noon, " anxiously trotting about his business, all besmeared with dust and sweat"; and the Spaniards had a saying that " no animal but a dog and an Englishman " cared to be abroad at midday.[2]

The sugar boom and its sudden collapse in the last years of the eighteenth century can hardly have improved

land. In Montserrat the negroes had " an Irish accent, which, grafted on negro English, forms the most diverting jargon I ever heard in my life."—Coleridge, *Six Months in the West Indies*, 1825, p. 176.

[1] A witness examined by a Committee of the House of Commons in 1832 admitted that the hospitality of a planter always included the offer of a black girl; and plantation accounts were found to contain such items as these : " Hire of Gracey, a mulatto, to Mr. —— at £20 per annum; hire of AnneClarke, a mulatto, to Mr. —— at £16 per annum." —*Anti-Slavery Reporter*, v. 77.

[2] Long, ii. 22, 262, 266, 287, 540, 546, 547, 922 ; Edwards, ii. 6, 9 ; Gardner, p. 376.

the moral atmosphere of Jamaica; but one source of
speculation, the most ruinous and the most demoralising,
was cut off when the slave trade was abolished in 1807.
The colonial legislatures were far from carrying out the
implications of that Act in the manner anticipated by
its friends; but, instead of adding to the misery of the
slaves as it did in the case of most other Powers, it made
for their better treatment. The British abolition, as compared with the American, French, and Spanish, may be
described—at least in the West Indies—as instantaneous
and complete. Henceforth the creole negroes no longer
received an annual infusion of the savage Africans who
had caused all the revolts and provided a pretext for
all the barbarous laws and punishments; and the relaxation of discipline was accompanied by an improvement
in their condition which one rather hopes than believes
to have been considerable. No doubt the difficulty of
keeping gangs at full strength without importation must
have caused them in some cases to be overworked; but
on the whole, as slaves could no longer be easily replaced,
it was the interest of their owner to keep them in health;
and the influence of this motive is appreciable in the
statistics of population.[1]

The plantations on a sugar estate usually occupied

---

[1] It is difficult to estimate the waste of life on the plantations before
1807, as importation was required for new as well as old estates; and
the statistics given in the Privy Council Report of 1789 are quite
unreliable. Moreover, we have to guard against exaggeration. Before
1807 the Abolitionists were always trying to minimise the annual
decrease of negroes in order to show that the planters could dispense
with the slave trade. After 1807, when their object was to denounce
slavery as destructive to life, they tended to magnify the decrease.
Pitt and Wilberforce proved to their own satisfaction that the annual
decrease in Jamaica in 1788 was only one per cent.; but another and
more competent authority put it as high as two and a half.—*Parl.
Hist.* xxix. 267, 307, 338. With the establishment of a triennial
registry in 1817 we are on comparatively firm ground. The number of
slaves then registered in Jamaica was 346,150, and in 1829 it was
322,421, which represents an average annual decrease for twelve years
of about five-eighths.—Commons' *Report on Slavery*, 1832, Appendix.
Allowance must be made for manumitted slaves—probably about 5000.

only about a third of its area, the remainder being reserved
for timber and pasture. The proprietor was of course in
charge when he happened to be resident ; but in most
cases he had delegated his function to an " attorney,"
who was so called, not because he was a lawyer, but
because he had a " power of attorney " to manage the
business. One attorney had usually quite a number of
estates under his control, and there was some advantage
in this as it left a freer hand to the overseer who was more
of an expert ; but, on the whole, it was a bad system,
tending to exhaust rather than to husband the soil ; for
the proprietor, who might never have seen his estate, was
dissatisfied with the attorney unless he received a large
annual return, and the attorney, who was paid by a
commission on the gross sales,[1] too often made this his
chief consideration in choosing an overseer. Estates,
however, so frequently changed hands that their permanent value was not likely in any case to be much considered. The overseer had assistants, who in Jamaica,
though they had nothing to do with accounts, were called
"book-keepers,"[2] and a staff of head negroes who supervised the drivers, sugar-makers, artisans, cattle-men, and
watchmen.

The slaves were divided, mainly according to age,
into three gangs. The first or " great gang " was
composed of men and women between the ages of sixteen
and fifty ; and one of our authorities writes with
enthusiasm of this force, which he describes as " composed of the flower of all the field-battalions drafted
and recruited from all the other gangs as they come of
age to endure severe labour " and " brigaded by its
chief field officer, the head driver." This officer carried
as an emblem of his authority a " polished staff or wand
with prongy crooks," and also for more practical purposes

---

[1] The evil of this system led in some cases to the appointment of
salaried attorneys.—Dallas, *History of the Maroons*, 1803, ii. 359.

[2] In the Windward Islands the book-keeper was called the overseer
and his superior the manager.

a short-handled whip, flung over his shoulder or wound round his neck. The second gang comprised men and women over fifty, and boys and girls from twelve to sixteen, who did lighter work ; and the third or " small gang," under a female driver or " driveress "[1] and comprising children from six to twelve years of age, was employed mainly in weeding. Women who had become too old or too infirm for field-work cooked or had charge of infants, and men in the same category were employed as watchmen—an occupation too hard for " many of these superannuated slaves." They were stationed at night on the lines, the cane-fields and the provision-grounds, to protect them from thieves and to hunt or trap rats, nothing being so injurious " to a piece of ripening canes as this gnawing, destructive little animal "; and they had also to guard the " moving pens " in which for the sake of their manure the cattle were confined. The slave who discharged this duty had a severe ordeal, especially when stationed, with only a fire to cheer him, on some lonely hill-top ; and he was severely punished for every instance of neglect or trespass, though " perhaps without a foot to stand upon or a hand to serve him." Nor is there much reason to believe that the good huts, which were often recommended for watchmen, were ever generally provided. A clergyman in 1824 found their huts " the most wretched abodes I ever saw."[2]

In addition to these regular slave gangs working on the plantations, there was a mobile corps of mercenaries known as jobbers. A planter who wished to relieve or supplement his own negroes could obtain a squad of these labourers, who were mostly the property of the

[1] In Demerara adults of both sexes were not infrequently driven by a woman, who was " sometimes peculiarly severe."—Pinckard, *Notes on the West Indies*, ii. 122.

[2] Roughley, *The Jamaica Planter's Guide*, 1823, pp. 80, 89, 99, 113, 115 ; Beckford, *Descriptive Account of Jamaica*, 1790, i. 198, 203, 204 ; Bickell, *The West Indies as they are*, 1825, p. 198. Stewart, *View of Jamaica*, 1823, p. 231.

contractor, but some of whom had usually been borrowed. They had to endure not only the hardest and most disagreeable work, but long journeys and indifferent shelter, for they could usually return only once a week to their homes. It was thought that the abolition of the slave trade would diminish the number of jobbers owing to the difficulty of forming gangs; but apparently it had no such effect; for in 1833 they were said to be very numerous, and as many as 30,000—though this must have been an exaggeration—in Barbados alone.[1] On some estates the head-negroes were permitted to own slaves; and here, at two removes from freedom, we have " the quintessence of the slave system." [2]

The production of sugar was much the most onerous of West Indian industries; and it was prosecuted with feverish energy in time of crop, extending from about the beginning of the year to May, when the cutting of the canes and the extraction, boiling, and potting of the juice were carried on simultaneously. Droughts were always to be feared in the dry season and heavy rains towards its close; but the high pressure then enforced was due also to an erroneous idea that sugar during the boiling process should never be allowed to cool. Rollers, driven by mules, wind, or water, were used to beat out the canes; and the juice, when thus " expressed " in the mill, was carried along a wooden gutter lined with lead into the boiling-house, where it was clarified in a series of copper cauldrons; and thence, after it had cooled and granulated, it was taken into the curing-house, where it was potted and drained. The process was suspended from seven o'clock on Saturday evening to five on Monday morning; but, with this exception, in the factory, where about twenty-five men and women were employed, it was carried on continuously by

[1] Hansard (1835), xxvi. 1055.
[2] Cooper, *Facts illustrative of the Condition of the Slaves in Jamaica*, 1824, p. 55.

" spells " or shifts working all day and either part of the
night or the whole of every second or third night. So
rapid was the motion of the mill, and so rapid also the
combustion of the dried canes or " trash " used as fuel
in the boiling-house, that the work of the millers and
firemen, though light enough in itself, was exhausting.
A French writer described as " prodigious " the galloping
of the mules attached to the sweeps of the mill ; but
"still more surprising" in his opinion was the ceaseless
celerity with which the firemen kept up a full blaze of
cane-trash. Those who fed the mill with canes were
liable, especially when tired or half-asleep, to have their
fingers caught between the rollers. A hatchet was kept
in readiness to sever the arm, which in such cases was
always drawn in ; and this no doubt explains the number
of maimed watchmen.[1]   The negroes employed as boiler-
men had a less exacting, but a heavier task. Standing
barefoot for hours on the stones or hard ground and
without seats for their intermissions of duty, they frequently developed " disorders of the legs." The ladle
suspended on a pole which transferred the sugar from one
cauldron to another was " in itself particularly heavy " ;
and, as the strainers were placed at a considerable
height above the cauldrons, it had to be raised as well
as swung. " How dreadful to think of their standing
twelve hours over a boiling cauldron ! "[2] wrote Lady
Nugent, wife of the Acting Governor of Jamaica, about
1802. " I would not have a sugar estate for the whole
world." [3]

The process of sugar-making would have been arduous
enough even if it had been prosecuted only during the

[1] See p. 62.
[2] This was an exaggeration. They were employed only when the
liquor required skimming, and are said to have been idle about one
half of their time.
[3] Beckford, ii. 9–13, 47–78 ; Stephen, ii. 144, 145, 175–179 ; Turnbull, *Cuba*, p. 287 ; Stedman, i. 328 ; Mary Gaunt, *Where the Twain
Meet*, 1922, p. 226.

day; but the exaction of night-work greatly intensified its hardships and was denounced by Dallas, himself a planter, as a flagrant abuse " which avarice cannot be tempted to forego." Any loss due to its abolition would, he believed, easily be made up if the works, instead of being allowed to go out of order at the end of the crop season, were kept properly equipped throughout the year. But he considered the practice uneconomical as well as cruel. " The languor after a sleepless night is evident to the eye and in its effects. The exertions of the fresh sink to the level of those made by the weary and sleepy whom they join and whose labours through a long dark night give a dullness to those of the day." [1]

It is difficult to reconcile what we know of sugar-making with the undoubted fact that the negroes were never so brisk, lively, and cheerful as during harvest. The popularity of this season on a sugar estate was the standing puzzle of the Abolitionists, and they were forced to content themselves with ascribing it to the effect produced on the health and spirits of the slaves by the dry season, and especially by the unlimited consumption of canes and cane-juice which was then allowed. It should, of course, be remembered that, whilst only about a fourth of their number were capable of working night and day, these benefits were common to all.

There can be no question that the sugar-slaves were worked too long, too continuously, and too hard during the crop season; and it must be admitted that they suffered from the first and second of these evils " out of crop "—that is, during about two-thirds of the year. The planter in Jamaica was forbidden by law to work his negroes before five in the morning and after seven in the evening. With half-an-hour for breakfast and two

---

[1] *History of the Maroons*, ii. 339. A writer of 1824 would have us believe that the introduction of steam-engines was superseding the necessity for night-work in Demerara; but as late as 1830 the Court of Policy extended the working day in harvest from fourteen to sixteen hours.—P.P. 1831–2, vol. xlvi.

hours at noon for dinner, this made a working day of eleven and a half hours ; but the actual seems to have been rather less than the legal maximum. In Demerara and Berbice work stopped at six, as may be seen from the absurd statement that it could not be made to stop earlier " without infringing the rights of property in a manner which could never possibly be contemplated by any legislature." [1] In the small and fully planted islands, where there was little pasture or fodder for the cattle, the slave before going home was required to pick a bundle of natural grass, which was seldom plentiful or close at hand. Sunday was a holiday on the plantations, but did not bring much relief to the slave, at least in those colonies in which he raised his own food. If the half-acre assigned for this purpose was within easy reach, he usually devoted to it about half of his noontide leisure ; but on old estates, where most of the level ground had been appropriated by the planter, it was usually in the mountains, some five to ten miles distant. In that case he could work for himself only on the twenty-six Saturdays " out of crop " which were prescribed for the purpose by law ; and he usually worked also on Sunday.[2] This, being market-day,[3] could not in any case be a day of rest ; for plantations and towns were generally far apart ; and, unless the slave had been able to collect his produce overnight, which was seldom possible during crop, he had to undertake two long walks, first in the early morning to his allotment, and then to market—in the latter case both going and returning with a heavy basket on his head.[4] The lack

[1] M'Donnell, *Compulsory Manumission*, 1827, p. 60.

[2] It was often said that Sunday was the only day available during crop ; but cultivation was impracticable during most of the dry season.—M'Queen, *The West India Colonies*, 1824, p. 223.

[3] Abolitionists, when they talked of Sabbath desecration in the West Indies, often forgot that there was no *general* Sunday market. The negroes were free to dispose of their produce, but they could supply their wants only from the Jews.

[4] The negroes had a cheerful facility in carrying " immense weights."

of genuine holidays, except three at Christmas [1] and one at New Year, Easter, and Whitsuntide, was probably a greater hardship than even the long duration of toil ; but in such a climate as that of the West Indies the slaves could not be always at work ; and we find a planter lamenting that they could not discover some sedentary occupation for their " many vacant hours in the rainy seasons." [2]

So far, the Abolitionists when they talked of over-work had a strong case ; but they spoiled it by asserting, or by letting it be inferred as a natural deduction from the driving system, that the exertion demanded of the slaves was not only prolonged but generally severe. The daily task assigned to them was more a matter of custom than of arbitrary exaction ; and, according to Stewart, it was " seldom more than they can go through with ease and without injury to their health." [3] They were not always dull and apathetic in the field. They might be merry and talkative or accompany every stroke of the hoe " with the chorus of contentment " ; [4] and whether or not they lacked " the fatigue which renders sweet the slumbers of the English labourer," [5] they had sufficient energy when released from toil to amuse them-

—Beckford, ii. 153. Lafcadio Hearn noticed in Martinique that young girls would walk right across the island and back before sunset under burdens difficult for a strong man to lift to his shoulder.—*Two Years in the French West Indies*, 1890, p. 392.

[1] " In England no idea of ' jolly Christmas ' can be imagined in comparison with the three days of Christmas in St. Vincent's. In every place is seen a gaiety of colours and dress and a corresponding gaiety of mind and spirits ; fun and finery are general."—Sir William Young's *Tour through the Windward Islands*, 1791–1792, in Edwards, iii. 259. The negroes danced in the proprietor's house, and Sir William opened the ball in a minuet with " black Phillis."

[2] Beckford, ii. 67, 152 ; Stephen, ii. 109, 118.

[3] *View of Jamaica*, p. 310. Stewart laid claim to " the most perfect impartiality," and with so much truth that Stephen is at pains to show (ii. 205) that he is not an Abolitionist.

[4] Beckford, ii. 2.

[5] Bridges, *A Voice from Jamaica in Reply to William Wilberforce*, 1823, p. 12.

keep up the field." Some estates in good seasons were actually independent of planting, and no estate, whatever its situation, depended exclusively on this source. Moreover, to a considerable extent, the plough was used, either as a substitute for holing, the plants being placed in the furrow and immediately covered in, or as a means of breaking up the land several months before it was holed. Many plantations, or parts of them, were indeed too stony, too precipitous, or too much cut up for draining to admit of the plough ; but in these cases it was usual for a planter to relieve his own negroes by having the work done by jobbers.[1]

Two cane-cuttings were deposited in each segment of a trench and were then frequently covered with manure. This was carried by the slaves in baskets on their heads, and the exertion might be great if the manure was wet or if the driver insisted on speed. Abolitionists naturally made the most of this grievance ; but they did not mention that this mode of manuring was far from general. A common practice in Jamaica was to manure the land by putting cattle on it for several months before it was planted and to move them from one enclosure to another. It not only saved labour but was more effective, and on flat land or gentle elevations was " universally adopted." [2]

It may be well at this stage to consider how it fared with the negro under industrial conditions so precarious as those of the " West Indian lottery." The Abolitionists had no difficulty in showing that he was liable to be overworked when there was a good market for sugar. In the case of free workmen high prices mean an increased demand for labour and a rise in its remunera-

---

[1] *Report of Commons' Committee on Slavery*, 1832 ; Edwards, i. 463 ; ii. 243–246 ; Beckford, ii. 190 ; Stewart, p. 103.

[2] Edwards, ii. 255 ; Beckford, ii. 190 ; Stephen, ii. 169. This writer claims to have based his indictment of slavery exclusively on the statements of its defenders ; but he uses these only where they tell against themselves. Ratoons, ploughing, and movable cattle-pens are good examples of his omissions.

tion ; but the slaves were not wage-earners ; and, as
their number could not now be increased by importation,
an extension of sugar-planting could be obtained—unless jobbers were employed, as indeed they often were
—only by severe or more protracted toil.[1] Prosperity,
with its attendant pressure, was, however, a rare phenomenon in this industry ; and the negro was certainly
exposed to greater dangers, if not to greater hardships,
when trade was dull than when it was brisk. A planter
who could not meet his obligations was liable to have
his slaves " levied upon " under a writ of execution.
" If an estate has no greater number of labouring hands
than are necessary to sustain it, the loss of twenty or
thirty, nay even of five or ten able slaves, must necessarily make the remaining number insufficient " ; and
not only did the produce decrease, but the slaves that
were left suffered " the diminution which must follow
their being overworked." [2] Depression of trade might,
however, bring other evils on the slave than the
bankruptcy or embarrassment of his owner. Unlike the
free workman, he could suffer neither dismissal nor
reduction of wages ; but his subsistence might be
endangered ; and this brings us to another question
raised by the Abolitionists—that of the sufficiency of
food.

In regard to the mode of providing for the slaves, the
colonies, with some exceptions, fall into two groups. In
Demerara and Barbados food was grown in the same
collective manner and under the same coercion as sugar ;
and this was a good system. It ensured food for negroes
too lazy to grow it in sufficient quantity for themselves,
and it occupied time which would otherwise have been
given to more arduous work on the plantations. Even
the Abolitionists admitted the *embonpoint* of the Barbadian slaves.[3] In general, however, the slaves were

[1] *Second Report of the Anti-Slavery Society*, 1825, pp. 21, 26.
[2] Long, i. 398.   [3] *Reporter*, iii. 427.

cards which had been sent by a negro as invitations to a supper party. Another instance of surprising affluence is thus described : " The historian is in the habit of seeing every day *a slave* who has slaves waiting upon him, horses and grooms at his command, whose table displays every luxury of the climate and whose clothes are fashioned and actually sent to him by a London tailor." [1] The dwellings of the slaves were more picturesque than substantial, and in general were poorly enough furnished ; but the planter who wished to make an impression on his guest had only to take him into the house of a head-man or artisan, where he was pretty sure to find four-post beds, sideboards, mirrors, and framed pictures, and might even be offered a bottle of wine. Though extravagance was a common characteristic of industrious negroes, they also showed many examples of thrift. We read of a proprietor in Jamaica hiring a mule-cart from one of his carpenters to convey his luggage to Kingston, and of another, when hard pressed for money, raising a loan among his slaves ; and a planter assures us that individual slaves had made him their banker for sums ranging from £50 to £300. These instances of well-being were apt to convey quite a wrong impression of the general condition of the slaves, and at one time the Abolitionists never liked to hear them mentioned ; but they cited them readily enough later when, on the eve of emancipation, they wished to show that the negro could be relied on to work for wages.[2]

Legally, as we have seen, the slave could not own property ; but the custom which secured to him his personal belongings gave him also a right to his cottage and to the garden in which he buried his dead. He was allowed to bequeath these as well as his other effects ; and a proprietor who had to provide immediate accom-

[1] Bridges, *Annals of Jamaica*, 1828, ii. 381.
[2] Stewart, pp. 267, 269 ; Whiteley, *Three Months in Jamaica*, 1833, p. 3 ; De la Beche, p. 48 ; *Quarterly Review* (1823), xxix. 492 ; Coleridge, p. 137 ; Hansard (1833), xviii. 489, 522, 523.

modation for a new gang says that he " hired some houses and seventeen rooms at one dollar a month for each room from the negroes upon my estate." [1]

It is rather remarkable that the indictment of slavery, in so far as it took account of industrial conditions, was based entirely on sugar ; and we are therefore prepared to find that the negroes who were employed in other occupations had a much easier lot. The product that came next in importance to sugar, though at a great distance, was coffee. We have seen that Parliament, in its anxiety that our colonies should live up to their reputation as " sugar islands," had stamped out in Jamaica a promising cultivation of indigo and cocoa ; and coffee, but for the open market in North America, must have suffered the same fate. In 1732 an almost prohibitive duty had been imposed on the importation of West Indian coffee ; but one of the many fiscal reforms of Pitt when he came into power in 1783 was to lower this duty from 1s. 6d. to 6½d. a pound ; and the industry at once revived. In 1791 more than a thousand coffee plantations in St. Domingue disappeared under the tidal wave of the French Revolution. For many years there was a shortage of supply ; and, though the price fell even below the former level during Napoleon's attempt to close the Continent to British commerce,[2] it recovered before the Peace of 1814. The export of coffee from Jamaica, which in 1784 was 2,000,000 lbs., had risen in 1820 to over 22,000,000 lbs.

The coffee-grower could count on a more equal and certain return and a larger average profit in proportion to his outlay than any other planter in the West Indies ; and the extension of his operations in Jamaica was both natural and beneficial. Two-thirds of the island were mountainous ; and the coffee-tree flourished best at an altitude of from 2000 to 3000 feet. Like the cocoa plant,

---

[1] Martin, Counter-Appeal to Wilberforce, 1823, p. 8 ; Edwards, ii. 163.
[2] It was said that 60,000 tons of coffee were lying unsaleable in London at 6d. a pound when the price on the Continent was 6s.

it was usually grown under shade. Hence it did not require much weeding ; and, being always kept low, it was easily pruned. Picking berries, mostly within reach, was a very different matter from cutting canes seven or eight inches thick. The harvest season, though it sometimes entailed night work, lasted only half as long as the sugar harvest ; and the curing of coffee—removing the outer pulp and separating the beans from their skins—involved no exertion comparable to what an old writer called " the sweat negociation of sugar." The air of a " coffee-walk " or, as it was sometimes called, a " coffee-mountain," was more wholesome for negroes as well as Europeans than that of the cane-lands ; and the work had a great advantage in method. The sugar-planter might marshal his " field-battalions " and flog them into action ; but the coffee-planter had to depend on individual effort. An acre and a half comprising about a thousand trees could be tended by one or two negroes ; and during the picking season the only incentive that could be applied was that of task-work. The Spaniards in Cuba set three tasks, to be done respectively before breakfast, dinner, and nightfall, so that the slave could gain only brief intervals of leisure ; but he was more fortunate in our colonies, where only one task was set—usually in a good season the picking of three baskets or 30 lbs. of berries. On some estates the negroes preferred to work continuously till their task was completed about half-past four in the afternoon ; and the more active or expert often contrived to finish two or even three hours earlier. Those who did not bring in the prescribed quantity were of course liable to be flogged, as indeed with little enough discrimination they too often were ; but most planters found it their interest to be lenient, as the slave, when hard pressed, was apt to pick unripe berries or to steal from the previous day's supply.[1]

[1] Edwards, ii. 339–358 ; De la Beche, p. 19 ; Stewart, pp. 118, 119 ; Bickell, p. 23 ; McDonnell, *Negro Slavery*, 1824, pp. 150, 157 ; Turnbull, *Cuba*, pp. 301, 308.

Cotton-growing, though precarious for the planter, was reckoned the most healthy, or the least unhealthy, occupation in the British West Indies ; but it was not of much importance and was confined mainly to the Bahamas, Barbados, and Demerara. Little or nothing appears to be known about the condition of the negroes on grazing farms or " cattle-pens " ; but their vital statistics placed them midway between coffee and cotton. The largest group of slaves next to the actual labourers on sugar-plantations was that of the " unattached " or personal slaves, whose condition depended on whether they belonged to rich or poor owners. All the authorities agree in drawing the sharpest possible distinction between the two sections of this class. The house slaves of wealthy planters, attorneys, and merchants were usually too numerous for the little they had to do and had an easy enough life, except for the cuffings and floggings which their carelessness, laziness,[1] and dishonesty often provoked. Closely associated with their masters, and frequently skilled mechanics, they always got the lion's share of manumissions, whether through favour or purchase. Very different was the lot of the one or two slaves belonging to a shopkeeper or artisan. They shared in the poverty of their owner and, more than any others of their unfortunate race, were over-worked, under-fed and ill-used. " Want and wretchedness are deeply stamped in every line of their persons ; and they may not inaptly be said to resemble the worn-out horse or the starved and jaded ass too often seen trembling under a heavy burden or reeling in an old tattered cart upon the roads of England." [2]

Those industries were always the easiest for the slaves in which they were least liable to be worked collectively under the coercion of a driver, and consequently they were best off in colonies where there was little or no mass

---

[1] Long (ii. 415) had seen them fall asleep, like the fat boy in *Pickwick*, whilst waiting at table. " At large dinners I have frequently observed them wholly engrossed by listening to any good stories and laughing loudly at them. If singing took place, it was impossible to keep them out of the room."—Martin, p. 17.   [2] Pinckard, i. 298.

production, such as the Bahamas and especially British
Honduras and the Bermudas. Slavery in the Bahamas
approximated to the type which had once prevailed in
Cuba and still survived in Porto Rico. The proprietors
were rather small farmers than planters, living frugally
on the produce of their lands and many of them quite
illiterate. They employed free blacks as well as slaves ;
and the latter, who numbered about 9000, participated
to some extent in the produce of their labour. For
example, in cutting wood, which was their hardest work,
they were allowed to retain and sell a portion of what
they brought in. In Honduras there were about 3000
slaves, and they were employed mainly in felling mahogany trees, cutting and hauling the logs, and floating
them down-stream. These gigantic trees were searched
for, much in the manner of game. They were widely
dispersed ; they could be detected only from a height by
the colour of their foliage ; and the leader of a gang,
whose function it was to locate and then to find them,
was known as " the huntsman." As other leaders were
apt to get on his track, he had to be cunning as well as
skilful. " Trucking " or carting timber was performed
at night owing to the great heat, and was thus described
in 1833 by Colonel Cockburn, the Superintendent of
British Honduras : " I have witnessed this species of
mahogany harvest home with the greatest pleasure ; a
more enlivening scene cannot be imagined. The roads
in many places over which the trucks must pass are cut
through luxuriant palm groves ; the cattle are of the
finest description, the men in the highest spirits, and the
whole scene most brilliantly illuminated by the numerous
pitch-pine torches with which it is accompanied. On
these, as on other occasions, the free labourer and slave
work together ; but, though with the gangs for months
together, it would be impossible to discover the one from
the other, unless they were separately pointed out."
Both classes had the same liberal allowance of salt pork,

flour, sugar, rum, and tobacco ; and on Saturday, which
was at their own disposal, the slaves worked for wages.
There were thus ample facilities for the purchase of
freedom ; and the annual rate of manumission was far
higher than in any other British colony. Though the
master was frequently isolated with his slaves " in the
depth of trackless forests," he never hesitated to trust
them with arms.

Conditions were even better in the Bermudas, where
about 5000 slaves were employed, for the most part as
ship-builders, fishermen, and seamen. They were usually
hired out, and were allowed to keep a third of their earn-
ings. During the American Revolution a number of
privateers were equipped in these islands. Many of the
negro sailors were taken prisoners, and the Governor
reported with pride that in the event of their release or
escape they invariably came back. In 1828 two vessels
arrived from the Bermudas at Belfast, and amongst their
crews were eleven slaves. They were judicially examined, but made no complaint against their owners or
captains, and, though all had been aware when they left
home that the completion of their voyage would make
them free, only three remained.[1]

Hitherto we have considered the condition of the
slaves mainly as it was affected by the industries in
which they were engaged. We now approach a more
important and more difficult question—that of the hardships and dangers to which from the mere fact of their
bondage they were all equally exposed. These, as we
shall see, were numerous enough ; but one of the most
serious and the first to attract attention was the liability
of slaves to be sold, apart from the estate, in payment
of their master's debts.[2] Long described it as " by far

---

[1] *Reporter*, i. 315 ; ii. 17, 44, 82, 326 ; Edwards, i. 516 ; iv. 235 ;
Henderson, *The British Settlement of Honduras*, 1811, pp. 61–72 ;
Bridges, *Annals of Jamaica*, ii. 497–505 ; P.P. 1835, vol. l.

[2] " The distress and terror among a gang of negroes, when the
marshall's deputy, with his dogs and other assistants, comes to levy in

the highest degree of cruelty annexed to their condition,"
and showed how injuriously they were affected by being
taken away from their homes and kindred and consigned
—as too often happened—to harsher masters and a less
congenial climate. " It is inconceivable," he wrote,
" what numbers have perished in consequence of the law
for recovery of debts." A slave, whose embarrassed or
bankrupt owner was unable to give security for his appearance at the end of forty days, was imprisoned. If
the gaol happened to be ruinous, as was commonly the
case, he was put in irons ; and, if not disposed of at the
first sale, as was also probable, he was detained till the
second. Certain merchants who petitioned against this
practice were said to have done themselves " infinite
honour " ; but their concern for the slaves seems to have
been limited to the fact " that during such unmerited
confinement they despond and contract diseases which
reduce their value at the day of sale very considerably." [1]

About 1730 some of the colonial legislatures were
prepared—so at least we are informed [2]—to remedy
this grievance by providing that slaves should be in-
separable from the estate, when the merchants of the
home country, and especially of Bristol, became alarmed
for the security of their capital and procured an Act of
Parliament which not only enabled them to take pre-
liminary proceedings in England for the recovery of their
debts, but allowed them for this purpose to seize " houses,
lands, negroes, and other hereditaments and real estates."
The " West Indian lottery " was then at the height of its
reputation ; but, forty years later, it had fallen so far
into disfavour with British capitalists that the sale of
slaves for debt in Jamaica was becoming more frequent
owing to " this door being shut against the new beginners

a large way, cannot be conceived by those who, happily for themselves,
have never been spectators of such scenes and can scarcely be described
by those who have witnessed them."—Bickell, p. 19.

[1] *Third Report on West Indian Justice*—P.P. 1826–1827, vol. xxiv.
[2] *Parl. Hist.* xxxiii. 834.

of settlements"; and Parliament, on the ground that sufficient loans could not be raised at home, encouraged foreigners to invest in the sugar colonies by relieving the subjects of a hostile state from their disability to sue in the British courts, and also provided that mortgages for the colonies should be valid when executed in this country at the colonial rate of interest.[1]

In 1797 Ellis assured the House of Commons that, when the Jamaica legislature consolidated its slave laws in 1792, it would have attached the negroes to the soil had not its humane intentions been frustrated by the British Act of 1732. A few weeks later, the repeal of this law was proposed and carried without opposition by Bryan Edwards—"a law which I blush to state was enacted by a British Parliament in favour of British creditors." But he soon had more reason to blush for the colonial legislatures; for, though he had expressed his confidence that they would speedily "redress the grievance and give sufficient security to the creditor without violating the rights of humanity," not one of them adopted this course, though it was pressed upon them in a circular despatch sent from the Colonial Office to all the Governors.[2] Considering indeed how few of the planters could afford to contract their means of raising money, we cannot but doubt whether the "humane intentions" attributed to the Assemblies in 1730 and 1792 had ever been seriously entertained.[3] The sale of slaves for debt continued, except in Tobago, till slavery was abolished in 1833;[4] but on large estates

---

[1] 5 Geo. II. 7; 13 Geo. III. c. 14; 14 Geo. III. c. 79; Long, *Jamaica*, i. 392, 399; ii. 435.

[2] *Parl. Hist.* xxxiii. 263, 831–834; Wilberforce's *Appeal*, pp. 29, 30.

[3] In the *Report on West Indian Justice*, which has been already cited, reform was deprecated as unsuitable to a state of things dependent on "the support of credit and the security of borrowed capital."

[4] It is a serious error in Dr. Cunningham's *Growth of English Industry and Commerce* (ii. 478) that he supposes the reform in question to have been effected.

it was not common and was seldom aggravated by the separation of families.[1]

We have seen that the power of the slave-owner was much less restrained by law in the British than in the Spanish colonies; but in most of the former attempts had been made in recent years to remove this reproach; and the only colony in which no concession, or practically none, had been made to the spirit of the age was Barbados. Too much stress was laid by the Abolitionists on the survival of barbarous laws, which were to be found in England as well as in the West Indies, and in both cases were mostly obsolete; but at the beginning of the nineteenth century an Act was not only unrepealed but tragically operative in Barbados which provided that, " if any master kills or maims his slave in punishing him or in ordering him to be punished," no fine should be imposed; " but, if any man of wantonness or only of bloodymindedness or cruel intention kill a negro or other slave," he should pay £15 currency or £11 4s. sterling. In 1804 several negroes were murdered; but Lord Seaforth, the Governor and himself a slave-owner, met with great opposition when he sought to have the law altered —" so horribly absurd are the prejudices of the people." The Bill he had recommended was thrown out by the Assembly; and he cannot have been satisfied with the shape in which it passed next year; for the death penalty was to be incurred only by those who should murder a slave not only wilfully—the usual term—but " maliciously, wantonly and without provocation,"[2] and the witnesses were to be not only free persons but whites.[3]

In 1822 the Government appointed two Commissioners to inquire into the administration of justice in the West Indies; and Barbados figured, little to its advantage, in the first Report, which was drawn up by

---

[1] Bickell, p. 18; M'Queen, *The West India Colonies*, 1824, p. 271.

[2] " Wantonly and without provocation " was omitted when the Act was renewed in 1817.　　　　[3] Wilberforce's *Appeal*, pp. 40–46.

Mr. Dwarris, the surviving Commissioner, in 1825. The Chief Justice of the colony admitted that he had not been "bred to the profession" and was no lawyer;[1] and he might have said the same of all the legal officials except the Attorney-General. He also admitted that there were sixty-seven laws in manuscript, and "in consequence they knew nothing about them"; but the Commissioners soon satisfied themselves that the unprinted Acts "kept in offices" were no fewer than 247.[2] Dwarris, who had a sugar-estate in Jamaica, was not disposed to expect much in the way of protection for the slaves; but he was evidently shocked to find that, except for the recent Act as to murder, the power of the master was absolutely untrammelled. "No man or set of men has legal power to call him to account for working his slave as long as he likes, for whipping him as much as he pleases; for chaining, for starving him." The master, in fact, was more privileged than the magistrate, who could inflict only a certain number of stripes. The slave was not tried, as in some other colonies, by a jury of whites, but by two Justices of the Peace and three freeholders who, if unanimous, could pass sentence of death, and, unless the *owner* appealed, could carry it out. The charge was not in writing and, though a record of the proceedings was supposed to be kept by the magistrates, it was not sent to any public office. No time was lost in executing the prisoner, who was suspended on the nearest tree unless, as often happened, the proprietor of the ground was present and objected. "In such case the miserable culprit is dragged from tree to tree, from

---

[1] This anomaly continued till 1837.

[2] Another characteristic feature of Barbados was that one and the same building housed the legislature, law courts, and gaol. It was a happy arrangement for the prisoners, who beguiled their enforced leisure by attending the debates.—Coleridge, pp. 48, 296. What with its composite legislature and gaol, its amateur lawyers, its white men living on the charity of slaves and white women taking in their washing, it must be admitted that "Little England" was not quite worthy of its name.

estate to estate ; and in one case of then recent occurrence the constable was at last forced to throw the exhausted sufferer off the town bridge, securing the rope
by a lamp-post." The Commissioner consoled himself
with the reflection that slaves were too valuable to be
readily prosecuted or condemned ; that they were well-
treated in general, and lived only in the present. " The
improvident negro, far from pining in misery, dances
and sleeps, trifles and dreams away life, thoughtless,
careless, and happily ignorant of his unprotected
condition." [1]

We shall see something later of the measures taken
in other colonies to bring the slaves under legal protection. If the colonists were much too proud of their
meliorating laws, the Abolitionists treated them with too
great contempt. Some of the provisions were valuable
and effectual, such as those which gave the slaves
twenty-six days in the year instead of seventeen for the
cultivation of their grounds and prohibited Sunday work
in the mills. But in matters less open to observation
they achieved little and merited the criticism of Burke
that they were destitute of " an executory principle."
Restrictions, which the good master resented as a reflection on his humanity or as diminishing in some
measure the impassable gulf between blacks and whites,
were evaded without scruple by those whose excesses
they were meant to restrain ; and a curious example
of this perversity is mentioned by Dwarris. In some
of the colonies an Act was passed restraining overseers
from giving more than ten lashes. Ten accordingly
were given, but, after a short interval, were followed by
more. It was then enacted that only ten lashes should
be given for the same offence, and this was met by

---

[1] P.P., 1825, vol. xv. Dwarris had not been long in Barbados when
" a dreadful case " occurred—the whipping of a slave to death. The
coroner's jury met and adjourned for three days, during which the
criminal, who was " a gentleman of property and influence," escaped,
" as must have been intended."—Samuel Parr's *Works*, 1828, viii. 28.

punishing for one offence and then alleging another. Hence another Act that only ten lashes should be given on the same day, which also failed, because the severity of the punishment depended much less on " the quantum of blows than the degree of force." And finally a fourth Act was passed that no new flogging should be inflicted till the victim had recovered from the effects of the last. It could seldom be necessary, however, to render even such mock homage to the law so long as the only persons likely to witness its violation were precluded from giving evidence. We have seen that the testimony of slaves was allowed only for and against each other ; and it was admitted even by so complacent a slave-owner as Sir William Young that the law of evidence " covered the most guilty European with impunity." [1] It would have been more correct to say that this impunity extended to every free person, whether white or coloured. Oaths, it was said, could not bind people incapable of understanding their religious character ; and many of the whites believed that they would soon be exterminated if they allowed slave evidence to be used against them before they had had " time to build up the sacred wall of Christianity between ourselves and an engine so powerful." [2] Their fears may well seem absurd when we remember that slaves were competent witnesses in courts-martial, and that even under the proposed reform a white person would still be tried by a judge and jury of his own colour, who, though bound not to reject slave evidence, would be little disposed to believe it ; and one at least of the planters was sufficiently in sympathy with the slaves to predict that it would one day be a wonder even in the West Indies " that the shadow and mockery of justice should have been held out to them, while an insuperable bar was placed between them and the reality." [3]

[1] Wilberforce, *Appeal*, p. 12.
[2] Bridges, *A Voice from Jamaica*, p. 20.   [3] Stewart, p. 226.

In Jamaica the justices and vestry of each parish were constituted a Council of Protection for the negroes, and the cruel treatment of a slave was punished with a fine of £100 currency or imprisonment for twelve months, whilst " in atrocious cases " the victim might be set free. But it was almost impossible to prove an outrage which did not amount to mutilation or had not been witnessed by a white or other free person ; and, groundless accusations being severely discouraged,[1] it was " three to one " that the slave who complained of a flogging got another. That cases of ill-treatment were fully investigated in " the grand courts," or even before a bench of justices, was not denied ; but too often they were slighted or hushed up by the local magistrates. The usual remedy for continued ill-usage was flight, and scores of runaway slaves were constantly advertised in the Jamaica newspapers. Many of them were branded —a practice which did not wholly cease with the slave trade.[2]

On the whole, we must conclude that actually in Barbados and practically elsewhere the slaves in anything short of murder were at the absolute disposal of their owners ; and the question of their treatment thus resolves itself into a personal equation depending on the provocation given on one side and the forbearance exercised on the other. It would be unjust as well as ungenerous to blame the negroes for vices which were the natural outcome of their degraded condition ; but we cannot overlook this point in considering their liability to punishment. They were " generally sad thieves." Their depredations were a greater trial to the decrepit watchmen than those of rats or cattle ; thousands of mules and oxen were lost every year in Jamaica owing

[1] This was much complained of by the Abolitionists, but, without some restraint on appeals, it is difficult to see how the negroes could have been kept to their work. Even as it was, they sometimes went off *en masse* to complain.—Barclay, p. 83.

[2] Bickell, pp. 31, 37–47, 199–201.

to the dishonesty of their keepers;[1] and the pilfering of sugar during harvest, apart from the legitimate consumption, was estimated at fully a tenth of the crop.[2] For this indeed the planters were largely responsible. They refused to sell sugar to the islanders, reserving it all for export; but, unable or unwilling to enforce this restriction, they allowed it to be sold in the negro market, where it was " all known to be stolen sugar."[3] There was as much thieving indoors as outside. Young bookkeepers were often imposed upon by the negroes, " supposing their humility and accommodating manners to be accompanied by innocency of heart." They arrived " with every article of use or comfort for a West India climate," and in a month or two had lost almost their whole outfit.[4] Not many of the planters would have agreed with Thomas Cooper, a Unitarian missionary, that the negroes were incapable of affection, fidelity, or gratitude; but few would have questioned his enumeration of their demerits—" low cunning and contempt of truth, a determined resolution to thieve, and the greatest aversion to every species of labour."[5] The last and least heinous of these defects was emphasised by another observer who described it as " indolence engrafted upon an obdurate and inflexible perverseness."[6]

One may safely assume that owners and overseers did not behave too well under this perpetual provocation —that, whatever kindness and patience may have been shown, there was also harshness and brutality; but it is

[1] Roughley, p. 85.

[2] De la Beche, p. 8. Beckford (ii. 79) remarks incidentally that, if a hogshead of sugar left the plantation full, it had a better chance of arriving so at the port. Magic was more effective than traps or spring-guns in protecting the gardens of the negroes, but lost its efficacy when applied to those of the whites.—Stewart, p. 279.

[3] Cooper, *Facts illustrative of the Condition of the Slaves*, 1824, p. 12.

[4] Williamson, i. 248.

[5] Cooper, p. 14. For similar evidence from other missionaries see Watson's *Defence of the Wesleyan Methodist Missions*, 1817, pp. 20–22. " Lying, theft, and sloth are habitual."   [6] Pinckard, i. 354.

difficult to say in what proportion these qualities were combined in the average planter. Slave-ships and sugar-plantations were long regarded in Britain as the main-stay of our colonial dominion ; but the public had no great opinion of those by whom they were managed. When Stephen in 1824 described British slavery as " pre-eminently harsh, uniting in itself every species of op-pression that has elsewhere existed under the sun, and with many aggravations as much beyond example as excuse," [1] we are apt to dismiss such a statement as idle words generated by the heat of controversy in an excited pamphleteer ; but exactly the same assertion was made by Burke [2] in 1757, and almost the same—the comparison being limited to European nations—by Dean Tucker [3] in 1785. " We are so fond of depreciating our own colonies," wrote Long, " that we paint our planters in the most bloody colours and represent their slaves as the most ill-treated and miserable of mankind " ; and he went on to say that, just as we should ridicule the foreigner who, because outrages occurred in England, should charge the whole people with being " a most bloody, inhuman and unfeeling race," so it was equally absurd to consider the occasional ill-treatment of a slave as indicating the general practice.[4] Whatever reason there may have been for this protest in 1774, it must have been much more needed later, when every crime that came to light on a plantation was blazoned in the Abolitionist press. There was, however, a difference between the two cases which Long overlooked. If out-rages occurred in England in spite of all the means avail-able for detecting, exposing, and punishing them, how much more, in the absence of such facilities, were they likely to occur in the West Indies ? Moreover in Eng-land there was no disposition to shield or extenuate such

[1] West India Slavery, i. 435.   [2] European Settlements, ii. 148.
[3] Quoted by Lecky, History of England, Cabinet edition, vii. 362.
[4] History of Jamaica, ii. 441, 442.

crimes, whereas in the colonies, though a cruel slave-owner might be looked at askance or even shunned by his neighbours, it was considered prejudicial to discipline that he should be exposed and punished. Again, it was a common argument to contrast the mild treatment of the slaves after 1807 with the more rigorous discipline which had been necessary when Koromantis and other half-savages were being constantly imported; but in those earlier days the imputation of cruelty or even harshness had invariably been repelled.[1] Naval officers, who had enjoyed colonial hospitality, and who thought that our maritime supremacy was bound up with the slave trade, were always ready to say a good word for the planters. Rodney, when examined by a Committee of the Privy Council in 1788, said he had been in all the islands, had often observed the treatment of the negroes, and could affirm that he " never knew the least cruelty inflicted on them " ;[2] and Admiral Barrington went so far as to say that " the slaves appeared to him so happy that he often wished himself in their situation." [3] In 1807 Lord St. Vincent told the House of Lords from his own experience that " the West India islands formed Paradise itself to the negroes in comparison with their native country." [4]

There was probably even less truth in these extravagant assertions than in the laboured and envenomed denunciations of Stephen. But we cannot pass lightly over the judgment of one who scorned to utter a " syllable " in defence of slavery and was to advocate gradual emancipation long before Buxton. " From much and careful observation," wrote Dr. Pinckard in 1796, " I am authorised to remark that the planters in general are humane and merciful." [5] We have also the striking, if not paradoxical, fact that the slavery of the

---

[1] " There has never been any present tense for cruelty in the statements of the planters and their friends."—*Reporter*, i. 192.

[2] Mundy, *Life of Lord Rodney*, ii. 426.   [3] *Reporter*, i. 257.

[4] Hansard (1807), viii. 669.   [5] *Notes on the West Indies*, ii. 459.

negroes, hard and degrading as it was, had not injured
but improved their intellectual and physical condition.
Captain Elliot was familiar with the west coast of Africa
as well as with the West Indies. He was not likely to
underrate the hardships of the slaves, being their Protector [1] in British Guiana ; and in an official report of
1832 he stated that " the difference between the full-
grown man at the period of his deportation from the
coast of Guinea and the slave of a like age born in the
West Indies affords a convincing and astonishing proof
of the capacity of this people for improvement." [2]   And
lastly we shall find that when the slaves were more or
less freed in 1834, their conduct was far from justifying
the fear of that great venture which even the Abolitionists had entertained. [3]

At the outset of this inquiry the moral and social condition of the slaves was represented as utterly degraded ;
but there is nothing in this view to affect the question
of their treatment—the question whether, though regarded as little better than beasts of burden, they were
as a rule well or ill-used ; and the reader may satisfy
himself on this point by turning to that vigorous and
piquant writer, the historian of Jamaica. Long had so
poor an opinion of the negro that he considered him as
closely allied to the orang-outang—merely " a different
species of the same genus " ; and yet he anticipated
some of the meliorating measures which were to be
proposed, half a century later, by the British Government. [4] The slave-owners had not the good sense to
adopt his suggestions ; but there is some evidence that

[1] We shall find that this office was established in the Crown colonies
in 1824.

[2] *Commons' Report on Slavery*, 1832, Appendix.

[3] " If, indeed, they had been subjected to a despotism so unmitigated
as that which they have been described to have borne through so
lengthened a period of misery, is it, my Lords, I ask, in human nature
that they could have been so soon qualified to receive their emancipation ? "—Bishop Phillpotts in Hansard (1838), xlii. 1.

[4] *History of Jamaica*, ii. 357, 491.

they shared his kindly, though contemptuous, spirit. No importance need be attached to the fact that in every colony there were slaves—and many of them— who disavowed all desire for freedom. This merely showed that they happened to have good masters and were so demoralised by servitude that they could not face the prospect of earning their own living and supporting themselves when sick or infirm. Far more significant is another fact emphasised by Long himself and one which surprised every visitor in our islands. " A planter smiles with disdain to hear himself calumniated for tyrannical behaviour to his negroes. He would wish the defamer might be present to observe with what freedom and confidence they address him, not with the abject prostration of real slaves, but as their common friend and father." [1] It would be unfair not to mention in this connexion a custom creditable to the good nature of the planters. When a negro had committed some offence, he frequently sought the good offices of a neighbouring overseer, who either gave him a letter or in more serious cases returned with him. It seems to have been a point of honour not to refuse the request, even at the cost of a troublesome journey, and the intercession was almost invariably successful.[2] Again, it was highly creditable to the negroes that in the three more or less serious revolts from 1807 to 1833 none, or almost none, of the whites were murdered ; but the immunity of the latter affords at least a presumption that their treatment of the slaves had not been cruel.

If we admit on these grounds the comparative humanity of the planters, we have to ask ourselves why it was that they did not remove the blemishes which disfigured their system of management. In regard to the duration of toil, they probably reflected that the

---

[1] *History of Jamaica*, ii. 270.
[2] Barclay, p. 8 ; confirmed by Williamson, ii. 225, Lewis, p. 60, and Hansard (1818), xxxviii. 309.

hours of work in Britain, where labour was much more efficient, were almost as long, and as to night work, it was always represented as unavoidable. But how is one to explain the denial, or practical denial, of a weekly day of rest ? We have seen that it was an exaggeration to say that the slaves must work for themselves on Sunday or starve. They could have spent the day in repose, as many of them spent it in dancing and dissipation, but only at the cost of dispensing with all but the bare necessaries of life.[1] Stewart, whilst lamenting the proneness of the slaves to abuse their Sunday leisure, acknowledged it to be " just that they should have one day a week to themselves for labour and another for rest." But here, as in the case of sale for debt, we are confronted with the obstacle that sugar-planting was dependent on borrowed capital. According to Stewart, an average estate yielding 200 hogsheads would bring in a net income of £1200 currency ; but if the proprietor had to pay the usual interest on a loan of £10,000, his income would be reduced to £600—" barely sufficient to enable him to keep up a decent establishment " ; and, if he had to surrender twenty-six more working days in the year—that is, one a week instead of one a fortnight—his income would suffer a further diminution of £364. But this calculation, fantastic in itself,[2] took no account of a probable improvement in the quality of labour ; and in point of fact the Jewish planters, who were at least as flourishing as their neighbours, gave their slaves every Saturday in addition to Sunday.[3]

The worst feature of a sugar-plantation was, of course, its discipline, which consisted mainly in the use of the whip both as a stimulus to labour and as a punishment. The negro driver was not only empowered to " touch up " the members of his gang, but for such offences as

[1] Hansard (1826), xv. 1336.
[2] It was based, not on the loss of twenty-six days' labour, but on the cost of replacing it by the hire of jobbers.—*View of Jamaica*, p. 345.
[3] Long, ii. 491.

coming late to work or persistent idleness could inflict as
many as ten lashes ; and one does not need to be told
that such a power in such hands was often grossly abused.
Negroes born in slavery being more docile than imported
Africans, the driving system was somewhat relaxed
after the abolition of the slave trade ; but Charles Ellis,
chairman of the West Indian Committee in London,
must have regretted, in view of subsequent disclosures,
that in 1823 he had assured the House of Commons that
the whip in Jamaica was merely a relic of barbarism and
survived " more as a badge of authority than as an
instrument of correction." [1] On some estates the whip
was little used, on others it was not even carried ; but
these were exceptional cases ; and Cooper, after living
for three years in the midst of sugar-plantations, could
say as late as 1824 that all the negroes he had seen in
the field were " as completely urged on to their duty by
the lash as any team of horses that runs in the mail." [2]
Bickell, an Anglican curate, and by no means a fanatical
Abolitionist, gives much the same account ; and he
attributed the sufferings of the slaves to the dullness and
apathy produced by continuity, if not intensity, of toil.
" This constant work, work, work is a principal cause
of one of the greatest hardships in West Indian slavery—I
mean the constant use of the whip ; for, seeing that work
is their only portion, they are inclined to be indolent."
He even thought that, with a very natural perversity,
they " take care not to put forth all their strength." [3]

Flogging was authorised by the criminal law of England ; [4] but the punishment could, of course, be inflicted
only after trial and conviction.   It was practised with

[1] Hansard (1823), ix. 304.　　　[2] *Facts*, etc., p. 48.
[3] *The West Indies as they are*, p. 12.   Overwork led to theft as well
as indolence.   Negroes " too improvident to work for themselves on
holidays " (!) naturally stole from the provision grounds of their
neighbours.—*Quarterly Review* (1823), xxix. 489.
[4] It was not till 1822 that the whipping of women was abolished in
England ; and during the seven years, 1816–1822, 6959 persons were
flogged.

far greater severity in the army and navy than on sugar-
plantations ; but soldiers could be flogged only on the
sentence of a court-martial ; and, though the captain
of a warship could order on his own responsibility as
many as forty-eight lashes, he had at least to make a
quarterly return of his punishments to the Admiralty.
No such restrictions, not even that of publicity, existed
in the West Indies ; and chastisements ordered by the
overseer, whose limit in Jamaica was thirty-nine lashes,
were a grievous addition to the discipline of the field.
It ought, of course, to be remembered that the slaves
comprised what in any other community would have
been called a criminal class, that the master's jurisdiction
supplanted to a large extent that of the magistrate, and
that flogging was often the penalty of crimes which in
this country would have been punished with transportation or death. We are told that to the greater number
of the slaves severe punishment was " in a manner unknown " ;[1] but we are also told that, when slaves were
seen uncovered in hot weather, they almost always
showed traces of laceration ;[2] and both statements may
" in a manner " be true ; for the lowest type of negro
had the least sense of decency ; and the whip was used
often enough on some of this class to produce " a cal-
losity of the parts " which rendered " its further application of little avail."[3] If the planters had been careful
of their reputation at home, they would have restrained
the cracking as well as the infliction of the whip ; but

[1] *Quarterly Review* (1823), xxix. 489.

[2] *Negro Slavery* (1823), pp. 50, 64. Sir William Young, a non-
resident proprietor, when he visited his estates, made a point of looking
at the backs of his negroes whenever he found them stripped to the
waist. His overseers had not informed him that negroes, unlike
soldiers, were usually flogged, as Stephen (i. 51) delicately puts it, " only
on a part of the frame from the fleshy texture of which the incisions,
however torturous, are not likely to be fatal."

[3] " A bad subject in good health will take any number of lashes, as
the registers of every regiment in the service will prove."—Jeremie,
Four Essays on Colonial Slavery, 1831, p. 85.

it was frequently used in this way, not only to accelerate man and beast, but even, in preference to bells or conch shells, to summon the negroes to their work ; and strangers were horrified by " the frightful sound which reaches our ears every minute in passing through estates by the crack of the lash." [1] Nothing could be done without this instrument. " If a boy was sent to drive chickens," said an ex-governor of Jamaica, " the first thing he did was to make a whip." [2]

All this does not help us to understand how the slave could approach his master with a confidence and familiarity [3] which, as we shall see, were a complete contrast to his attitude in the United States ; and, distasteful as it is to minimise the horrors of slavery, one is forced to conclude that there must have been more good masters, or fewer very bad masters, than the Abolitionists were willing to admit. The latter at this period could not fail to attract an attention disproportionate to their number. On a well-managed estate the headdriver was usually an old negro who had been promoted for intelligence and good conduct ; and, as the following description shows, he was by no means a mere whipperup of recalcitrant slaves. " Go to a field of labourers in Jamaica and you will see a venerable old man standing behind them, leaning over his staff and engaged in conversation with some one of the gang, among whom as many jokes are passed . . . and as much noisy mirth prevails as in a field of labourers in the mother country ; generally, indeed, much more." [4] Again, the average

---

[1] Williamson, ii. 223.   [2] *Reporter*, v. 481.

[3] Blacks and whites exchanged salutations when they met ; in the churches they often communicated indiscriminately ; and a planter, on entering his house, might find a slave seated beside his wife. " The slaves will come up with a degree of frankness and boldness that would astonish you."—*Commons' Report on Slavery*, 1832.

[4] Barclay, p. 41. I put this aside as a fanciful picture, till I found it confirmed by Roughley (p. 81), who says that the head-driver was too often " an elderly or middle-aged negro," and implies that he was inclined to tolerate " freedoms " from those under him.

negro, who dreaded being debarred from his evening amusements, preferred flogging to imprisonment [1]—a fact which seems to show that the floggings, as one would expect, were rather frequent than severe.[2] Even the maximum of thirty-nine lashes was not enough to overcome this preference ; for a West Indian proprietor stated in Parliament that he had sometimes been solicited to use his influence with the master of a slave to have this punishment substituted for solitary confinement or detention in the stocks.[3]

As any master could safely maltreat his slave so long as he took care not to be seen by a free person, we may take it for granted that such violations of the law did occur in all the colonies—not to mention Barbados, where there was no law ; but admittedly the slaves were better protected by public opinion in Jamaica than in the smaller islands. To these we must turn if we wish to see the British slave-owner at his worst ; and the reader must have a very poor opinion of our countrymen if he is not astonished to find how bad he could be.

Little more than a century ago there was living in Tortola a certain Hon. Arthur Hodge, member of His Majesty's Council for the Virgin Islands, " a man of liberal education and of the most polished manners," whose treatment of his slaves was appalling. How many murders he had perpetrated or superintended was never known ; but the estimate of his manager was that in three years he caused at least sixty men, women, and children to be flogged or otherwise tortured to death. In 1811 he was tried and convicted on the first of several charges ; but the jury recommended him to mercy ; and

[1] " They cannot bear it, and the memory of it seems to make a lasting impression upon their minds, while the lash makes none but upon their skins."—Lewis, p. 173.

[2] " For this the need of the slave's return to work is his security." —P.P. 1814–1815, vol. vii.

[3] Hansard (1818), xxxviii. 294.

so great was the indignation aroused by the execution
of a white man for the murder of his own slave that the
Governor thought it necessary to proclaim martial law,
to call out the militia, and to obtain the assistance of a
frigate. About the same time another ruffian was
making the first of two remarkable appearances in Nevis.
This was Edward Huggins, a sugar planter who had
amassed a large fortune by acting on the maxim that
it was cheaper to buy negroes than to breed them.
Several of his slaves were supposed to have been
murdered, and two to have committed suicide. The
legislature of the Leeward Islands had passed an Act in
1798 prohibiting night-work except during crop. But
Huggins made his slaves carry out manure to the cane-
fields by moonlight, and this caused frequent desertions.
The same Act which forbade night-work also provided
against the cruel punishment of slaves ; but Huggins
cared as little for the one provision as for the other ;
and in 1810, disdaining to avail himself of the privacy
of his plantation, he marched thirty-two of his slaves
through the streets of Charlestown to the market-place
and there, in view of several magistrates, had them
mercilessly flogged.[1] He was tried before a packed jury,
including his own overseer and the overseer of his son-
in-law, and was acquitted. For at least sixteen years
Huggins had been notorious for cruelty, and seven years
later, in 1817, he was again prosecuted—this time for
giving a hundred lashes each to two boys accused of
receiving a stolen pair of stockings, and thirty and
twenty lashes in mere spite to two girls, and was again
acquitted. The question whether the lord of a plantation had a divine right to govern or misgovern his black
subjects was hotly debated in Nevis ; but Huggins
was a duellist and a marksman and nobody could

---

[1] In Dominica, in 1817, a coloured proprietor, resenting the acquittal
of some of his slaves on a charge of mutiny, had them as publicly,
though less severely, flogged.—Hansard (1818), xxxviii. 298–303.

meddle with him without being prepared to receive a challenge.[1]

The Briton, unlike the Spaniard, was practically an absolute ruler of slaves ; and, just as despotic kings thought it impious that one of their sacred order, however bad, should be made amenable to law, so the average British slave-owner demanded a similar immunity for his fellows. We have seen that in the case of Hodge, atrocious as it was, public opinion in Tortola resented his execution ; and a similar spirit manifested itself later in the Bahamas. "General kindness to their slaves" may or may not have been characteristic of Mr. and Mrs. Moss ; but, if so, it underwent a surprising lapse in 1826. A girl, one of their house staff, was kept in the stocks for seventeen days. She was flogged five or six times, and, in order to keep her awake, red pepper was rubbed in her eyes. When taken out, she was again flogged, though suffering from a fever then prevalent, and was sent to field-work ; and, soon after the driver had taken upon himself to administer a final flogging, she died. The perpetrators of this enormity were fined and imprisoned for five months ; but "the most respectable persons in the place" made a point of visiting them in gaol, and, when the husband was released, they entertained him to a public dinner. Even the Governor, General Grant, whose humanity was afterwards proved in Trinidad, was induced to intercede for "the unfortunate Helen and Henry Moss."[2]

Three years later, a case of cruelty occurred in Jamaica, which, owing to the office and prominence of the accused, made a great sensation. One of the colonial clergymen at this period was the Rev. R. W. Bridges, who had endeared himself to the planters by publishing a pamphlet in reply to Wilberforce ; and on May 11,

---

[1] *Fifth Report of African Institution* ; Hansard (1818), xxxviii. 304–317 ; Edwards, iv. 455–460.

[2] Hansard (1830), xxv. 1186–1189, 1213.

1829, the magistrates of St. Ann's parish assembled in a so-called Council of Protection[1] to hear a complaint brought against their rector by his cook, Kitty Hylton. In the story as told by the girl there was probably a good deal of exaggeration; but more than enough of it was fully corroborated and not denied. It appeared that on April 2 Bridges had reason to reprimand her for a dinner so "shamefully cooked" that part of it had to be sent away. Next day he found that she had killed a turkey. She pleaded that she had been told to kill it, but Bridges denied this and was furiously incensed. He violently struck and kicked her and then had her flogged with bamboo rods. She escaped during the night and was seen by several persons in the neighbourhood, four of whom testified to her disfigured as well as lacerated condition; and the magistrate to whom she had appealed said that she had been switched from the nape of the neck to her posteriors, that her face and thighs were dreadfully bruised, and that he had "never seen anything so severe of the kind." Nothing could have been fairer or more thorough than the investigation, and the only disappointing feature was its result— "carried by a majority of 13 to 4 against the prosecution." The matter was taken up by the Colonial Office on information supplied by the Anti-Slavery Society; and, after more than a year had elapsed, Bridges was indicted by the Attorney-General, when, as might have been anticipated, the grand jury threw out the bill.[2]

Good masters contribute as little to the justification of slavery as bad masters to its condemnation; but they are less unpleasant to contemplate; and we are fortunate in being able to turn for this purpose to the journal of "wonder-working Lewis," as Byron called him, the author of romances, plays, and poems which, though now forgotten, had a great vogue in their day. His reputation had been established by "The Monk,"

[1] See p. 86. [2] *Reporter*, iii. 377; iv. 140–143.

which appeared when he was no more than twenty years
of age. On the death of his father in 1812 Lewis had
inherited two large estates—Cornwall and Hordley—
in Jamaica. He had every reason to believe that these
were in good hands; but he wished to see for himself
the condition of his slaves, and left England to visit them
in November 1815. As it happened, the Cornwall estate
was then well managed; but, a few years earlier, as
Lewis was yet to learn, it had been reduced to such a
condition—under an absentee attorney who was supposed to be resident—that the negroes had one and all
absconded and got rid of their brutal overseer by com-
plaining of him to a magistrate. His feelings on landing
at the town of Black River were those of agreeable surprise. It was New Year's Day and a general holiday,
and he " never saw so many people who appeared to be
so unaffectedly happy." Negroes were everywhere, not
drunken or quarrelsome, but laughing, singing, and
dancing and displaying their fine clothes; and almost
every white man he met put to him the same question :
What would Wilberforce think if he could see this scene ?
When he reached Cornwall, the pleasantness of this
first impression was by no means diminished. " I never
witnessed on the stage a scene so picturesque as a negro
village." The dwellings were two-roomed huts, wattled
and plastered without and white-washed within, and
had "a hermitage-like appearance," each standing in
its own umbrageous garden ; and the whole village was
" intersected by lanes bordered with all kinds of sweet-
smelling and flowering plants."[1] The negroes kept pigs
and poultry, and had, of course, allotments on which they
grew provisions both for their own support and for sale.
They appeared to be healthy and contented, addressed
their owner with much more familiarity than would
have been used by an English farmer to his squire, and

[1] See Pinckard, i. 199, for the description of a similar "negro-yard"
in Barbados, and also Coleridge, p. 221.

performed their tasks in so gay and unconcerned a fashion that " I can hardly persuade myself that it is really work they are about."

Lewis at first thought it almost worth the sacrifice he had made in leaving home to be surrounded by such light-hearted creatures as the negroes ; but in a few weeks he had begun to " doubt whether they are the greatest thieves or liars," and found them most " perverse." They had long been praying for a sight of their master and had welcomed him with transports of joy ; but less and less sugar had been made since his arrival and the quantity purloined was " enormous." And on some neighbouring estates they had a " vile trick of poisoning people." Yet he was more amused than seriously annoyed at the conjunction of effusive gratitude and devotion with persistent misdoing. " I verily believe that every negro on the estate is extremely anxious that all should do their full duty except himself." At all events he continued to practise the utmost humanity and forbearance ; and before leaving Jamaica on April 1, 1816, he had digested his principles of management into a code. Labour was to be exempt from the lash. Punishments were to be entered in a register and a copy given to the delinquent lest he should wish to complain. Striking or cuffing was forbidden ; and two book-keepers accused of this offence had already been dismissed. The negroes were to have every Saturday for the cultivation of their grounds ; and Sunday, so far as the public markets would permit, was to be a day of relaxation.

Many non-resident proprietors had made rules for the management of their slaves, and some had come out to enforce them ; but Lewis was perhaps the only one of their number who not only went to the West Indies for this purpose, but returned, after a brief interval, to see that his regulations were observed. He stayed only a year and five months in England ; and in January

1818, after a long and perilous voyage, he was again on
the Cornwall estate. To his great relief he found that
not one of the negroes had even an imaginary grievance.
Few of them had been flogged, and these only for " absolute crimes " ; and, despite the mildness of their treatment, they had attained to their old standard of work.
But population under the most favourable conditions
was still decreasing ; and the attempt to introduce
ploughing had been abandoned owing rather to the
obstinacy than to the awkwardness of the few labourers
required, who had broken one plough after another and
" ruined beast after beast." On this occasion Lewis
found time to visit his other and distant estate of
Hordley ; and here, instead of the paradise he had been
led to expect, he found " a perfect hell." Eight petty
tyrants had almost excited a revolt. " All the blacks
accused all the whites ; all the whites accused all the
blacks ; and, as far as I could make out, both parties
were extremely in the right." This discovery must
have heightened the regret with which he parted
from the wayward but lovable negroes of Cornwall.
" I only wish that in my future dealings with white
persons, whether in Jamaica or out of it, I could but
meet with half so much gratitude, affection and good-
will." [1]

The condition of Hordley and the previous condition
of Cornwall may lead one to suppose that there could be
no security for the good management of an estate without the residence or occasional presence of its proprietor ;
but those absentee proprietors—many of them nobles
and wealthy commoners—who held their estates by
inheritance, and not by purchase or mortgage, were the
best of their class, and so, it may be assumed, were the

[1] *Journal, passim.* Lewis fell a victim to his humanity. He died
early on the voyage home of yellow fever. In a codicil to his will he
directed that whoever succeeded to his estate of Cornwall must reside
three months in Jamaica every third year, or at least must devolve this
duty on some near relative.—*Life*, ii. 158.

agents they employed.[1] The estate now to be mentioned is that of Halse Hall, one of the oldest in Jamaica, dating from the reign of Charles II and belonging to Sir Henry de la Beche. His attorneys had prohibited first the use and then the carrying of the whip, and in this way had abolished it on most of the estates under their control. There was a register of punishments, and flogging was resorted to only in extreme cases, and never in the case of women. There were 207 negroes on the estate. Only 10 of these were Africans and 111 were females; yet population had decreased till the year ending March 1824, when the births just equalled the deaths. Every Saturday out of crop was allowed to the negroes for cultivation. They had ample provision grounds within five minutes' walk of their dwellings; but, as the lowlands of Halse Hall were subject to drought, they had other grounds in the mountains, and were allowed the use of a waggon to carry up their plants and tools.[2] De la Beche visited his estate in December 1823, and lived there for a year. Like all resident proprietors, he spent much of his time in listening to the complaints of his negroes, and found that they always went away contented if he had been able to make them laugh. "An old woman once occupied me a good hour with a complaint against a person who after all turned out to be dead; the offence, moreover, was given five years previously." [3]

Most of the points raised by the Abolitionists in their indictment of slavery have now been reviewed; but a charge remains to be considered which they regarded as putting the seal of confirmation on all the rest. There still continued to be more deaths amongst the slaves

---

[1] As the slaves were admittedly best off on the large estates, the evil of non-residence would seem to have been exaggerated. The *small* resident proprietor had a bad reputation.

[2] It is characteristic of Stephen that he mentions (ii. 269) only the *distant* provision grounds.

[3] *Notes on the Condition of the Negroes, passim.*

than births ; and, whilst in a modern civilised state
such a phenomenon would be ascribed to a high standard
of comfort, it was attributed in this case to the enforcement of a low standard, or, in other words, to ill-treatment.
Before we deal with this aspect of the case it will be well
to consider how far the decrease can be explained on
other grounds. Really in great measure it was due to
the operation and subsequent effects of the slave trade.
We have seen what miserable recruits the planters got
under that system ; but for our present purpose it is
more important to notice that two-thirds of the negroes
imported were males. Ten years after 1807 the dispro-
portion of the sexes in all the colonies except Demerara
had disappeared ; but there still remained another
obstacle to reproduction ; for the slaves when imported
had been nearly all adults, and until these had died out
there would necessarily be an over-proportion of persons
beyond middle life. Thus in 1824 in a gang of 182 slaves,
nearly all creoles, the number over forty years of age
was 29, whilst in a gang of 376 slaves, of whom 110 were
Africans, the number over forty was 149.[1] Other causes
inimical to life or reproduction affected creoles only less
than Africans—infantile diseases, such as tetanus, neglect or mismanagement of infants, rum-drinking, exposure
and over-fatigue in night dancing, sorcery, polygamy,[2]
and, above all, a " depopulating promiscuous intercourse."
De la Beche during a year's residence on his estate could
not prevail upon a single couple to marry. The women
were more reluctant than the men, and " too many "
of them procured abortions.[3]

There were thus causes conducing to lower the birth-
rate and others to raise the death-rate ; and the sugar
industry must be included amongst the latter. A table
was compiled by the Abolitionists showing how the

[1] Barclay, p. 339.
[2] It was computed that in Jamaica alone 10,000 head negroes had
from two to four wives.—Edwards, ii. 176.
[3] *Notes on the Condition of the Negroes*, p. 17.

increase or decrease of population in each colony from
1818 to 1824 was affected by the amount of sugar exported in proportion to the total number of slaves. It
is only a very rough test owing to the varying proportions
of Africans and creoles, and also because some colonies
exported little or nothing but sugar and others a considerable quantity of coffee or cotton ; but, on the whole,
it establishes the conclusion that, the greater the output of sugar by the slaves, so much the greater was the
decrease in their number. Trinidad, a rich and undeveloped colony, had the worst record, the annual output
being 11·80 cwts. per head and the decrease 2·75 per
cent.[1] A large increase of population was shown in the
Bahamas, where no sugar was grown, and a slight increase
in Barbados and Dominica, where the amount produced
was comparatively small.[2]

The Abolitionists did not fail to point out that, whilst
the negroes were decreasing under British rule in the
West Indies, they were rapidly increasing in the less
congenial climate of the United States ; but here we
must distinguish between the demand for slave labour
in North America, the expansion of which was sudden
and unexpected, and the means by which it was supplied.
Of the thirteen States which formed the Union of 1787,
ten had interdicted the slave trade and seven had abolished or were about to abolish slavery. The chief products for which slave labour was deemed indispensable
were sugar, cotton, and rice. None of them were widely
cultivated, and America could not compete with the
cheaper labour of India in the production of cotton
owing to the tedious process required to separate the
fibre from the seed. The statesman who negotiated a
commercial treaty with Great Britain in 1794 was not

---

[1] Much of the mortality in Trinidad was, however, due to the clearing
and draining of pestilential swamps, which would have affected free
labourers as much as slaves. Coleridge in 1825 found the island only
half cultivated, and large tracts encumbered with the charred remains
of trees.   [2] *Reporter*, ii. 12.

even aware that his country exported cotton; and a
few years earlier eight bags of American cotton had
been seized by the British authorities on the ground that
so great a quantity could not have come from the United
States. But in 1793 Whitney invented the saw-gin
which enabled a workman to prepare more cotton fibre
in a day than he had formerly prepared in six or seven
weeks. The export of cotton was then only 187,000 lbs.;
but it rose in the very next year to 1,601,760 lbs.; and
this invention, coinciding with the utilisation of steam-
power in the British cotton-mills and followed in 1803
by the purchase of Louisiana [1] from France, made slavery
the most cherished institution of the Southern States.[2]

More remarkable, because less easily explained, than
this expansion of the demand for slaves in America was
the increase in the supply. In the thirty years 1790–
1820 the slave population of the United States was much
more than doubled, increasing from 697,686 to 1,543,688;
and the Abolitionists did not hesitate in their official
organ [3] to ascribe this phenomenon to " the superiority
of the United States in the physical treatment of their
slaves." If we cannot dismiss this statement as wholly
unfounded, it is only because the vast majority of the
American negroes were employed in the cultivation of
cotton, which ranked as the lightest occupation, and a
very limited one, in the British West Indies. In some
respects, such as their incapacity to give evidence against
whites, their condition was as bad as that of our slaves.
In most respects it was worse. The killing of a slave,
whether deliberate or impulsive, cost the perpetrator
at this period, and much later, no more than a fine; and
in 1816 the grand jury of Charleston declared that the

---

[1] The present State of Louisiana, which was admitted into the
Union in 1812, is only a small part of this vast territory, which comprised the western valley of the Mississippi and almost the whole valley
of the Missouri.

[2] Rhodes, *History of the United States*, 1893, i. 25–28.

[3] *Reporter*, ii. 12.

frequency of negro homicide had for many years brought upon their city the reproach of the civilised world. In neither case were the slaves attached to the soil; but with us after 1825 they could not be sold out of the colony, whereas in America they were driven in gangs from one State to another, and little if any care was taken to prevent the separation of families. Demerara was the only British colony in which manumission was restrained by more than a tax; but in Georgia, the Carolinas, and Louisiana it required an Act of the legislature, and in almost all the Southern States the freed slave was deported. There was no law in our colonies which prohibited the teaching of a slave to read or which forbade him in any but staple products to trade on his own account or, except in Barbados, to hire himself out; but such restrictions, though often disregarded, existed in America. Sometimes the Abolitionists admitted the greater severity of the American law, but complimented the slave-owners on conduct much milder than their principles. Here too, in their eagerness to discredit the British planter, they overshot the mark. The American slaves were badly, or at least irregularly, fed and miserably housed. They were usually, if not always, excluded from the churches; they were treated with an aloofness, with a haughty disdain, which were unknown in our colonies; and " the chilly indication of a crushed spirit " was evident to travellers in " the cowering humility, the expressions of servile respect with which the negro approaches the white man." In 1817 the treatment of the slaves in North and South Carolina was found to be " as villainous as can well be imagined " ; and in 1833, when indeed the system had become worse, it was described as one " to which West Indian barbarity is mercy and mildness." [1]

[1] Hall, *Travels*, 1818, p. 319 ; Fearon, *Sketches of America*, 3rd edition, 1819, p. 60 ; *Correspondence between John Gladstone, M.P., and James Cropper*, 1824, p. 71 ; Abdy's *Journal*, 1835, i. 388 ; Buckingham, *The Slave States of America*, 1842, p. 106.

The Abolitionists had advocated the registration of
slaves in the West Indies on the ground that there could
be no security for an improvement in their lot so long
as the possibility of importation was not cut off; but
in ascribing the increase of the American slaves to good
treatment they suppressed what must have been well
known to them as members of the African Institution—
that illicit importation was almost as great a scandal
and curse in the United States as in Cuba. The foreign
slave trade of the Southern States was prosecuted on a
large scale down to the outbreak of the Civil War; but
during the first eighteen years of abolition, 1807–1825,
the activity of the law-breakers, though far exceeded in
later days, was then thought prodigious. The annual
importation at this period was estimated at about 15,000;
and Judge Story, in charging a jury, said, " American
citizens are steeped to their very mouths (I can hardly
use too bold a figure) in this stream of iniquity." But
there was an internal as well as a foreign slave trade.
The Middle States, which had more slaves than they
could profitably employ, made a business of breeding
them for sale. It was said in 1829 that for the last
twenty years Virginia had drawn an annual revenue of
not less than a million and a half dollars from the exportation of its slaves; and in 1832, according to a
statement made in the legislature, it had become " one
grand menagerie where men are reared for the market
like oxen for the shambles." The number annually
despatched south was estimated at about 6000.[1] The
district of Columbia, under the direct rule of the Federal
Government, was the chief seat of this traffic, and Washington was one of the most frequented slave marts in

[1] The tricks of the African trade were reproduced in this inland
commerce. Old men had their whiskers shaved off and their grey hairs
either plucked out or, when too numerous, dyed. " These slaves were
then taught how old they were . . . After going through the blacking
process they looked fifteen years younger."—*Johns Hopkins University
Studies in History*, Series xxii, No. 2, p. 48.

the world. A few years later, more money was said to
be made in slave-trading within the United States than
in almost any other business. It was considered good
policy on the sugar plantations to work off the negroes
about once in seven years and buy a new gang ; and
Louisiana, despite its natural decrease, doubled its slave
population in the ten years 1810–1820.[1] The internal
slave trade could not, of course, in itself augment the total
number of negroes, but indirectly it had that effect,
slaves being reared faster in one part of the country than
they were used up in another. If in America, as in the
West Indies, there had been no foreign slave trade and
no reserve of slavery beyond the bounds of its profitable
employment, population in both cases would have shown
the same features—a decrease on sugar plantations,
which in the United States were confined to Louisiana,
and an increase on cotton plantations.

The slave-owners of America and of the British West
Indies present a curious contrast in regard to Christianity,
the diffusion of which amongst the negroes would have
raised their condition by promoting marriage, putting
down sorcery, and exempting them from the frequent
floggings inflicted for theft. In America the planters,
though they refused to worship under the same roof
with people of colour, were religious,[2] if not moral ; and
their slaves might have received religious instruction on
Sunday, had it not been forbidden to teach them to
read. In Jamaica the instruction of the slaves with a
view to baptism had been enacted as early as 1696 and
re-enacted in 1788 and 1826, and here and elsewhere the

---

[1] Du Bois, *The Suppression of the African Slave Trade to the United
States*, 1896, pp. 124, 143 ; *Gladstone and Cropper Correspondence*, p. 45 ;
M'Queen, p. 324 ; Rhodes, i. 308, 316 ; Buckingham, i. 235 ; Sturge,
A Visit to the United States in 1841, pp. 74, 75, 83.

[2] Their pietism had originated in the reaction against the French
Revolution. Lieut. Hall says that, instead of improving the condition
of their slaves, they paid " a more personal compliment to the Deity "
by building churches.—*Travels*, p. 412.

churches were open to all ;[1] but Sunday was " a day of marketing, labour, dancing, and excesses of every kind " ; and it was affirmed by a friend of the planters that they showed a contempt for religion " of a nature so culpable and criminal that to that cause principally are we to ascribe the destructive line of conduct followed by our negroes, affecting their lives and health."[2] There were twenty-one parishes in Jamaica ; but their average area was about 140 square miles, and the clergy were far from earning their substantial stipends and enormous fees. Their incomes are said to have ranged from £1000 to £3000 a year.[3] A society for the conversion and education of the negro slaves had been founded under the auspices of Bishop Porteus in 1794. A brief account of its operations was published in 1823 ; and it was then represented in the West Indies by eight missionaries and one schoolmaster. Greater efforts were required to satisfy the Evangelical movement, which made rapid progress in England after the Peace ; and the Assembly of Jamaica, in response to this pressure, sought to encourage the twenty-one parish clergymen by giving each of them a curate and providing that baptism should be paid for at the rate of 2s. 6d. a head. The Act came into operation at the beginning of 1817 ; and, six months later, one of the clergy was able to announce that he had baptised more than a fifth of his 24,000 negro parishioners, and had adopted " preparatory measures for the speedy baptism of the whole." At least two other clergymen had been almost equally successful. Instantaneous conversion was no novelty to religious people at home ; but they were not prepared for the form it was to assume in the West Indies. " The usual practice has been to assemble numbers of the negroes either at the churches or on the estates, sometimes from fifty to a hundred or

[1] In St. Christopher Coleridge received the sacrament after a negress.—*Six Months in the British West Indies*, p. 219.

[2] Williamson, ii. 284. See also Bickell, p. 202.

[3] Gardner, p. 331.

more ; they are merely asked what their names are to
be and then baptised *en masse,* the rector receiving half
a crown currency for each person." [1]

Sunday trading and Sunday labour were serious
obstacles to the religious instruction of the slaves ; but
a good deal had been accomplished by more zealous
emissaries than those of the Church. The pioneers in
this work were the Moravians, who in 1754 extended
their ministrations from the Danish to the British West
Indies. The first and always the principal scene of their
efforts was Antigua, where in 1821 they had four settlements, comprising as actual members of their community
one-fifth of the 37,000 slaves. At the same period in
St. Christopher, where they established themselves in
1777, they had 2774 members. No religious denomination was, however, to obtain so great an influence in this
region as the Wesleyan Methodists. Their starting-point
was also Antigua, which Dr. Coke, the leader of their
first mission in 1786, called " the favourite of Heaven " ;
and during the next thirty years they obtained a footing
in most of the other islands. Of about sixty missionaries
at work in 1817 two-thirds were Methodists. Speaking
in Parliament in 1823, Sir George Rose estimated the
Wesleyan community among the slaves at about 63,000
adults and 17,000 children ; and, allowing 20,000 to
all other denominations, he reckoned that 100,000, or
about one-seventh of the whole number, were more or
less Christian.[2]

The Moravians were never suspected of spreading
disaffection among the slaves, and it might have been
supposed that the Methodists would be equally trusted ;
for in the mother country they prided themselves on

---

[1] De la Beche, p. 27 ; *Edinburgh Review* (1824), xl. 226. Fees for
baptism were abolished in 1826.

[2] Hansard (1823), ix. 315 ; Brown, *History of Christianity among
the Heathen,* 2nd edition, 1823, i. 383, 389 ; Watson, *Defence of Wesleyan
Methodist Missions,* 1817, p. 125 ; Coke, *History of the West Indies,*
1810, ii. 441.

inculcating a " spirit of subordination and of willingness
to work in the lower class," and indeed were denounced
by Cobbett as " the bitterest foes of freedom in England."
Nevertheless, in several islands, and notably in St. Vincent, Barbados, and Jamaica, they were exposed to both
popular violence and legal repression. A large chapel
was erected at Bridgetown in 1789, but was constantly
besieged and invaded by a gang of hooligans who behaved
" more like fiends than human beings." Some of them
were apprehended and convicted; but the magistrate
found himself incompetent to punish an offence which
had been " committed against Almighty God." At
Kingston the two missionaries were personally in as
much danger as their chapel, and one of them had to
escape from his persecutors " disguised in a suit of regi-
mentals." A planter in St. Vincent declared that the
Methodists were " odious to all the respectable persons
of the island." It was noted as a unique phenomenon
in Barbados that " even the negroes themselves were
prejudiced against us "; and the legislatures of Jamaica
and St. Vincent tried so persistently to silence Methodism
that in 1809 the Governors of all the colonies were forbidden to give their assent to any Bill affecting religion
till it had been sanctioned by the Crown.[1]

Slavery was not protected in the West Indies by the
economic and constitutional difficulties which made for
its continuance in the United States; and those of the
planters who had not resigned themselves to its eventual
abolition may well have dreaded the diffusion of Christianity amongst their negroes, knowing that the more
fitted they became for freedom, the greater must appear
to be the injustice of detaining them as slaves. It is
difficult indeed to believe that what they objected to
was the spirit and manner of the Wesleyans and not
their purpose. These men were often crude and uncultivated and relied too much on the influence of religious

[1] Coke, i. 421; ii. 146, 147, 153; Williamson, ii. 371.

terrorism ; [1] but they were directed not to interfere in
the civil relations of master and slave except to incul-
cate the duty of obedience and, so far as consistent with
their mission, to conform to the regulations and even to
the prejudices of the whites ; [2] and in every island there
were owners and managers who had satisfied themselves that these and far higher obligations would be
scrupulously discharged. When the Methodists preached
to the negroes it was always with the consent of their
master and often with his warm encouragement and
support. Sometimes indeed he entertained them " with
a degree of elegance and grandeur " which they feared
might become " a snare." Planters subscribed to chapel-
building, supplied timber, lent their carpenters and
masons, and in some cases even built the chapel at their
own expense. In one case we find them pledging themselves to provide a stipend for the preacher. At least
two of the clergy in Jamaica subscribed to the erection
of chapels, and in one parish the vestry evinced their
appreciation of a deceased missionary by giving £100
sterling to his widow. These were testimonies to a work,
the harmlessness of which was certainly its least merit.
The Methodists had a social as well as a religious message.
Not only did drunkenness, brawling and immorality dis-
appear under their influence, but the slaves lived in
greater cleanliness and comfort, saved money or spent
it more wisely, and " the effect may be discovered in
the neatness of their habitations." " Our negroes," said
a planter to one of Coke's colleagues, " are now twenty
times better servants and consequently need not one-
twentieth part of their former punishment " ; and Sir

---

[1] One negro thought he was safe from the devil's clutches only when
singing hymns, and " kept singing so incessantly day and night that at
length terror and want of sleep turned his brain," and he died insane.—
Lewis, p. 89.

[2] Dr. Coke in his three volumes on the West Indies sometimes
carries reticence to the verge of indiscretion, as where he says (ii. 141)
that the negroes of Barbados were less amenable than those of any
other island " for reasons which are concealed."

George Rose said in the speech already quoted that, of two estates under his charge, the negroes on one, though baptised, were grossly depraved and immoral, whilst on the other, which was close to a Methodist station, only ten males and one female out of 250 slaves had been punished during the year 1821. Public order and security were also promoted by the Methodists. In the Virgin Islands they succeeded, where the magistrates had failed, in suppressing a negro festival, often attended with bloodshed, in which the spirits of the dead were supposed to indicate persons who had injured them when alive and on whom they desired to be avenged. It was another triumph for the missionaries that the guard of whites formerly required to maintain order in Nevis during the Christmas holidays was no longer needed, and a still greater triumph that in several islands during the French Revolutionary War " the religious negroes "—and these only—were entrusted with arms.[1]

We have now to trace the course, if not the progress, of a movement for inducing the colonial legislatures to ameliorate the conditions of slavery with a view to its eventual abolition ; and, when the object of that movement was rather abandoned than achieved in 1833, it will probably be found that a handful of missionaries, whose devotion too often cost them their lives,[2] had done more to avert the dangers of emancipation than had been accomplished in ten years of popular agitation and parliamentary effort.

[1] Watson, pp. 109, 120, 121, 124–127, 132, 133 ; Coke, ii. 438 ; iii. 65 ; Brown, ii. 72.

[2] In the first thirty years twenty-six Wesleyan missionaries succumbed to their exertions and the climate.—Watson, p. 66.

CHAPTER II

The Colonial Trade Bill, which reduced the disabilities but not the protection of the sugar colonies, was passed in 1822; and the controversy it excited between the East and West Indians was waged at intervals in Parliament till 1834, when a promise was obtained by the former that the duties would as soon as possible be equalised. We have seen that Huskisson was of opinion that this fiscal grievance could not be agitated without raising "the fearful and delicate question of negro slavery"; and his prediction was speedily fulfilled. In January 1823 a society was founded in London for the mitigation and gradual abolition of slavery; and on March 19 the first anti-slavery petition was presented to Parliament. It came from the Quakers who, forty years earlier, had been the first to petition against the slave trade; and Wilberforce, who had acted for them on that occasion, was again their agent. Shortly before this, he had launched a campaign in the press by publishing "An Appeal on behalf of the Negro Slaves"; but he was now too infirm, if not too old, to think of repeating his former triumphs in the House of Commons; and, when asked by Canning whether he meant to follow up the Quaker petition, he replied that a motion on the subject would be brought forward by Thomas Fowell Buxton.

Wilberforce and Buxton, the two men whose names are associated respectively with the abolition of the slave trade and the abolition of slavery, had grown to manhood under very similar conditions. Both were of ancient but not distinguished ancestry; both were the grandsons of merchants who had acquired landed property by marriage; and both were educated for independence under the guardianship of their mothers. Wilberforce, having an ample fortune, devoted himself from the first to public life. Returned for Hull in 1780, when he had barely completed his twenty-first year, he represented for many years the great constituency of Yorkshire; he was the intimate friend of Pitt; and he identified himself with the opponents of the slave trade rather as patron than as leader; for, though their society had been founded in 1787, he did not become a member till 1794, two years after the House of Commons had declared for gradual abolition.

Thomas Fowell Buxton, the second of that name, was the son of a popular landowner in Essex, and High Sheriff of the county. Curiously enough, he had the chance of entering the House of Commons at the same age as Wilberforce; for he acquitted himself with such distinction as a student at Dublin that at the close of his academic career in 1807 he was invited to stand for the representation of the University in Parliament. Happily he declined the honour; for the wealth of his family had been dissipated in law-suits and speculation; and he soon "longed for any employment that would produce me a hundred a year, if I had to work twelve hours a day for it." In 1808 he entered the brewery of Truman, Hanbury and Co., in which one of his uncles was a partner; and, three years later, the business under his management was entirely remodelled. Buxton, like Wilberforce, was an Evangelical; and the philanthropic tendency of that religious type was strengthened in his case by the circumstances of his birth and marriage. His mother and his wife both belonged to the Society of Friends; and he was the brother-in-law of Elizabeth Fry. His first public speech was delivered at a meeting of the Norwich Auxiliary Bible Society ; but he made his mark with the public by an appeal at the Mansion House in 1816 on behalf of the Spitalfields weavers who were then in great distress—a speech which brought him the congratulations of the Prince Regent and a letter from Wilberforce in which the latter anticipated " the success of the efforts which I trust you will one day make in other instances in an assembly in which I trust we shall be fellow labourers." This hope or prediction was fulfilled in 1818, when Buxton was returned to Parliament for Weymouth and advocated prison reform, to which he was already committed, and a mitigation of the criminal law. A speech on the latter subject in which he seconded a motion proposed by Sir James Mackintosh established his reputation in the House ; and in 1821, immediately after another speech, which Mackintosh described as " the most powerful appeal " he had ever heard in Parliament, Wilberforce besought him to " commence the war " on slavery, should he himself be unable to undertake the task, or to continue it should he be compelled to desist.[1]

To annul the right of property in slaves was obviously a more formidable undertaking than to prevent their importation from Africa ; but those who essayed the former task were the heirs as well as the successors of those who had accomplished the latter. Humanitarianism

[1] *Memoirs of Sir Thomas Fowell Buxton*, pp. 1–119. This work is a good enough portrait, but the account given of the anti-slavery movement is meagre and inaccurate. Wilberforce and Buxton were strikingly dissimilar in personal appearance—the one small, frail, and a martyr to ill-health, the other of towering height and massive figure and an enthusiast for all country sports. Abraham Plaistow, the gamekeeper who had taught him as a boy to ride, shoot and fish, was Buxton's friend for life ; and as a student we find him writing to his mother that he meant " to visit Weymouth before returning to Ireland to see how my horses and my relations do." Buxton had several hair-breadth escapes, and on at least two occasions showed conspicuous courage— once in securing a mad dog and again in rescuing a ship-wrecked sailor. He wrote of the dog : " I was determined not to kill him, as I thought, if he should prove not to be mad, it would be such a satisfaction to the three persons whom he had bitten."

evils likely to be produced in the West Indies by the
agitation of this subject," and showed forcibly enough
that every project of reform, however trivial, had excited
the same alarm ; but his recital of past controversies
was a needless provocation ; and, in arguing that " the
furious passions of the negro " could not be aroused by
proposals for his relief, he missed or evaded the point of
his opponents' case, which of course was that Parliament could not admonish or coerce the planters without
unsettling their slaves. The House soon learned that
the scheme of gradual emancipation offered for its approval was that of Dundas—all slaves born after a certain
date to be free and to be educated at the cost, not indeed
of their masters, but of the State. Under this system
slavery would not be abolished—" it will expire, it will,
as it were, burn itself down into its socket and go out."
We had no more right to enslave negroes at birth than
to kidnap them as adults in Africa, and the former was
" even a greater crime " than the latter, because the
African had had his twenty or thirty years of freedom,
whereas the infant slave would know nothing but " servitude and misery." Having thus argued or talked
himself into the paradoxical position that slavery was
more iniquitous than the slave trade, Buxton read to
the House a summary of regulations for the present race
of slaves, which he had communicated to Earl Bathurst,
the Colonial Secretary. The negroes were to be in-
separable from the estate, were to be admitted as witnesses, were to have a week-day at their disposal, and
were to be allowed to purchase their freedom in the
Spanish manner by instalments of a day at a time. All
obstacles to manumission were to be removed. Religious
instruction, marriage, and the observance of Sunday
were to be introduced ; some measures—" but what
I cannot say "—were to be taken to restrain the punitive
discretion of the master, and some substitute was to be
found for the driving system. The negroes had suffered

more than enough to permit of these reforms being
presented as a measure of reparation ; but the idea
was not calculated to commend them to the planters,
especially when it took the form of a peroration on the
horrors of the slave trade.

The leader of the House of Commons at this period
was George Canning, Foreign Secretary in Lord Liverpool's Cabinet, and in earlier days, unlike his chief, a
stout opponent of the slave trade. He rose immediately
after Buxton ; and the policy of the Government, whatever we may think of its merits, could not have been
announced in better temper and taste. Slavery for
Canning was " this most fearful question," in the discussion of which great harm might be done by " one
rash word, perhaps even one too ardent expression."
He expressed the uneasiness it gave him to see religion
brought " as it were bodily " into a political discussion ;
and in reference to Christianity and the British constitution, both of which had accommodated themselves to
slavery, he deprecated the putting forward as a belated
principle of action what had never been more than an
antagonism of spirit—a course which he described as
" confounding what is morally true with what is historic-
ally false." Buxton had admitted that an evil which
had been authorised by the community must be redressed
at its expense ; but Canning, without noticing this
admission, was at pains to impress upon the House that
property, even human property, must be considered as
" the creature of the law." He did not allude to manumission or to facilities for the purchase of freedom, and
on the question of evidence, though favourable to the
claims of the negroes, he declined to commit himself ;
but he acknowledged the necessity of enforcing their
Sunday leisure, of securing to them by law the possession
of their property, and of attaching them to the soil ;
and he must have surprised the Abolitionists by telling
them that he went even further than they did on the

To emancipation in the manner advocated by Dundas and Buxton he was quite opposed, and indicated the very gradual manner in which he hoped this process would be accomplished by citing the decay of villeinage in England, where " it was not ploughed up by revolution or mown down by the scythe of a legislative abolition, but was plucked up, stalk by stalk, by the progressive hand of private and voluntary enfranchisement." These words were quoted from the Report of the African Institution for 1815 ; but the writer had no doubt intended only to encourage " particular manumissions " in the West Indies ; and it was naturally asked in the course of this debate whether we had " no additional lights to guide us in 1823 beyond those which were possessed in 1400," when the trade in slaves between Bristol and Ireland had scarcely ceased. The other West Indians who followed Ellis were occupied mainly in skirmishing with the Abolitionists, but they all declared their satisfaction with the Government scheme. Buxton before withdrawing his motion endeavoured to extract from Canning an admission that negro children must eventually be declared free ; and the latter, whilst refusing to commit himself to the date or mode of emancipation, was induced to say that " the progeny of slaves must not be eternally slaves." [1]

On May 22, a week after this debate, Whitmore moved for a Select Committee to inquire into the duties on East and West Indian sugar.[2] His motion was defeated by a majority of 161 to 34 ; but the question was reopened by the same speaker at a meeting of the Anti-Slavery Society in 1825, and was discussed at great length in its Second Report. Whitmore and his philanthropic friends denounced the commercial privileges

[1] Hansard (1823), ix. 257–307, 311, 336, 359.

[2] Several West Indian planters and merchants in Glasgow who petitioned against the raising of the slavery question could not " but notice the curious coincidence of the time for its discussion with another question relative to the comparative rate of duties on East and West Indian sugar."—*Commons' Journals*, March 15, 1823.

enjoyed by the West Indian planters as "a system of pauperism," as that "pampering and protecting system which has hitherto kept them from all effective efforts at improvement" and had discouraged even the use of the plough. The withdrawal of these privileges would benefit the slaves because sugar would no longer be grown on inferior soils, and it would be advantageous, though less agreeable, to their masters, who under the spur of competition would be forced to become resident and would thus be saved the "heavy cost of agency." The Report even went so far as to suggest that fiscal reform might solve the West Indian problem more effectively than the direct interference of Parliament; and it appears that Wilberforce had once hesitated whether to choose Whitmore or Buxton as his successor.[1] But no one, it was urged, had more to gain from the abolition of this monopoly than the British consumer. It was estimated that the increase in the price of sugar due to the bounty alone was costing him yearly £1,200,000; and this sum was as much applied to the support of colonial bondage as if it were distributed amongst the 1800 sugar planters at the rate of £700 a head. "The people of England are the real upholders of negro slavery."

All this was good material for the platform and the press, but it was not allowed to pass without criticism in Parliament. Whitmore's "first point" in supporting his motion was that "the consumer was entitled to the greatest competition that could be produced in the market." It was at once pointed out that he proposed only such a readjustment of duties as would admit Indian but not foreign sugar. Nor was it clear why the "pampering and protecting system" should be so much worse for sugar-growing than for other British industries. And, if sugar, being a re-exported commodity, was only nominally protected, what became of the argument that

[1] *Life,* v. 129.

then recommended that its consideration should be deferred till the 28th. No meeting of that date is recorded, and on August 4 the Governor introduced the subject with some rather extraordinary remarks. He said that it would be "matter of serious deliberation" how far the measures contemplated in Canning's speech "could be introduced and acted on "; but, "whether the system therein laid down should not be put in progress here," he conceived that members would best consult the interests of the colony by "showing a disposition to meet the wishes of the mother country." No decision was reached at this meeting, and a long discussion on the 6th was equally inconclusive. Next day resolutions in accordance with the despatch were indeed passed ; but, in order to allow time for devising the best and safest means of carrying them out, their further consideration was adjourned to the 28th.[1] Thus to some four weeks of delay and suspense were to be added three more. Though the new regulations had not been published, they could not be kept secret, and those of the planters who had not patience to await their official disclosure showed either submission or defiance. Some took away the whip from their drivers : some, in a spirit of bravado, sent them out with two whips.

All this could not but unsettle the field-negroes, especially as sensational reports were being circulated by the house slaves and by sailors who had arrived from England. They were all soon convinced that the King had conferred upon them some benefit which was being kept back ; and many believed that this " good thing " was no less than their freedom. Such a rumour must have quickened the disaffection which was always latent in Demerara. It was the only colony in which there was still a preponderance of African negroes over Creoles, and a considerable proportion of the latter had been snatched from their homes in the islands ; for the inter-colonial

---

[1] *P.P.*, 1825, vol. xxvi.

slave trade was not abolished till 1825. Demerara had been in our possession for only nine years. The British planters disclaimed the harshness of their predecessors ; but most of them were non-resident ; and many of the overseers were still Dutch. The sale and dispersion of slaves belonging to bankrupt owners were of course no novelty ; but the victims seem to have been unusually numerous about the middle of August, when as many as seventy or eighty were advertised in a single gazette ; and the diffusion of Christianity amongst the " east coast " [1] negroes had long been viewed with suspicion. In 1811 the holding of religious meetings on estates after sunset had been prohibited. The Home Government, having " no disposition to look with jealousy and distrust upon the conduct of the missionaries," had recalled this proclamation ; and Lord Liverpool, who was then at the Colonial Office, had authorised meetings till nine o'clock, provided they were held with consent of the planters. General Murray, who had no love for " sectaries," understood this to mean that permission was essential even for attendance at chapel on Sundays ; and in May 1823 he not only circularised the magistrates to this effect, but recommended that the negroes should be accompanied by their overseer or some other white person as a means of " enabling the planter to judge of the doctrine held forth to his slaves." [2] Some planters adopted this precaution, some gave only a limited number of passes, and some gave them too late in the day. On

---

[1] The east coast or bank of the River Demerara.

[2] Of the manner in which this injunction was carried out, we have the following description : " Fancy to yourself a white man on a mule going a gentle trot, surrounded by thirty or forty slaves of all ages, in all manner of dresses, running to keep up with him ; and as many of the young and lazy ones as can lay hold of the mule's tail being dragged along in that manner. Arrived at the chapel, all out of breath, they take their respective seats ; and immediately after service they muster ; the overseer mounts his beast, the negroes being around him ; two or three grasp the mule's tail and away they trot."—*Imperial Magazine*, January, 1823.

so long as he was not recognised as a legal witness, it was recommended that he should be admitted in this capacity " in all except perhaps certain cases," if he produced a certificate from his religious teacher that he understood the nature of an oath. A register was to be kept of certificated witnesses ; and the " certain cases " were defined as those in which the master was directly concerned and such as would affect the life of a white person. Marriage could not be established too soon, and mothers with a certain number of children might be exempted from field work. All unnecessary obstacles to manumission must be removed ; but the colonial authorities might satisfy themselves that the slave who was to be freed was in good health and not under six or over fifty years of age. Outside these limits a bond of maintenance might be exacted, but the penalty was not to be enforced unless the freed person became incapacitated within ten years of his release in the case of children and fourteen years in the case of adults. Elaborate suggestions were made for amending the law in regard to sale for debt ; and husbands and wives, and children under fourteen, were not to be sold separately. No master was to flog his slave till the day after the offence, and then only if a free person was present in addition to himself or his overseer. If more than three lashes were inflicted, all particulars of the punishment must be entered in the plantation-book, the accuracy of which was to be certified quarterly on oath before a magistrate. In order to guard against the possibility of a slave being flogged in the absence of a free person or of certificated witnesses, it was proposed to be enacted that traces of punishment should suffice to convict the master if he could not repel the charge. Savings banks were to be established, and the depositor was to be allowed to name his heir. Governors were required to urge upon their Assemblies the importance of complying as soon as possible with the wishes of the Government in " a spirit of perfect and cordial co-operation " ; and the Colonial Secretary was to be informed at once of any serious opposition in order that it might be brought before Parliament. There were obvious defects in the scheme ; but these will be discussed more appropriately when we come to consider the edict in which it was subsequently embodied.[1]

This despatch of July 9, though it assumed the existence of legislative bodies, was sent to all the slave-holding colonies. The Government had anticipated that all would concur at once in abolishing the driving system and the flogging of women ; but, before proceeding further with their programme of reform where it could be carried out on their own authority, they wished to allow time for its adoption in the self-governing colonies. If in their case there should be hesitation and unnecessary delay, " a disagreeable contrast " would be presented between them and the Crown colonies ; and Ministers did not wish to be responsible for " the reproach which under such a state of things they would be liable to from their own population." [2] It soon appeared that the colonial Assemblies were prepared to take this risk.

In Jamaica the first despatch had excited a storm of indignation which raged more furiously than ever on receipt of the second. Meetings were held in every parish ; and resolutions—probably the least violent— which had been adopted by the parishioners of St. David's were sent to a London newspaper and republished by Cobbett. In this document the colonists declared that their lives and property were endangered by the anti-slavery agitation in Britain, protested against the right of Parliament to infringe upon their legislative inde-pendence,[3] and expressed their confidence that " the

---

[1] The despatch will be found in the *Annual Register* for 1823.

[2] Hansard (1824), x. 1051.

[3] In this connexion it may be mentioned that the Stamp Act of 1765 met with no opposition in the West Indies, except in St. Christopher and Nevis, where the colonists, incited by New England sailors, burnt

their accusers as " great nuisances to the estate " ; and
the Duke in this case could find no trace of " concert or
combination amongst the negroes for any criminal purpose." In the remaining parish of St. George three
negroes were executed and eleven transported on the
testimony of two miscreants, Mack and Corberand, who
were afterwards banished from the island as " persons
of a most dangerous character." Mack was an informer.
Corberand had turned King's evidence and seems indeed
to have been a veritable Titus Oates. At each of the
five trials he added something new to his " story of a
diabolical plot for the overthrow of the Government
and the massacre of the white inhabitants " ; and there
was one circumstance which, though not mentioned in
the papers laid before Parliament, did more than anything else to destroy his credit. A silver coin was
believed amongst the negroes to be a charm against
the evil consequences of perjury ; and Corberand was
detected giving evidence with this talisman in his mouth.[1]

Plots which came to nothing, and one of which turned
out to be " a mere hoax," were reported from St. Lucia
and Trinidad ; in the latter island as in Jamaica there
were wrathful meetings ; and the nine hundred whites
in Dominica threatened to avenge themselves on Parliament by declaring their independence.[2] In Barbados
the Assembly was politely uncompliant ; and " a party
of respectable gentlemen " found a vent for their anti-
Abolitionist ardour in demolishing the Methodist chapel
at Bridgetown and chasing out of the island its " villainous
preacher."

Insurrection in Demerara, plots in Jamaica, riots
in Barbados, defiant or evasive Assemblies—this was
an alarming response to the mild admonitions of Parlia-

---

[1] Froude in 1888 found the practice still prevalent.—*The English in
the West Indies*, p. 249. The Parliamentary Papers relating to the
Jamaica plots are well summarised in *The Slave Colonies of Great
Britain*, 1825. See also Hansard (1826), xiv. 1007-1075.

[2] *Christian Observer*, 1824, p. 217.

ment on behalf of the slaves ; and Zachary Macaulay
was far from expressing the general opinion when he
assured Wilberforce and Buxton that the disturbances
were " the work of Canning, Bathurst and Co., and not
of your firm." Ministers could not be expected to accept
this view ; many who had acquiesced in the resolutions
of May 15 now declared them unwise ; and the Abolitionists in more than one popular journal were over-
whelmed with abuse. Cobbett in republishing the
colonial resolutions declared that Jamaica had been
driven almost to a declaration of independence ; and
this result he attributed to " from ten to fifteen thousand
impudent sleekheaded blackguards bawling aloud in the
conventicles and all making a merit of being humane
at the expense of the planters in the colonies." He had
an utter detestation of Wilberforce, whom he accused
of preaching liberty in the West Indies whilst supporting reactionary measures at home, of overlooking the
factory slaves of Lancashire in favour of " a fat and
lazy negro that laughs from morning to night " ;[1] and
on December 13 he devoted himself in this spirit to what
he called a " thorough ransacking " of the philanthropist's
" Appeal." But Cobbett hated the Methodists—" the
vilest crew that God ever suffered to infest the earth "
—even more, if possible, than he hated Wilberforce ;
and, three weeks later, he hailed with enthusiasm the
destruction of their chapel at Bridgetown. He was
delighted that " the West Indians, men as gentle, as
generous and as good as ever breathed," had given this
proof of their spirit, and declared that " the impudent
vagabonds in Barbados richly merited the pulling down
of their den." [2] Little more congenial to the Abolitionists

[1] A Yorkshire manufacturer who had personal experience of both
factory workers and plantation slaves thought the latter much the
worse off.—Whiteley, *Three Months in Jamaica*, 1833. He was associated with Oastler in philanthropic work.
[2] *Political Register*, xlviii. 514, 559, 583, 591, 673, 677 ; xlix. 31, 34,
41.

was the atmosphere of Parliament. Buxton thought himself the most unpopular man in the House, and wrote to a friend, " The degree, I will not call it of opposition, but virulence, against me is quite surprising." [1]

Parliament met on February 3, 1824 ; and the King's speech must have confirmed the suspicions of those who had been dreading that the Government would shrink from enforcing its measures for improving the condition of the slaves. No allusion was made to the attitude of the colonial legislatures, and the only reform announced was " an extended plan of religious instruction." The question was said to be " perplexed with difficulties which no sudden effort can disentangle." To raise " exaggerated expectations " among the slaves would be as fatal to them as to their masters ; and Parliament was admonished that " the correction of a long-standing and complicated system in which the fortunes and the safety of large classes of His Majesty's subjects are involved " could be accomplished only by means which should be consistent with justice and " in which caution shall temper zeal." Evidently the coercion which had been threatened should the Assemblies prove contumacious was not to be applied ; but the Abolitionist leaders were reluctant to accept a conclusion so unflattering to their hopes. On February 14 they had an interview with Canning at the Foreign Office and were told that the Government had resolved to " do nothing except in Trinidad where there is no colonial Assembly." [2]

The second general debate on slavery took place on March 16, when papers relating to the Government policy and its reception in the colonies were laid before Parliament, and a statement was made in the Lords by Bathurst and in the Commons by Canning. If the West Indian peers were not satisfied with the speech of the Colonial Secretary, they must have been hard to please. The resolutions of May 15, which he read, were an express

[1] *Memoirs of Buxton*, p. 143.   [2] *Ibid.*, p. 144.

avowal that the condition of the slaves ought to be
improved with a view to preparing them for freedom.
Yet Bathurst said that the Assembly of Barbados had
hesitated to adopt the reforms because they thought
that in doing so they would commit themselves to a
plan for emancipation ; and he added that one of the
great difficulties with which the Government had had
to contend was " the unfortunate mixing of these two
questions." Summarising his two circular despatches,
but omitting the proposed abolition of the driving whip,
he said that the Assemblies in general were prepared
to adopt the great majority of the reforms " had not
events and circumstances occurred to delay that intention." He excused " the very intemperate manner "
in which the instructions had been received in Jamaica
by referring to the attacks made on its Assembly and
people by " various publications in this country " ; and
he even minimised the necessity for reform by asserting
that the existing slave laws were not only good but " in
general fairly executed." Canning rather exaggerated
the lapse of time which the House of Commons had contemplated for the fulfilment of its resolutions ; but on
the whole he was much happier than his colleague in
his mode of vindicating the policy of forbearance. He
admitted that it would be easy to cite passages from
the Jamaica newspapers which were calculated to put
members in " a towering passion," but urged that the
spirit of resentment should be disarmed by the conscious-
ness of superior power. The supremacy of Parliament
was " an *arcanum* of empire which ought to be kept
within the *penetralia* of the constitution," and, far from
being used to chastise " petty refractoriness," should be
brought forth " only in the utmost extremity of the
State where other remedies have failed to stay the raging
of some moral or political pestilence." He proposed,
therefore, to persevere in his policy of " temperate but
authoritative admonition " ; and he assured any member

of the Jamaica Assembly who might be conning the
speeches of Washington and Franklin in order to prepare
himself for denouncing the encroachments of the mother
country that he would have no lofty pretensions to
repel, but would be left " to found his insurrection, if
insurrection he will have, on an abstract admiration of
the cart-whip." But the policy of the Government
was not wholly one of inaction ; and both Canning and
Bathurst announced that the religious instruction of the
negroes was to be promoted by the founding of bishoprics
in Jamaica and Barbados, and that the programme of
reform, whatever might become of it elsewhere, was to
be carried out at once in the Crown colony of Trinidad.

Lord Holland, a West Indian proprietor, was the
only person who commented on Bathurst's speech ; but
Canning was bitterly reproached. Buxton declared that
he and his friends had given up the question into the
hands of the Government on the express understanding
that measures for the benefit of the whole slave population were to be adopted and enforced, and that this
pledge would be violated if it was to be " frittered down,
at present at least, to a single island." And he reminded
Canning of his promise that, if the Government encountered any serious opposition, they " would not
hesitate to come down to Parliament for counsel."
Wilberforce referred to the mischief caused in Demerara
and Jamaica by the raising of false hopes, and asked
whether they were not exposing the colonists to a far
greater danger by not making good the expectations
they had raised. He maintained that Parliament must
depend on itself to abolish slavery and that, by trying
to work through local legislatures which neither liked
the measures recommended nor approved of their ultimate object, it was merely " exciting irritation." Ellis,
speaking for the West Indians, said that the Assemblies
would give way if they were not coerced, and especially
if they were not called upon to adopt " measures of

doubtful prudence till they had seen them elsewhere in successful operation." [1]

Though the number of anti-slavery petitions had risen from 225 in the last session to nearly 600, the Abolitionists were too conscious of their weakness to challenge a division. But there was soon to be a reaction in their favour; and this change was foreshadowed on April 13, when Sir James Mackintosh presented a petition from the London Missionary Society in regard to John Smith, a minister of the Independents, who had been sentenced to death—and had since died—in connexion with the negro rising in Demerara. As the official account of the trial was not yet before the House, Mackintosh did not discuss the petition; and Wilmot Horton, the Under-Secretary for the Colonies, contented himself with affirming his belief that on some points the petitioners had been grossly deceived. On June 1 Brougham moved that the House should express its condemnation of " those unexampled proceedings " in an address to the King. Great eloquence and animation and a vast array of legal erudition, both Dutch and English, were displayed in the debate, which lasted till half-past one in the morning and was resumed at equal length on the 11th. Wilmot Horton made an able reply to Brougham and declared his dissent from the motion " without any qualification "; but Canning on the 11th, thinking it " utterly impossible to come to a completely satisfactory judgment," was content to move the previous question, and even this was carried by a majority of no more than forty-seven.

Whatever may have been the legal aspect of this case, its personal history was extremely sad. Smith was consumptive and had been on the point of leaving " the steaming swamps " of Demerara for a healthier climate when he was arrested on August 21, 1823.

[1] Hansard (1824), x. 1048–50, 1061, 1105, 1106, 1113, 1114, 1140, 1148, 1153, 1154.

Before and during his trial, which did not begin till
October 13 and lasted for six weeks, he was closely con-
fined. The court recommended him to mercy; but
General Murray referred this request to the Home
Government; and before a reply could be received
Smith died in the common gaol on February 6, 1824.
It was only in defiance of the Governor's orders that
Mrs. Smith was present at her husband's burial. Two
negro artisans had begun to rail in and brick over the
grave when their work was demolished by order of a
magistrate; and at a public meeting Lord Bathurst
was censured for having advised the King to remit the
death penalty.

Smith was tried by court-martial, which was said
to be illegal; but his prosecution, whether under military or civil auspices, was inevitable. The planters,
with some exceptions, had the worst possible opinion
of missionaries; and in the *Guiana Chronicle and
Demerara Gazette* of February 11, 1822, we read: " Let
them be looked after now more strictly than ever, and
we pledge ourselves to do for them in proper colours
whenever we may be furnished with the authentic particulars of any immoral or illegal wanderings from the
path of their duty." We have seen that a few weeks
before the revolt General Murray had advised planters
to satisfy themselves as to the doctrine which was being
taught to their slaves; and his suspicions must necessarily have been confirmed when he found that the
rising had originated amongst the negroes who were
under Smith's influence and that several of the leaders
were connected with his chapel.[1] The Governor and the
missionary had never been on good terms. When the
latter presented his credentials in 1817, Murray is re-

---

[1] The register of Smith's chapel was subsequently examined, and it
was found that out of about 2000 baptised negroes only five or six were
convicted, and only one communicant out of about 200. But, if the
rebels numbered 13,000, there must have been a great many who were
not convicted.

ported to have said that he would be expelled if he taught the negroes to read. During an epidemic of small-pox in 1819 Smith had reopened his chapel to negroes on other plantations sooner than the authorities approved ; and in his journal under date October 21, 1822, he wrote : " Oh that this colony should be governed by a man who sets his face against the moral and religious improvement of the negro slaves ! "

The court found that the tendency, though not the intention, of Smith's religious teaching had been to foster discontent among the slaves,[1] and in particular that he had dissuaded them from adding to their resources [2] by working their grounds and going to market on Sunday. It was also found that on the eve of the revolt and during its progress he had communicated with one of the rebels ; but the third charge, that he knew of the intention to rebel and did not give information, was the only one that was wholly sustained ; and this was the position most keenly assailed and defended in the parliamentary debate. Smith was able to prove that several weeks before the outbreak he had warned Stewart and Cort, the overseer and the attorney of an adjoining plantation,[3] that the negroes were excited about the new instructions and that some of them had asked him " whether their freedom had come out." Indeed, had not Cort dissuaded him, he would probably have undeceived them from the pulpit. But one of the slave prisoners, who must all have been sorely tempted to propitiate the authorities by incriminating Smith, said that the latter had been

[1] Walpole and other modern writers mention the text of one of Smith's sermons as injudicious : " If thou hadst known, even thou, at least in this thy day, the things which belong unto thy peace ! but now they are hid from thine eyes." These words referred, not to the suppressed despatch, but to the fact that those negroes who were to be sold would no longer have the opportunity of religious instruction. See p. 129.

[2] In Demerara, food for *subsistence* was grown by the gang and distributed by the masters.

[3] The plantation Success, of which Mr. Gladstone, father of the statesman, was the non-resident proprietor. Jack Gladstone, a negro on this estate, was the chief leader.

informed by Quamina, one of his deacons, on the day before the revolt, when the witness was the only other person present, that two of the negroes were advocating an attempt to take their liberty by force. This evidence was inconsistent with that of no fewer than four other slaves who also claimed to have been present ; [1] and their testimony corroborated that of Smith himself, who said that at the interview in question he had rebuked Quamina for saying that " it would be good to send our managers to town to fetch up the new law." Smith had heard before of this design. He seems to have gone on the assumption, not likely to be approved by his judges, that he was not bound to disclose an agitation—especially as he was honestly trying to discourage it—which did not contemplate an actual appeal to arms ; and it was not till six o'clock on the following evening, when the news had travelled as far as Georgetown, that he was shown a letter, written to another negro by " Jack Gladstone and the rest of the brethren at Bethel Chapel," in which they announced their intention to rise that night at seven o'clock. Writing to a friend two days later, Smith said that the negroes had risen, " though not unexpectedly, yet in a way that neither I nor any one else, I believe, ever anticipated " ; and one can readily understand that he wished to be very sure of his ground before he informed against members of his own congregation and thereby exposed them to such retribution as subsequently befell the plotters in Jamaica.

The Governor declared in a despatch to Lord Bathurst that his object in having Smith tried by court-martial was to give him a better chance of justice than he would have had from a jury of planters ; and we find that, whilst the court which tried the negro prisoners was composed mainly of officers belonging to the local militia, Smith's judges, with two exceptions, were officers of the

[1] See Lushington on this point.—Hansard (1824), xi. 1213-19.

regular army. The London Missionary Society said in its petition that the object was to secure for the prosecution the advantage of slave evidence ; but Brougham admitted that this would have been available under Dutch law in the civil court.[1] The fifteen officers, however, proved to be by no means impartial, though one of them was the Chief Justice of the colony, who sat as a militia colonel. Extracts from Smith's private journal, which had no bearing on the case except in so far as they disclosed his repugnance to slavery[2] and his religious antipathy to the Governor, were used against him—a species of proof which had not been admitted in England, according to Sir James Mackintosh, since Lord Jeffreys had presided at the trial of Algernon Sydney and which had been condemned by the legislature in reversing Sydney's attainder. Jeffreys was believed to have tampered with his record, and the military judges in Demerara had at least made deletions in theirs. The minutes laid before Parliament fully supported Brougham's assertion that hearsay evidence was admitted for the prosecution " three or four deep " or, as he elsewhere expressed it, " to the third, the fourth, aye, even to the fifth degree." But another and complete report of the trial, which had been drawn up by the prisoner's " advising advocate," was published by the London Missionary Society ; and from passages in this version which had been suppressed in the other it appeared that, when the accused offered hearsay evidence, the court first ruled that such testimony would not " in future " be admitted, and then did admit it, but only when it suited their purpose. Thus one witness for the defence was not allowed to relate a conversation in which he himself had taken part, whilst another was compelled to answer a question

[1] Slave evidence may have been legal against whites when Demerara was a Dutch colony, but according to Stedman it was never admitted in practice. See p. 56.

[2] " March 22, 1819 : While writing this, my very heart flutters at hearing the almost incessant cracking of the whip."

L

bearing implicitly on a confession [1] which from its manifest absurdity had been suppressed.

These and other features of the trial made an impression very unfavourable to the colonists; but what did more than anything else in their own opinion to prejudice them in the eyes of the British public was the part taken in this affair by Mr. Austin, the only Episcopal clergyman in Demerara and chaplain to the garrison at Georgetown. He was a member of the board of evidence appointed to investigate the revolt. With no predilection in favour of Smith, who was known to him only as a Dissenter and suspected incendiary, he became convinced of his innocence, and, defying a storm of obloquy and abuse which was to culminate in his expulsion from the colony, strove gallantly to save him. About the end of 1823 an extract from a letter written by Austin to a friend appeared in a missionary journal. Its authorship was suspected and soon discovered in Demerara; and the *Guiana Chronicle* then expressed itself with its accustomed vigour: "To find language sufficiently expressive to denote our abhorrence of the conduct of this individual is impossible. There is no language in the known world capable of supplying us with words sufficiently strong for the purpose." The extract with the author's name was placed before Parliament by the London Missionary Society in its petition; and Austin in this passage declared that in the late rising "nothing but those religious impressions which under Providence Mr. Smith has been instrumental in fixing, nothing but those principles of the gospel of peace which he had been proclaiming, could have prevented a dreadful effusion of blood here and saved the lives of those very persons who are now, I shudder to write it, seeking his life." Austin testified at the trial that,

[1] The confession of Paris, one of the condemned negroes, according to which Smith blessed the revolt as "begun in Christ" and as a reward for such complaisance was to be Emperor of Demerara.—Hansard, 1824, xi. 1039.

when it was remarked to one of the insurgents that they had shed little or no blood, the reply was, " It is contrary to the religion we profess : we cannot give life and therefore we will not take it." [1]

We have seen that Canning and Bathurst had announced that two bishoprics were to be founded in the West Indies. The former had explained that the object was to widen the basis of the Church by bringing blacks as well as whites under its care ; and he sought to commend the scheme to the planters by assuring them that " for a time at least " the colonial treasuries would not be called upon to contribute. For two years the interest of a sum appropriated, but not immediately required, for church-building at home would be applied to this purpose, and further assistance might be expected from a West Indian pension fund. Bathurst had brought himself to believe—" a hope might be entertained "— that proprietors and overseers would show less hostility to the religious instruction of the negroes when it was undertaken by clergy of their own Church, and that " a community of feeling " would be produced when the slave was admitted to the religion of his master instead of having to content himself with what Lord Holland had once called " an inferior article."

This not very robust optimism must have been shaken when Bathurst was informed more than a year and a half later what was being done in the diocese of Jamaica. Bishop Lipscombe was able to report that the proprietors and their representatives had shown great readiness to co-operate " for the benefit of the Church " ; but for the benefit of the negro he had ventured only to propose that the children of three or four contiguous estates should be assembled twice a week for oral instruction, no method " in the present state of public

---

[1] *P.P.*, 1824, vol. xxiii ; *Report of the Case*, 1824, Preface and pp. 182, 189, 197 ; *Substance of the Debate* (with " some new facts " in Preface), 1824 ; Hansard (1824), xi. 961–1076 1206, 1313 ; *Edinburgh Review* (1824), xl.

in future. Woodford pleaded for a reconsideration of this article which had "really created great consternation," urging that female slaves were "allowed by all to be the most prone to give offence," that now for the first time it had been forbidden to strike them, and that a planter who succumbed to this temptation might ruin not only himself but his family and creditors. Bathurst refused to alter the clause, though it had not been included in his own list of reforms, and did not pacify the Governor by directing that the penalty should not be enforced till it had been referred to the Home Government. In spite of all appeals for revision and delay, the Order was proclaimed on May 24 and came into force on June 24.[1]

The Abolitionists had warmly welcomed this edict when it was submitted to Parliament, but on closer inspection they found that it had serious defects. It was manifestly a compromise between Bathurst's general instructions of July 9, 1823, and the usage of Trinidad ; and, Spanish slavery being much more humane than British, this compromise had been arrived at, partly by supplementing the instructions, but much more by contracting the basis of custom. The outstanding addition to Bathurst's scheme, more important even than the institution of a Protector, was compulsory manumission ; but this article of the Spanish code had been adopted without reviving the facilities for earning money which had made it so great a boon to the slave. When Trinidad was a Spanish colony, the slave had had 134 days in the year that he could call his own, viz. one day a week in addition to Sundays and thirty Church festivals.[2] In 1800, three years after the British occupation, an ordinance was issued which reduced the week-day allowance of time to seventeen days—Saturday afternoon during six months of the year and four annual holidays.[3]

---

[1] *P.P.*, 1825, vol. xxvi.　　　　　　　[2] See p. 37.

[3] It was not till 1827 that the Abolitionists succeeded in getting this ordinance printed. They had previously assumed that the slaves had twenty-six days. The ordinance was issued by General Picton, the dis-

In the debate of 1823 Buxton had proposed that the slaves should have another day instead of Sunday for cultivating their grounds. Canning had assented to this and so provisionally had Ellis. But the point was not mentioned in Bathurst's despatch ; and it is astonishing that the Order in Council, which not only professed to make Sunday in Bathurst's own words " really a day of rest and religious instruction," but offered freedom to all who could earn it, should have left unchanged an ordinance so illiberal as that of 1800. But the Government in this matter incurred a much graver responsibility than their failure, serious as it was, to provide facilities for earning freedom. Their first object ought to have been to break up the continuity of labour imposed upon the negroes by their masters and by the necessity of providing for their own subsistence. We have seen that the mortality amongst the slaves in Trinidad was greater than in any other British colony, whilst the production of sugar per head was also greater ; and a planter of twenty-five years' standing indicated the main cause of this sinister pre-eminence when he said, " It is the sugar that kills them." [1]

As the instructions had been enlarged to include compulsory manumission, so the basis of custom had been narrowed almost to the exclusion of slave evidence. By an Order in Council, issued as recently as September 16, 1822, for establishing new courts of justice, it had been declared competent for the criminal court to admit as witnesses persons not free but otherwise competent under the law of England ; and it is a singular coincidence that, when Bathurst wrote on July 9, 1823 to recommend a limited admission of slave evidence, the Council of Trinidad on that very day was stating, in answer to a question, that it had always been received there

tinguished soldier and administrator, whose subsequent prosecution for cruelty caused as great a sensation as did that of Governor Eyre of Jamaica in 1867.

[1] *Further Progress of Colonial Reform*, 1827, p. 59.

The Government had announced that the Trinidad
Order would be extended to the other Crown colonies ;
and Demerara, which, but for the revolt, would have
staged the first experiment, was to be the scene of the
second. Indeed, on March 18, 1824, a week before the
Order was returned for promulgation to Trinidad, it
had been sent to Demerara for the purpose of being
adapted to the Dutch law. Meanwhile Governor Murray,
presumably as a sequel to the Smith case, had been
recalled, and another Major-General reigned in his stead.
Though personally unconnected with the planters, Sir
Benjamin D'Urban seems to have readily assimilated
their views. That the slaves were totally unfit for
emancipation, and yet at the same time too intelligent
to admit of the question being safely discussed, was no
paradox to their owners ; and D'Urban, in acknowledging the Order which had awaited his arrival from Antigua,
said that the negroes were described to him as " remark-
ably well informed " and as having early information
of all that affected their interests in Parliament and the
press. "Many of them read, most well understand
what is read." The task of remodelling the Order
occupied the Court of Policy for about seven weeks ;
and on June 25 it was despatched to the Colonial Office,
much altered and reduced from forty-three clauses to
thirty-five. Punishments might be witnessed by six
slaves as an alternative to one freeman. Flogging, where
it did not exceed six lashes, might be immediate and
without witnesses. Magistrates were to be allowed to
authorise the flogging of females, and they could also
" in special circumstances " permit Sunday work on the
plantations. Slaves were not to marry without consent of their owners, because marriage under the Dutch
law conferred privileges which would be inconsistent

revised and finally adjusted by James, afterwards Sir James, Stephen,
who was then counsel to the Colonial Office. His father, the most
extreme of Abolitionist writers, described the Order as "a parcel of
trash."—Hansard (1826), xiv. 1081.

with a state of slavery. Only on the same condition
were they to be allowed to hold property, and actions
for its protection were to be brought, not by the slaves,
but on their behalf by the owners. The clause which
required the master to prove a negative should his slave
allege that he had been punished illegally and without
witnesses was omitted, and so were the clauses for compulsory manumission and the forfeiture of slave property.
The usage which required voluntary manumission to be
sanctioned by the Governor and the Court of Policy was
to continue ; and, most remarkable of all, the Governor
was to be empowered to suspend at his discretion the
whole or any part of the proposed law.

It was not till November 20 that this draft was
returned by Bathurst, who then rejected almost all the
alterations and insisted that his demands should be complied with before publication. The Court of Policy
again set to work ; but their new draft, which they
defended in marginal notes, fell so far short of the required approximation that the Governor did not venture
to promulgate it ; and on March 14, 1825, it was remitted
to the Home Government. Marriage, shorn of its civil
rights, was indeed conceded ; the judicial flogging of
females was given up ; and, in lieu of the forfeiture
clause, it was to be enacted that the master who had
been twice convicted of cruelty should incur double the
penalty of his former offence and be incapacitated for
managing slaves—his own, if he had any, being placed
under trustees. The Court had not again inserted their
provision for suspending the law ; but in an address to
the Governor, which at their request he forwarded to
the Colonial Office, they said that they were still " impressed with the same fears of danger from the measures
now to be adopted "—which indeed they had prepared
" with trembling hands "—and implored the King to
protect them " by arming his representative in this
colony with those suspensive powers."

Though Dutch institutions may have been less amenable than Spanish to the royal authority, there was nothing to prevent Ministers imposing their will on Demerara as they had imposed it on Trinidad; but, having used the legislative council as their instrument, they were unwilling to weaken its authority by interposing between this body and the slaves; and they were no doubt anxious that the benefits intended for the latter should be no longer withheld. Consequently they decided to authorise the draft as an Act of the Court of Policy; but Bathurst in intimating this decision on July 9, 1825, the second anniversary of his famous despatch, declared that the Government did not mean to abandon any of their Trinidad reforms and that nothing would satisfy them but complete compliance. Writing on February 25, 1826, when the Order had been nearly six months in force, he again insisted on the omitted reforms and especially on compulsory manumission, which he declared to be essential to the desire for gradual emancipation avowed by the House of Commons;[1] and he intimated to the Court of Policy that, if they disregarded this final warning, the reforms would be enacted without their concurrence. In justice to these " trembling " legislators it should be mentioned that in two respects their draft was an improvement on the Trinidad Order. A record of punishments was to be kept not only on plantations but by all persons having gangs of over six slaves; and the evidence of slaves was admitted both in civil suits affecting their owner and in capital charges against whites. In August the Court of Policy reconsidered their handiwork, but still refused to make any alteration.

The obstinacy shown in Demerara was carried much further in the adjoining colony of Berbice. Here the

---

[1] It is difficult to reconcile this statement with Bathurst's speech in the Lords (see p. 139) and with the fact that compulsory manumission was not mentioned in his circular despatch.

Council took the same line as the Court of Policy, that
is to say, they resolved on August 12, 1823, to abolish
the driving whip and the flogging of women, but persuaded the Governor not to publish their decision. In
January of the following year the Governor suggested
that the contemplated enactment might now be made
without danger and represented that the situation had
become anomalous, as he had prohibited the magistrates
from flogging females, whilst no such injunction had
been laid on the slave-owners. The Council replied
that in their opinion the disturbances in Demerara were
still too recent to permit of an alteration in the law ;
and in May, when this excuse could no longer be pleaded,
they proved equally obdurate. On July 23 Bathurst
sent out the Trinidad Order and intimated to the
Governor that, as the Council would not move, commissioners would be sent to assist him in adapting it
to the Dutch law. The Governor had hopes that the
Council would at least co-operate ; but on October 30
he reported that he could not discover in them " any
friendly feeling towards the measures." Nothing further
was done for nearly a year and a half ; but in March
1826 Bathurst ordered the refractory Council to be dissolved ; and the new Council, from which planters are
said to have been excluded, adopted the Trinidad Order
on September 25, having been told that, if they did not
do so, it would be established by a proclamation of the
Governor. It came into force on November 1.[1]

The Government met with considerable opposition
in extending the Trinidad Order to St. Lucia, an island
which, after changing hands more than a dozen times,
had been captured finally from the French in 1803 and
ceded in 1814. It had recently been devastated by
hurricanes ;[2] during the previous fifteen years scores

[1] *P.P.*, 1825, vol. xxvi ; 1826–27, vol. xxvi ; McDonnell, *Compulsory
Manumission or an Examination of the Actual State of the West India
Question*, 1827, p. 74 ; *Further Progress of Colonial Reform*, p 25.
[2] The Government buildings were blown down in 1817, when the

of plantations had been abandoned ; and the authorities pleaded with some reason that they were not in a position to deal liberally with their slaves, who, moreover, were said to be the least intelligent in the whole British West Indies, having " no instructor whatever." There seem to have been five Catholic churches, but only two of them had priests. Nine-tenths of the island were cut off from Castries by the want of roads ; troops could be moved to these parts only by sea ; and outside the capital there were but 275 whites capable of bearing arms. Nevertheless Bathurst insisted that French customs must be adapted to the Trinidad Order in its " entire spirit " ; and at last on February 8, 1826, the Council of the colony completed a draft which was in several respects, and notably in regard to the regulation of labour, an improvement on its model. The slave was to have one day in the week out of crop for the cultivation of his grounds, and half a day during crop, in addition to Sundays ; and, if he did not receive the customary dole of salt fish—which many planters could not afford to give—he was to have another whole day weekly throughout the year. Compulsory manumission, hitherto unknown in St. Lucia, was thus freed from the difficulties which clogged its operation in Trinidad ; and we are told that many slaves were able in a few years to save enough money to purchase their freedom.[1]

In view of the reluctance, and even the positive refusal, to accept the reforms where the Crown had authority to enforce them, we may imagine how they were likely to be received by those colonial Assemblies which did not acknowledge even the supremacy of Parliament. The Order in Council had barely come into operation in Trinidad when it was being sent round for imitation to the self-governing colonies ; and in

Governor was killed. They were rebuilt and in 1819 again blown down.—Hansard (1823), vii. 687 ; (1824), x. 971.

[1] P.P., 1825, vol. xxvi.

their case example was to prove as fruitless as precept. Jamaica had the first offer, the despatch to this colony being dated July 14, 1824, to all the others July 26. We have seen that shortly after the Jamaica Assembly had rejected Bathurst's reforms in the previous autumn there was a discovery of negro plots ; and this cause of alarm had recently revived. In June 1824 military intervention was supposed to have averted a rising of the slaves in the parish of Hanover. They seem to have been provoked by the exaction of an hour or two's labour on some of the Saturdays set apart for the cultivation of their provision grounds ; and informers alleged that they had agreed among themselves to strike for freedom. Surprised by militiamen on the day before the intended outbreak, they fled into the woods and did some damage to property, killing several horses and mules and burning a trash-house. Some were captured, some committed suicide, and the rest in a few days gave themselves up. Mutiny rather than rebellion would seem to have been their purpose, but thirteen of them were sentenced to death. Probably they were not all executed. A Committee of the Assembly reported that the slaves throughout the island had " imbibed notions that the King and Wilberforce had made them free," and suggested that Parliament should acknowledge its responsibility for the late disturbances by paying their cost, which was estimated with commendable accuracy at £15,270 12s. 11½d. As further debates on slavery were to be expected, there should also be " an ample indemnity against future losses." [1]

This " alarming insurrection," in which the casualties were seven horses and three mules, was speedily suppressed ; but the planters had not recovered their equanimity, imperfect enough at best, when Bathurst's despatch, enclosing the Trinidad Order and notifying the appointment of colonial bishops, reached Jamaica

[1] *P.P.*, 1825, vol. xxvi ; Bickell, pp. 151–73.

to conciliate his audience by denouncing " the diabolical falsehoods and infamous aspersions of a few interested and designing hypocrites moving in terrific phalanx to the total annihilation of the whole inhabitants of the West Indies," and by referring to " that detestable Institution which, keenly and immovably bent on your destruction, has with consummate ingenuity erected and set in motion against you a tremendous machinery throwing out at each evolution misery and woe." Whatever may have been the immediate effect of these words, they were far from pacifying the clamour out-of-doors, where the Speaker by his own account was so unpopular as almost to endanger his life. The Bill passed the Assembly on August 27, 1824, and, though the Trinidad Order had only just arrived, was said to include as many of its points as could safely be adopted ; but the Council were by no means enamoured of a measure which, its originator declared, " would endear their remembrance to posterity." They objected that Sunday markets and fines on manumission were not abolished ; that every negro or coloured person against whom nobody had proved a right of property was not assumed to be free ; that the death penalty—optional for the first offence, absolute for the second—was imposed on a slave who struck or offered to strike his master ; and, above all, that immunity was assured to any white person who killed a slave in the attempt to offer violence—a clause which they considered would defeat almost any prosecution for murder. When the Bill was returned to them unaltered, the Council rejected it, believing that they would better protect the slaves by maintaining the existing law, defective as it was, than by passing a measure which contained such a clause. Next year, after a violent quarrel between the Council and the Assembly, the Bill passed and was transmitted to London, where it was promptly annulled ; and the two Houses in their address to the Governor at the close of the session showed no disposition to accept the reforms. The Council affirmed that some of them would not in their opinion promote either the welfare of the slave or the interest of his master ; and the Assembly declared, " If it is determined that we shall be the victims of fanaticism, prejudice and injustice, we must submit ; but neither threats nor persuasion will ever induce us to put the finishing hand to our own political, perhaps natural, existence." [1]

Jamaica, Barbados, Trinidad, St. Lucia, Demerara and Berbice comprised about two-thirds of the slaves ; and, the rest being distributed over a number of small islands, it would be a tedious and unprofitable task to consider in detail how far they had been admitted to the measures prescribed for their relief. Happily we are able to take a general view of this process in so far as anything had yet been done; for Brougham on March 3, 1826, moved for a list of Acts passed in favour of the slaves since May 15, 1823 ; and the return, which was presented a month later, embraced the colonies of Jamaica, Barbados, the Bahamas, Grenada, Tobago, St. Vincent, Dominica and St. Christopher, and tabulated their legislation under the following heads : religious instruction and Sunday observance ; evidence ; marriage ; manumission ; sale of slaves detached from the estate ; separation of families ; regulation of punishments ; right of property and right of action. Barbados having legislated in vain, its schedule was entirely blank. Jamaica was better only in these respects, that the protection of slaves from seizure for debt had been made to include Saturday as well as Sunday, that the power of manumission had been granted to owners having only a limited interest, and that the right of slaves to receive legacies, though not to defend them at law, had been recognised. None of the colonies had sanctioned

---

[1] *P.P.*, 1825, vol. xxvi. ; *Second Report of the Anti-Slavery Society* ; Hansard (1826), xv. 1300.

found that the colonies, whatever might have been the measure of their disobedience, were to be brought sharply to book. Hitherto they had been subjected to two "gradations" of pressure. First they had been furnished with the proposals of the Government for giving effect to the resolutions passed by the House and recommended to carry them out in their own way. Then, when that plan failed, the Government had itself legislated for Trinidad and sent round its edict as a model for imitation. And now there was to be a third stage. An Act comprising the whole Trinidad Order was to be drawn up under the direction of Ministers and submitted by the Crown officials to each of the colonial legislatures, so that the latter would be compelled to accept or reject it in the course of their next session. And, in order that this final effort should be made under the weightiest possible sanction, the resolutions of 1823 were to be submitted for approval to the Lords.[1]

On the same evening the House was called upon to express its sorrow and indignation at "the perversions of law and violations of justice" which had been displayed in the recent trials of slaves in Jamaica; and Denman, who introduced the motion, declared that in these proceedings judicial oppression had "reached the highest pinnacle of its power—a height indeed far beyond anything they could possibly conceive." A counter-resolution, condemning the law but not admitting its abuse, was moved by Horton and supported with obvious reluctance by Canning. It was shown in the debate that freedom had been offered to all slaves who would give evidence; that the accused, though scarcely able to speak or even to understand English, were in all but one case undefended by counsel; that the witnesses, without being cross-examined, contradicted both themselves and each other; and that the first batch of

---

[1] Hansard (1826), xiv. 968, 971, 974, 976-79, 982.

prisoners was tried by the magistrate who had avowed
his anxiety to have executions before Christmas.[1] Hearsay evidence, only too plentiful in the Smith case, was
here the predominant feature ; and the following choice
specimen was culled by Buxton. A constable was
asked whether he had not found guns amongst the
conspirators. " No, but he had found a place where he
was told guns had been." Had he not found bayonets ?
" No, but I was shown a basket in which I was told a
great number of bayonets had been." And what Lushington called " hearsay evidence with a vengeance "
was given by a Mr. Movier, who said " that Mr. Hole,
a non-commissioned officer of the Hanover troops, and
others, informed him at Flint River that the overseer
at Magotty, Mr. Macdonald, had informed them that
the driver on the Magotty estate had stated to him,"
etc. But perhaps the severest comment on these trials
had been made in the preceding debate by Canning, who
said that, in view of the readiness to admit slave evidence
against slaves and the refusal to legalise it against whites,
" he was free to confess that, when he first looked upon
this picture and then upon that, the contrast did appear
to him most disgusting and most revolting." Horton's
amendment was carried by 103 to 63 ; but, on the suggestion of Brougham, all but the first sentence was
struck out ; and the House thus resolved unanimously
that the trials were " a further proof of the evils in-
separably attendant upon a state of slavery " and
an additional argument for the resolutions of 1823.
Supporters of the Government must have been relieved
to find that they were not called upon to affirm even
the technical legality of colonial justice. " On the
question of the trials," wrote a West Indian member
to a friend in the colonies, " there was only one feeling
in the House that such a state of law was utterly

---

[1] See p. 135.

as contending for " the prize of vituperative eloquence to be awarded by pious and sympathising ladies," he acknowledged with respect the cry of indignation which had come " from every corner of the kingdom, from every city, corporation, town and village," and declared that the public feeling, whether right or wrong, was too powerful to be disregarded. " Monopoly was unpopular, slavery detestable ; and the united odium of both was more than the colonies could bear." Lord St. Vincent followed the Lord Chancellor in emphasising the responsibility of Parliament for the slave trade, and was severe on the Duke of Devonshire, who at a public meeting had denied the right of the planters to compensation on the ground that they were receivers of stolen goods. " Who stole those goods—who sold them—who pocketed the money for them ?—who but the people of England ? " [1]

Canning's announcement that another turn of the screw was to be applied to the colonial legislatures caused some embarrassment to Brougham, who had intended to propose that their day of grace should now be cut short. But he soon came to the same conclusion as Lord Ellenborough—that to send back the twice-rejected demands without making their adoption compulsory would be a mere waste of time. On May 19, 1826, he moved that the House, as there had been no satisfactory response to its resolutions, should consider early in the next session such measures as might be deemed necessary to effect their purpose ; and he added that he had refrained from suggesting any specific measures only because the present session was too far advanced. Speaking rather as a prosecuting counsel than as a statesman, and not always either accurate or fair,[2] he filled

[1] Hansard (1826), xiv. 1140, 1143, 1144, 1150, 1157, 1158, 1160–64, 1172.

[2] Brougham was less than just to Tobago. It is evident from this and other debates that the speakers had not always mastered their Blue Books.

twenty-five columns of Hansard in endeavouring to
prove that the colonies had incurred that degree of guilt
which, as defined by Canning in 1823, was to bring down
upon them the intervention of Parliament.   St. Vincent
and Dominica, two of the more tractable colonies, had
legalised the evidence of a slave, but only under the fatal
proviso that it should not be admitted against his
master.   Nothing had been done in at least four colonies,
next to nothing in Jamaica, and worse than nothing in
Barbados, where there had been more bad legislation than
good.   For example, an Act of 1749, which subjected
to the maximum number of lashes a slave convicted of
disorderly behaviour or of riding or driving faster than
" a gentle trot," had been not only re-enacted but made
more arbitrary and severe.   In dealing with this island
Brougham showed what a hash of modern humanity
and ancient brutality was involved in the process of
consolidating the slave laws ; and the fondness of the
colonists for this method of amelioration was explained
incidentally, if not inadvertently, by Horton, the Under-
Secretary and himself a West Indian, who said that,
when such an Act was presented for approval, the Crown
could not reject the relics of barbarism without sacri-
ficing the " salutary new provisions."   Horton put
forward a strange plea for the colonists, urging that they
had been actuated by " other motives beyond those of
obstinacy and resistance "—as if defiance of Parliament
could be censurable only when indulged in for its own
sake as a pleasure.   Ellis, the West Indian leader, still
clung to his idea that slavery should be left to fade away
through the same age-long process which had brought
about the extinction of villeinage in England, and consequently he attacked compulsory manumission.   He
was complimented, but happily he was also controverted,
by Canning, who declared with his usual felicity and
force that this item was the most essential feature of
the Government programme.   All the other clauses went

but to mitigate slavery. " *This* clause is the way *out* of that system, the opening by which slavery itself may *escape* gradually, and as it were imperceptibly, without the shock of a convulsion." It was high time that the coercive power which Canning had described as lurking in the *penetralia* of the constitution should emerge from its retreat ; but Ministers took refuge in the " previous question," and Brougham's motion, which would unquestionably have strengthened their hands, was defeated.[1]

Meanwhile Bathurst was applying the third " gradation " of pressure to the West Indian legislatures, and, as usual, he began with Jamaica. On March 13, 1826, he wrote to the Duke of Manchester, directing him to dissolve the existing Assembly which had twice refused compliance. In order to bring the whole question before the new Assembly " in a more distinct shape," he would shortly send out the substance of the Trinidad Order classified under separate heads ;[2] and Ministers would then be able to decide " whether it will be necessary to take any other course." Bathurst, unknown to himself, had a coadjutor in this appeal. It so happened that on the same day a member of Parliament was sending to his friends in the West Indies a report of the debates on the London petition and the slave trials and of the slavery debate in the Lords. " You will observe," he wrote, " that in the whole course of these debates there is not one person who did not admit the extinction of slavery to be the whole object of Parliament and the country—an object which they were determined to accomplish, and that the only difference was as to the means and time of its accomplishment." Even Lord Eldon was amongst the emancipators ; and public

---

[1] Hansard (1826), xv. 1295, 1306, 1307, 1310, 1319, 1347, 1363. Stapleton, the private secretary and biographer of Canning, supposes (*Political Life*, iii. 108) that this was the only debate of 1826 on slavery in which Canning took part. He was in sympathy with the slave-owners ; but, apart from this defect, his account of the movement is quite inadequate.

[2] This was a modification of Canning's proposal. See p. 166.

opinion would have welcomed " any measure of rigour "
for enforcing the Trinidad regulations. The Abolitionists
wanted this question to be settled over the heads of the
colonists, whilst the Government desired " to leave it
in their hands on the condition of their carrying into
effect what is the wish of the whole English nation."
And the writer expressed his hope that, when the
Assembly realised that there was " no middle alternative,
they will not commit such an act of suicide as to refuse
their compliance." On May 26 this letter was printed
and strongly commended in the *Jamaica Gazette*, and
the editor was so impressed with its importance that he
also published a private letter to himself from M'Queen,
editor of the *Glasgow Courier*, who had been long in
Jamaica and was the apologist of the planters. " I
deeply regret to say," wrote M'Queen, " that prospects
are not mending for you ; Government, rest assured,
are bent upon general and ultimate emancipation."
Nothing but the hastening of this result would satisfy
" a vast portion of the population " ; and the apathy
of the West Indians in Parliament was " sickening and
distressing." By this time Bathurst had sent out eight
drafts of legislation,[1] which the law officers of the colony
were required to digest into Bills ; and in his covering
despatch of May 11, 1826, he said that he was " not
disposed to anticipate the continued rejection of enactments so earnestly and anxiously looked for by both
Houses of Parliament and by every class of society in
this kingdom."

The result of all this pressure, official and confidential,
was not known at the Colonial Office till the end of the
year, when it appeared that the Assembly of Jamaica
had declined to endanger their lives and property by
adopting an experiment which, as they asserted, was

[1] These drafts may be roughly indicated as follows : (1) appointment
of guardian ; (2) evidence ; (3) manumission ; (4) marriage ; (5) Sunday markets ; (6) property and savings banks ; (7) non-separation of
families under judicial process ; (8) punishment.

not a success in Trinidad, and had returned to their perennial task of amending the slave laws. Under this new scheme slave evidence was at last admitted, but on a most precarious basis, the witness having always to satisfy the court that he understood the obligation of an oath. Vainly was it proposed to substitute the cat for the cart-whip and to prohibit merely the *indecent* flogging of women; but on this occasion the voice of enlightenment did at least make itself heard. One of the members, a Mr. Barrett, declared that on his estate he had abolished both the cart-whip and the cat, and would not allow the former to be used even on his cattle. " I do not hesitate to declare to all who hear me that the cart-whip is a horrible, detestable instrument when used for the punishment and torture of slaves. Honourable members may raise a clamour against me, but they will do so in vain. They are afraid to hear the truth respecting this odious, this detestable instrument." [1]

On May 21, ten days after the date of his Jamaica despatch, Bathurst sent out the eight drafts of legislation to all the other chartered colonies; and the preamble of a Bill received from the island of Nevis, though it had passed in the previous year, may be cited as an indication of how in general they were received. Here the two Houses declared that, after having examined the question in all its bearings, they were " humbly, but firmly, of opinion that the pre-existing laws of this island may by means of certain alterations and amendments be rendered fully adequate to all the objects of those recommendations and of the said Order in Council which can be pursued with due regard to the civil existence and welfare of this colony." [2] The effect, and no doubt also the object, of thus amending old laws instead of enacting new ones was not only to mingle severity and

---

[1] *Reporter*, i. 206–213, 299, 306 ; *P.P.*, 1826–27, vol. xxv.

[2] Nevis, being thus careful of its " civil existence and welfare," had recognised marriage with the proviso that it should not " give any rights whatsoever, except those of a religious nature."

mildness in the manner indicated by Horton, but to make it impossible to judge accurately how much or how little had been done in the way of reform. Everything depended on the extent of modification. In Barbados there seems to have been a race for time between the Assembly and the legal draftsmen ; for the latter had not completed their work when a Consolidation Bill was sent up to the Governor. Sir Henry Warde knew that members meant this to be taken as their reply to Bathurst's demands, of which they had been fully, though unofficially, cognisant ; and, knowing also that they would be greatly offended if he carried out his instructions without first submitting their Bill to the Government, he gave it his provisional assent.[1]

None of the other colonies succeeded in thus evading the question which it was the whole object of the Government to bring to a decisive issue. If the Bills were not everywhere thrown out, it was only because in some cases they were not even allowed to be brought in ; and, in face of this insult to the British Parliament and people, Bathurst showed great weakness in not dismissing with contempt all further tinkering at the slave codes.[2] An instance may be cited to show the extent of his forbearance. In Grenada we find the Solicitor-General, who had framed the Bills, lamenting the failure of his " humble efforts " to bring them under consideration ; but the Consolidated Act was to be revised ; and Bathurst condescended to write that he hoped his " very sincere regret at the successive rejection " of all the measures might be qualified by the results of this revision.[3]

---

[1] The Act will be referred to later.

[2] No doubt, on this occasion, as in 1824 (see p. 139), he had to conform to the temper of the Cabinet, and especially of Lord Liverpool. Even so zealous an Abolitionist as Stephen acknowledged that up to this point he had not " been wanting in decision and firmness in maintaining his ground."—*England Enslaved by her own Slave Colonies*, 1826, p. 11.

[3] We have seen that Tobago had instituted a Guardian. Curiously enough, the office was now abolished in Grenada, the only colony in

A model system of slavery, framed and supervised by the British Government, had now been in operation for two years in Trinidad, and it may be well at this point to consider how it had worked.[1] We have seen that one of the worst defects of this system was that it did not secure to the negroes—overworked as they were in this colony—a weekly day of rest. Sunday markets were indeed sooner or later to be abolished, and meanwhile were to close at ten in the morning, and by a supplementary decree the slave was forbidden even to hire himself out on Sunday ; but on this day, owing to the want or deficiency of other time,[2] he had still to cultivate his provision grounds. Bathurst recognised the necessity, but tried again and again to obviate it by appealing to the moral sense of the slave-owners. Where the planter supplied his slaves with food, he was entitled to exact from them six days labour in the week ; but where the slaves grew their own food, as in Trinidad, he must be satisfied with as much less than six days as would enable them to discharge this task without working on Sunday. Argument was useless. Not only were

which it had previously existed. The legislature of the Bahamas declared that flogging was not only authorised but regulated in " holy scripture." This was an obvious allusion to M'Queen, who had said that the maximum punishment permitted to a slave-owner in the British West Indies was the same as that prescribed by the Jewish law —" forty stripes save one." The same writer referred to Exodus, xxi. 20 : " If a man smite his servant or his maid with a rod and he die under his hand, he shall surely be punished. Notwithstanding, if he continue a day or two, he shall not be punished ; for he is his money." Abolitionists who rebuked slave-owners for their inhumanity " would do well to remember this sacred law and tremble at their own presumption. Man is not wiser than his Maker." Similarly, if they objected to a slave being sold to discharge his master's debts, they were referred to Isaiah, l. 1—" Which of my creditors is it to whom I have sold you ? "—*The West India Colonies*, 1824, pp. 250–52, 270. The Jamaica Assembly voted a sum of £3,000 currency to their pious champion. A text less favourable to West Indian commentators is Exodus, c. xxi. v. 16 : " He that stealeth a man and selleth him, or if he be found in his hand, he shall surely be put to death."

[1] *P.P.*, 1826–7, vol. xxvi. ; 1828, vol. xxvii.
[2] Seventeen days instead of the usual twenty-six.

the slave-owners content that Sunday labour should continue for want of a substitute, but, when this pressure failed, they did not hesitate to violate the Order in Council by resorting to compulsion. When the new code had been in force for two years, Sir Ralph Woodford reported to Horton, who wanted to know " by return of post " what practical difficulties had arisen in the execution of the Order, that hiring out could not be prevented on Sunday, and that " all industrious negroes " worked in their grounds ; and he added this significant admission—" But the idle avoid it and by *some* masters are not forced to it." [1]

The right of the slave to purchase his freedom had presumably continued to some extent in Trinidad after the British conquest ; [2] but the Order in Council had restored it to vigour. In the three and a half years before the Order came into force on June 24, 1824, the number of slaves who had been manumitted was 377, and of these 210 had been freed by grant or bequest of their owners and 167 by purchase. In the next three and a half years the total number of manumissions was 588—gratuitous 179, purchased 409. That the number of the latter should have increased by no fewer than 242 is satisfactory enough ; but the second return, unlike the first, enables us to distinguish the plantation slaves from the favoured class of personal or domestic slaves ; and we find that the former, though twice as numerous (16,000 to 8000), obtained only a third of the purchased manumissions, and of the whole number only 170. This need not surprise us when we remember how hard it must have been for the field-worker with only seventeen week-days at his disposal to work his way to freedom.

---

[1] One rather wonders how anybody could be prosecuted in Trinidad for Sabbath desecration ; but it appears from the register of punishments that one negro in two years had contrived to commit this offence.

[2] M'Donnell says that it continued ; but the rate of manumission in Trinidad, 1819–25, was only three per cent., the same as in Antigua.

Nevertheless, though the Order had not enlarged the fixed allowance of spare time, there was one of its provisions which made it possible for individuals to gain more of this margin ; for the abolition of the driving system had forced upon masters the necessity of finding a new incentive to labour. Sir Ralph Woodford in recording his impressions of a visit to the sugar estates in 1826 said that he found task work adopted wherever it could be introduced and that, though there might sometimes be a difficulty in getting a labourer " to make good a task imperfectly performed," yet the advantages in general were " so great as to be admitted by all as affording great relief to masters as well as slaves." The system, though it hardly needed explanation, was described by Horton to the House of Commons. A certain amount of work, calculated on his average achievement, was assigned to the slave, who was told that the sooner he finished it the more time he would have for relaxation, for labour on his own account or for hire.[1] Task work proved far more effectual as a stimulus than the driving whip ; but it had certain drawbacks ; and these were thus dealt with on an estate which had been sequestered for a debt to the Crown and was managed under the Governor by a neighbouring planter. It seems that this man, a Mr. Peschier, did not " altogether " object to task work, but found that, when the task was given out by the day, the slaves over-exerted themselves and neglected their regular meals. It might have occurred to him that, as the King in Council had provided what Canning called " a way of escape " out of bondage, he ought to lessen the daily task and thus enable these " royal slaves " to qualify for compulsory manumission without injuring their health. But the plan he adopted was to deprive them of all prospect of continuous leisure by setting three tasks daily, which were to be done respectively before break-

[1] Hansard (1826), xiv. 990.

fast, and before and after dinner ; and the result was so far satisfactory that he had " now scarcely any sick," whereas previously many slaves were in hospital. Woodford reported this procedure to the Under-Secretary without a word of disapproval ; and owners could hardly have adopted a cheaper form of humanitarianism than one which both preserved the health of their slaves and prevented their release.

From Sunday labour and compulsory manumission we pass to another aspect of the Order in Council—the admission, if such it can be called, of slave evidence. We have seen that only slaves who had obtained a certificate of competency from their religious teachers were to be admitted as witnesses, but that a clause had been added reserving to the criminal courts any power they already possessed to receive the testimony of slaves. How these two clauses, the 35th and the 36th, were to be reconciled was a question which had been raised by opponents of the Order before it came into operation, and subsequently it gave rise to a complete difference of opinion between the Attorney-General of the colony and the Chief Judge. The former held that the only difference between the two classes of witnesses was that the one must be received without inquiry and the other only if found fit to be sworn. The latter, whilst admitting that the courts had the fullest discretion to receive or reject slave evidence, laid down, strangely enough, that in this matter they must conform to the standard of competency set up by the Government or in other words must insist on certificates ; and this ruling had unfortunate results ; for in Trinidad there were no religious teachers outside the towns, and not enough even there, and in two years only one certificate had been produced in court. Two very serious charges —one of rape, the other of murder—had to be abandoned ; and it seemed only too probable that " crimes would increase and that offenders would escape punishment

take possession of unoccupied land and by exacting a
rent compel the negro to work.[1]

The Privy Council took more than two years to dispose of the plea against compulsory manumission ; but
on March 18, 1829, it decided on the report of a committee that no sufficient cause had been shown for
rescinding this clause in the Berbice Ordinance ; and on
February 2, 1830, the four Orders in Council for the
regulation of slavery in Trinidad, St. Lucia, Demerara,
and Berbice were consolidated into one code.   The
new law had many defects, but it had the great
merit of removing all restrictions on the evidence of
slaves.

Compulsory manumission was the only one of
Canning's proposals which had not been sanctioned by
the West Indian community in London ; and it was
well known that the colonial Assemblies were composed
for the most part of their " attorneys " or agents.   Their
apathy was denounced and their sincerity questioned
in this country, whilst in the colonies they were held
up to execration as the real authors of a policy which
the Government without their support would not have
ventured to adopt.   Their power was doubtless overrated ; for popular opinion in the colonies was violently
hostile to reform ; and the attorneys, besides being not
very amenable to pressure,[2] could retain their political
influence only by humouring the lower class whites.
It now appeared that the non-resident proprietors
meant, not only to oppose compulsory manumission,
but to identify themselves in general with the colonial
Assemblies.   In 1826 appeared a pamphlet, written by

---

[1] *P.P.*, 1826–7, vol. xxvi ; 1828, vol. xxvii ; Hansard (1828), 1026,
1028, 1033 ; *Reporter*, ii. 184, 258 ; *Edinburgh Review* (1827), xlv. 379 ;
M'Donnell, *The West India Legislatures Vindicated*, 1826, p. 102 ; and
Compulsory Manumission, passim.

[2] They received six per cent. of the gross produce.   Dallas thought
it an " enormous commission " and referred to " the high airs and rapid
flights to fortune of the six per centers."—*History of the Maroons*, ii.
361, 370.

Alexander M'Donnell, Secretary to the West Indian
Committee, and professing to express their views, which
bore the significant title, " The West India Legislatures
Vindicated from the charge of having resisted the call
of the mother country for the amelioration of slavery."
M'Donnell occupied the latter half of his space in
denouncing compulsory manumission—a theme which
he amplified rather than developed in a subsequent
tract ; but in the first half he had a more difficult task,
having to justify his clients, first in siding with the
Government, and then in supporting the practical
rejection of demands which, with one exception, they
had themselves approved. We are told that, when
Buxton opened his campaign in 1823, the non-residents
were greatly alarmed, dreading an insurrection of the
negroes and feeling their inability as interested parties
to stem " the overwhelming tide of clamour " by showing
how greatly conditions had improved since the abolition
of the slave trade. They welcomed Canning's offer to
take command of the movement as an assurance both
of these good offices and of compensation for the planters ;
and they were " bitterly disappointed." The Government did nothing, as they thought, to allay the agitation ; and, instead of wielding the influence ascribed to
them in the colonies, they were " mercilessly run down."
It might have been supposed that they could not honour-
ably recede from the position they had assumed ; but
M'Donnell got rid of this difficulty by asserting—what
at best was an incomplete apology—that " the only
regulations of importance which the majority of the
colonies had not adopted to the extent contemplated"
were the abolition of the driving whip and the flogging
of women.[1]

It will be well at this point to indicate the succession

[1] *The West India Legislatures Vindicated*, pp. 5, 7, 8, 10, 18. At a
meeting on February 24, 1830, the West Indian Committee declared
its identity in interest with the colonial legislatures and its implicit
confidence in their proceedings.

of Ministries with which we shall have to deal. Canning, who had been the leading member of Lord Liverpool's Government in the House of Commons, became Prime Minister on the illness and resignation of his chief in April 1827; and Bathurst as Colonial Secretary was succeeded by Lord Goderich. When Canning died in August, Goderich obtained the premiership, and his place at the Colonial Office was taken by Huskisson. In January 1828 the Duke of Wellington formed a Ministry which lasted for nearly three years; and in the following May Huskisson was replaced by Sir George Murray.

Nothing of much importance to the Abolitionists occurred during the brief administration of Canning; but a question was raised which enabled them to retaliate on those who impeached their discretion. They were often accused of bringing forward measures which they would have shrunk from suggesting had their position been as perilous as that of the scanty and isolated white population of the West Indies; and the nervousness which we have seen to be characteristic of the planters makes it the more difficult to understand their racial exclusiveness. There were 25,000 whites in Jamaica and 340,000 slaves; but the free community was completed by 30,000 browns or " people of colour " and 10,000 blacks; and the former of these two classes had more reason than the latter to resent the hardships which were common to both. In the original charters of all the West Indian colonies it was declared that the children of whites born in the island should have the same privileges as free-born subjects, and for about half a century these privileges were accorded to the offspring of white men by brown or black women; but early in the eighteenth century the legislatures began to discriminate against persons of mixed blood; and, when Bryan Edwards published his " History of the British West Indies " in 1793, the position of these people in Jamaica had become so intolerable as to make them

" wretched to themselves and useless to the public." [1]
They could not give evidence in criminal cases against
whites and in this respect were worse off than the slaves
whose masters, if they were assaulted, could recover
damages. They could not serve on juries ; they were
excluded from both the Assembly and the franchise,
from all official and almost all business posts ; they could
not hold commissions even in their own companies of
militia ; they could not receive a bequest or make a
purchase of more than £1400 sterling ; they were not
allowed to navigate their own vessels or to drive their
own carts and coaches ; and their children were excluded,
with one partial exception, from all the public schools.
The men could seldom afford to marry, and the women
were " universally maintained by white men of all
ranks and conditions as kept mistresses." Despising the
blacks and cringing to the whites, the mulattos were
always loyal ; and after the Maroon War of 1796 they
were allowed to give evidence against whites in cases
of assault. In 1813 they were admitted in all cases as
witnesses, and their financial and some of their commercial disabilities were removed ; but they were still
excluded as jurymen, though it often happened owing to
the scarcity of whites that a coroner's inquest could
not be held without having recourse to soldiers or sailors.
In 1823 full citizenship was demanded and partially
obtained by the coloured people of Grenada ; but a
similar movement in Jamaica failed ; [2] and, three years
later, when a number of whites petitioned in their favour,
relief was refused to the coloured Christians who had
asked for it, but was bestowed, unsolicited, on the Jews.[3]

[1] Edwards, ii. 33.

[2] Two of the petitioners were deported on pretence of being concerned in the negro conspiracy. See p. 135.

[3] The leading members of the Jewish community in Jamaica were
both wealthy and popular. The Jews were expelled from the French
colonies by the *Code Noir* of 1685, and this measure of the French was
said to be almost as beneficial to Jamaica as their persecution of the
Huguenots had proved to England. Jews were most desirable immi-

As owners of property the mulattos had now almost as good a claim as the Jews to the franchise. Many of the coffee plantations and all but one of the pimento plantations were said to be in their hands; and four of them had recently left fortunes ranging from £120,000 to £250,000.

Resenting the attitude of the Assembly, though it had begun to emancipate them individually by private Bills, the coloured people of Jamaica applied to the House of Commons; and on June 12, 1827, a petition was presented on their behalf by Lushington and supported by Brougham. Canning declared that the injustice complained of belonged rather to the sphere of manners than of legislation and could be remedied only by the progress of opinion; and the course he recommended was that which had been pursued with so little success on the question of slavery—appeals to the local legislature and only in the last resort intervention by Parliament. But he did not fail to point out the position of the coloured population as "neutrals whom the governing part of the society might win to themselves by indulgence and conciliation and whom it would be absolute madness and the most incredible folly, with their eyes open, not to conciliate and thereby gain a most important acquisition." [1]

When Huskisson entered on his duties at the Colonial Office in the autumn of 1827, two very important slave codes—those of Barbados and Jamaica—were still under consideration. The Barbadian code certainly fared better than its framers were entitled to expect. This was the Act which had been passed, as we have seen, rather in place than in fulfilment of Bathurst's eight

grants, their chief object being, according to Voltaire, "the getting of money and children." In Jamaica they were reputed to be lax in ritual, especially as to pork, and "indeed," says Long, "the West India pork is of so exquisite a flavour that, if Moses had ever tasted it, he certainly would not have been so unkind towards his followers as to include it in his catalogue of non-eatables."—*History of Jamaica*, ii. 294-7, 922.

[1] *Journals of the Commons*, June 12, 1827; Hansard (1827), xvi. 1242-56.

drafts. The Council of the colony believed that the measure had no chance of receiving the royal assent as it left out some of the chief recommendations for which Ministers " stood pledged to the people of England," and they had passed it only with a view to following it up with a " Supplemental Bill," abolishing the driving whip and the flogging of females over fourteen, which the Assembly rejected. Nevertheless Huskisson confirmed the Act, though unable to regard it, as one can well believe, " with unqualified satisfaction " ; and it is evident that a similar compliment would have been paid to Jamaica if its legislators could have refrained from gratifying their spite against missionaries. There were three clauses of this nature in the Act, one prohibiting slaves from assuming the office of a religious teacher, another forbidding meetings for worship between sunset and sunrise, and a third making it punishable to collect money from slaves for religious or charitable objects. It was mainly, but not wholly on these grounds, that the Act was disallowed ; and the Governor was warned that no law which needlessly infringed religious liberty would ever be sanctioned by the Crown. In reply to the conciliatory, if not apologetic, terms in which Huskisson announced this decision, the Assembly occupied eleven and a half folio pages of print in expressing their indignation that so much respect had been shown to " mendicant sectarians " and so little to the constitution of the colony. Huskisson filled eight pages in trying " rather to allay than to foment the excitement " ; and one cannot but sympathise with the Abolitionists when they asked how long the Government meant to " engage in this unceasing conflict of clauses and enactments, this strife of words which leads to no useful result." [1] In 1828 the Bill was reintroduced and

---

[1] We shall find that Lord Grey's Government in 1831 put an end to this controversy on the sufficient ground that " to leave the choice of the words to any body of men is to place the substance and essence of the law at their discretion."

passed " precisely in the same words as the old law, with
the difference of dates " ; and next year it passed again,
this time somewhat improved as a slave code, but
" creating a more marked and invidious distinction
between sectarians and ministers of the Established
Church." [1]

In the other islands no real progress had been made
since the period of our survey,[2] with the notable exception that in Grenada and Tobago all restrictions on
the admission of slave evidence had at last been removed.
We have seen that Tobago had promised little and done
much ; but there was an instance in which this attitude
had been reversed.   If there was one colony in the whole
British West Indies which might have been expected
to welcome the proposals of the Government, it was
Antigua.   Here was a community which had warmly
encouraged the religious instruction of its slaves, which
had been the first to give them the right of being tried
by a jury, which had never imposed a tax on manumission, and the liberal character of whose institutions
was extolled even by Stephen.   The law-makers of
Antigua were fond of congratulating themselves on the
humane disposition they had inherited from their
ancestors, and indeed had done nothing but expatiate
on this theme up to August 1826, when the Governor
expressed " the strongest doubts " as to their delibera-
tions " terminating in a manner at all answerable to
the expectations " of Ministers and Parliament. Next
summer, when called upon to consider Bathurst's eight
Bills, which had been postponed owing to the dissolution
of the preceding Assembly, they claimed, as usual, " the
honour of having on every occasion of this sort led the
way towards improvement " ; but no answer was returned to the Governor when in May 1828 he complained

---

[1] *P.P.*, 1826–7, vol. xxv. ; 1828, vol. xxvii ; *Reporter*, ii. 349. The
new Jamaica slave code was at last accepted by the Crown in 1831.
    [2] See p. 163.

that he had heard nothing of these Bills for over ten months, and in August he had to report that they had all been rejected. A Slave Consolidation Act was indeed " now in slow progress " ; but at the end of the year it was " little advanced " ; and Sir George Murray had the " painful duty " of intimating to this colony the King's displeasure at its " extreme backwardness."

Speaking in Parliament on March 5, 1828, Brougham said that " the progress of the colonies was so slow as to be imperceptible to all human eyes save their own " ; but Ministers were unable or indisposed to contemplate direct action by Parliament and consequently were bound to magnify every symptom of compliance. Huskisson permitted himself to say that, certain instructions having been distinctly communicated to the colonies, " the acquiescence which had taken place amounted to nothing less than implied adoption " ; and Wellington declared that, on the whole, " considering the prejudices naturally interwoven with West India views of this subject, it was more wonderful to behold the progress already made than (sic) to express any strong censure for what remained to be done." [1] These apologies were more likely to harden than to soften the hearts of the slave-owners ; [2] but in justice to the Wellington Government it should be mentioned that Sir George Murray did make an attempt to bring them to reason. In a despatch of September 1828 which was intended to be laid before the Assemblies he emphasised and illustrated " the settled purpose " of Ministers to adhere strictly to the resolutions of 1823 ; and in a confidential despatch to the Governors he declared that, unless the colonial legislatures should strengthen the hands of their friends in this country by giving some practical proof of their concurrence in the principle of amelioration, " it will soon

[1] Hansard (1828), xviii. 978, 979 ; xix. 1466.
[2] In the colonies, and especially in St. Lucia, there was a feeling that the Government was inclined to favour the planter.—Jeremie, p. 101.

soon as possible be abolished.   Buxton readily accepted
a suggestion that all British children born on and after
the first of January next should be declared free ; but
Brougham naturally objected that this was not the
sort of project which could be carried at the close of
a session ; and Parliament, whilst still called upon
to emancipate infants, was left free to fix the date.
Denman moved that all opponents of slavery should be
exhorted to exert themselves " for uniting every heart
and hand in petitions to Parliament for its early and
universal abolition " ; and Lushington, in seconding
the motion, recommended that the petition of the Society
should be entrusted to Brougham.   " He spoke the truth,
lamentable as in itself it was, that scarcely a decent
hearing could be obtained in that House by any other
member on this subject.   He alone was possessed of
that power and that influence which Parliament did not
seem capable of resisting."   The colonists, if we may
judge from one of their newspapers, affected to regard
this meeting as " the last expiring effort of an exhausted
faction."   But for them as slave-owners it was the
beginning of the end.

On July 1, 1830, when Parliament was on the brink
of dissolution, the petition of the Society was presented
by Brougham, who described it as coming " from a
meeting which was equalled by none that I ever saw " ;
and on the 13th he called on the House for " a solemn
pledge " which should influence both the election and
the attitude of its successor.   He insisted that Parliament should take up the task which the colonial legislatures had moved " not by a hair's breadth " to
accomplish ; and he advocated the abolition of slavery
in a manner, if not with an intention, which could not
but alarm the planters, asserting as a lawyer that man
could have no property in his fellow creatures.   " Talk
not to me of such monstrous pretensions being decreed
by Acts of Parliament and recognised by treaties."

Such language would have dismayed Canning; but the present Ministers seemed rather to have receded than advanced from his position. Both Murray and Peel declared that they were not prepared to pledge themselves to that ultimate abolition which had been contemplated in the resolutions of 1823; and the latter said that he hoped the colonists, prompted by this and other motions, would " begin to improve and ameliorate " the condition of their slaves, and invited them to do so in the full conviction " that there was no intention on the part of the Legislature here to interfere so as to interrupt their efforts "—a contingency which Canning had expressly recognised. Brougham's assertion that there could be no property in slaves did not necessarily debar their owners from compensation, since, if Parliament had deluded itself on this point, there was the more reason that it should indemnify its victims; but, three days later, the interpretation which might have been put on Brougham's speech was frankly avowed by Otway Cave, who had discovered that the slaves, being British subjects, were *ipso facto* free. The Anti-Slavery Society had in his opinion been " carrying on a petty war of outposts." They ought to have attacked the enemy in force by showing that slavery had never been sanctioned by law; and he even made the extraordinary assertion that, if the planters had been legally entitled to their human property, he would have left them undisturbed—as if the validity of a bad law could be any reason for not demanding its repeal. He also said with more truth than discretion that, if Parliament refused freedom to the slaves, they would be justified in taking it by force.[1]

Wilberforce retired from Parliament at the general election of 1830, and his place as one of the four members for Yorkshire—all pledged to abolition—was taken by Brougham. The opponents of slavery were highly

[1] Hansard (1830), xxv. 1172–92, 1201, 1208, 1210, 1227–30.

gratified by the evidence afforded on this occasion of the popularity of their cause ; but they could not fully realise at the time how greatly they and all other friends of reform had benefited from the " July Revolution " in France. Charles X paid for his attempt to make himself absolute by having to make way for his cousin, Louis Philippe, as " King of the French " ; and great was the enthusiasm in Britain when it was seen that a people could assert itself, and even rise in arms, and yet be content with no more extravagant reward than the establishment of constitutional rule. The embargo which public opinion had imposed on political agitation since the days of Thomas Paine was insensibly removed ; [1] and the news from Paris arrived in time to influence some of the urban and all of the county elections in favour of parliamentary reform. The Tories had still a majority in the new Parliament ; but soon after it met on October 26 Wellington delivered the famous speech in which he described the representative system as so good that it could not be improved ; and on November 17 the Whigs came into office under Earl Grey. Both parties were committed to the amelioration of slavery with a view to its ultimate extinction ; but the Tories had merely been called upon in virtue of their official position to manage a movement which derived all its energy from the Whigs ; [2] and the events of November 1830 had this significance for the planters that, though the Government still tried to hold the balance between them and the Abolitionists, it was now in sympathy with the latter.

Buxton, though he credited the new Ministry with a

---

[1] " The battle of English liberty," said the *Edinburgh Review*, " has really been fought and won at Paris " ; and English liberty meant liberty also for the slaves.

[2] Buxton, Brougham, Lushington, Denman, Lord Suffield, and almost all the leading members of the Anti-Slavery Society were Whigs. The Nonconformist element was very strong in this party ; and, of 2,600 petitions presented in the autumn of 1830, 2,200 were said to have come from Dissenters.—Hansard (1830), i. 1052.

detestation of slavery equal to his own,[1] was well aware
that they could do no more than mitigate this evil till
they had settled the more urgent question of parliamentary reform ; but he and his friends could not recede
from the position which had been taken up by Brougham,
now Lord Chancellor, in the previous summer ; and on
April 15, 1831, four days before the first Reform Bill
was lost in Committee, he moved that the House should
consider the best means of abolishing slavery. The
motion was seconded by Lord Morpeth, the son of a
Cabinet Minister,[2] and only one other member had spoken
when the attitude of the Government was defined by
the Chancellor of the Exchequer, Lord Althorp. They
refused to go beyond the resolutions of 1823 and consequently would have nothing to do with immediate
emancipation ; but, unlike their predecessors, they
dismissed as wholly inadequate the proceedings of the
West Indian legislatures and were thus compelled to
take action. " It is impossible in my opinion," said
Althorp, " that the House can stand still." Even now,
after eight years of contumacy, the colonies were not
to be coerced ; but a reward was to be offered for their
compliance ; and he announced that the duties on slave-
grown products would be so adjusted as to give an
advantage to those colonies which had adopted the
resolutions. So far there was nothing to prevent a
recurrence of the interminable disputes as to what did
or did not constitute adoption ; but a different complexion was put on the matter by Lord Howick, son of
Lord Grey and Under-Secretary for the Colonies, who
outlined a stringent revision of the recent consolidated
Order in Council [3] which was then in preparation, and
intimated that colonies desirous of participating in the
proposed fiscal benefit would have to adopt it " word
for word." This was the mildest possible application

---

[1] *Memoirs*, p. 256.
[2] The Earl of Carlisle, who was for several years in the Cabinet
without office. [3] See p. 186.

of Canning's suggestion that, if the colonies proved obdurate, restraints might be put on their commerce ; but it was too severe for his Tory successors. Horace Twiss,[1] who had served under Sir George Murray at the Colonial Office, was so ill-informed as to threaten Parliament with a powerful opposition in Jamaica " owing to the union between the free people of colour and the whites " ; and, when this fable had been disposed of by Lushington, Peel thought it a still more alarming situation that the free blacks and mulattos should be " ready to use their utmost efforts to compel the refractory whites to obey the orders of the Government." He said that Althorp was appealing to the avarice of the planters, but " might find there were more serious and more powerful passions to be conquered. He might find there was pride to be overcome." These utterances reflected little credit on the late Ministry. Their attitude had indeed been naïvely disclosed by Sir George Murray shortly after they left office : " I have always supposed until this moment that to abstain from any extraordinary activity in the measures to be carried into effect with respect to the colonies was a merit rather than a defect." [2]

The Crown colonies must have reckoned with a revision of the Consolidated Order in Council ; for Murray in transmitting it to the Governors on February 4, 1830, had informed them that certain topics, such as the slave's hours of labour, his food, clothing, and religious instruction, had been omitted, though of more importance than some which were included ; and, a fortnight later, he had required them to furnish information on these points with a view to completing the code. Nevertheless

---

[1] " Of all the Under-Secretaries who had ever laid the weight of their authority upon the transactions of the Colonial Office, the fleshiest incubus."—Sir Henry Taylor, *Autobiography*, i. 117.

[2] Hansard (1830), i. 1060 ; (1831) iii. 1418, 1426, 1444, 1454, 1456, 1459 ; *Reporter*, iv. 252. The debate, which had been adjourned, was cut short by the dissolution of Parliament.

Lord Howick's announcement that a new and Whig edition of this edict was not only being prepared, but was to be established throughout the West Indies created " the greatest consternation and alarm " amongst the non-resident proprietors ; and their fears were by no means allayed when the Government consented to let them have copies of the draft and offered to receive written objections. It then appeared that the existing regulations were to be stiffened as well as enlarged. The Protector was no longer to act only when appealed to by his clients. He was to have the right of visiting estates, of entering the huts of the negroes and of conversing with them ; and the medical officer of a plantation was to keep a journal for his inspection. Of the new rules much the most important were those which fixed the duration of labour. These clauses did not abolish night work ; but they provided that no slave should be compelled to work more than nine hours in twelve " out of crop " or more than nine hours in twenty-four during crop. In both cases he was to have respites of one hour and two hours ; but in the former case they were fixed at eight in the morning and at noon, whilst in the latter they might be given at any other time, provided they were separated by intervals of not less than three or more than six hours. Slaves under fourteen or over sixty years of age and pregnant females were never to be employed at night or for more than six hours during the day.

Lord Goderich, who had been Colonial Secretary during the four months of Canning's administration in 1827, held the same office under Lord Grey ; and the Order in Council, as finally adjusted on November 2, 1831, was sent out by him on the 5th. A few changes had been made [1] in consequence of representations from proprietors and merchants connected with the Crown

---

[1] The chief change was that slaves were to be severely punished for complaints found to be groundless.

colonies ; but these representations, copies of which were
enclosed, had been used mainly as a means of anticipating the objections most likely to be raised in the
West Indies ; and this was done in a long and elaborate
despatch which ought to have convinced the slave-
owners that their term of probation was almost at an
end. Goderich admitted that the Government had been
influenced by general principles in so far as they took for
granted that unrestrained power must and will be abused
and that an unpopular law will never be voluntarily
executed ; but he denied that they had been " floating
on the tide of popular prejudice or impelled by vague
theories " ; and, in reply to the old argument that they
were not sufficiently well informed to legislate on this
question, he referred to the mass of materials which had
been accumulating for eight years and said that, if ignorance still existed, it must be incurable. He also denied
that " an exact knowledge of the particular society in
which a law is to operate " was sufficient for legislation,
especially where the society was so isolated, prejudiced,
and uncultivated as that of the West Indies and so dis-
tracted by pecuniary embarrassments of which slavery
itself was " the great and permanent source." The
Protector had been represented as a spy coming from
a distant country to report upon the actions of the
colonists ; but " at this distance from the scene the
colony and the colonists may be recognised rather in
the myriads of slaves than in the hundreds of managers
and owners " ; and, in reference to the complaint that
the Order was " vague, loose, and contrary to the most
approved principles of legislation," inasmuch as it
penalised modes of ill-treating slaves which were not
clearly defined, " nothing is more obvious than the
answer : What power is so vague, so loose, and so contrary to approved principles as that with which the
law invests the owner ? " In a subsequent despatch
it was stated that the discretionary power allowed to

Governors under the previous Order had in this case been reduced to the narrowest limits.

The apprehension of trouble evident in these arguments and injunctions was not belied. The first of the Crown colonies to receive the Order in Council was St. Lucia, and it was proclaimed there on December 24, 1831. Planters, attorneys, and merchants at once organised themselves for resistance under the leadership of a Mr. Muter who, as he belonged to all these three classes and was also a shipbroker, was able to conduct a quite ubiquitous campaign ; and the colony was soon in " an unexampled state of agitation." A Dr. Robinson resigned his office of Medical Examiner, and he and nine other doctors refused to submit to " such unwarrantable degradation " as was involved in their subjection to the Protector. The store-keepers endeavoured to procure a suspension of the Order by closing their premises for a week, and Muter succeeded in frustrating an attempt of the Governor to obtain provisions from Martinique. In Trinidad there was also resistance, though not so general and persistent ; and in British Guiana the Court of Policy sought to avert the publication of the Order by representing " utter ruin and desolation " as its inevitable result. The reduction in the hours of labour, which had attracted no great attention in London, was vehemently attacked by the colonists ; and here they had some reason to complain. That the slaves were overworked in the crop season had long been notorious ; but, as the firemen and boiler-men were not continuously employed, this grievance might have been remedied without fixing the same number of hours for both the cultivation and the manufacture of sugar.[1] If the Lancashire cotton manufacturer could legally exact twelve hours of labour from persons under sixteen, it was naturally asked why the planter should be prohibited

---

[1] Jeremie had suggested nine hours of field-work and during crop eleven hours of in-door work.—*Essays*, p. 80.

from exacting more than nine hours from a full-grown negro. The Government subsequently explained that they did not mean to prevent the slave working longer if his master could induce him to do so by the offer of wages.

A measure which had encountered so much obstruction in the Crown colonies was not likely to be adopted where it could not be authoritatively imposed; but Jamaica had been hurling defiance at " a tyrannical Government " ever since the speeches of Lords Althorp and Howick were received there in the previous summer. Parochial meetings, usually with a magistrate in the chair, had been held all over the island, at which misrepresentation was even more conspicuous than abuse. Lord Grey's Government was the fifth in succession which had declared that its immediate object was not the abolition but the amelioration of slavery; and it had gone beyond its predecessors only in this respect, that it had put forth a scheme for inducing the colonial legislatures to adopt reforms which had long been approved by both Houses of Parliament. But no one who read the resolutions of the planters could have supposed that this was their grievance. The Cabinet, they declared, had surrendered to a faction whose desire it was " to see the knife at our throats—to stand by and cheer on the blacks to our destruction "; they were to be deprived of their property in a manner which could not " fail to create a servile war of too horrible a nature to contemplate "; they were required to yield " uncompensated emancipation "; British slavery, repudiated by its own Government, could be preserved only under the protection of the United States; and by way of preparing for secession they even proposed to raise a permanent militia. Committees of correspondence were formed in some of the parishes, and a meeting of delegates was held at Spanish Town on November 28. The agitators were mainly overseers and attorneys. Consequently it was not their own but other people's property that they proposed to put under a foreign flag ; and the immediate, though not the worst, effect of their resolutions was to intensify the quarrel between the whites and the free people of colour. The latter had been fully enfranchised in 1830 ; but they were enthusiastically loyal, and, knowing how people of their complexion were treated in the Southern States of the Union, they had so great an abhorrence of America that they " hated its very name."

The blustering of planters was too familiar a phenomenon to be taken seriously in Britain ; and the policy of the Government was unchanged when Goderich, after having transmitted his instructions to the Crown colonies on November 5, addressed himself to the autonomous islands on December 10. He began by recalling the earnest appeals for submission to the wishes of Parliament which had gone forth year after year— " the expression of hopes which had not been fulfilled and of confidence which had not been justified," and declared that " His Majesty's present advisers have resolved to pursue no further this course of warning and entreaty." Canning had suggested in 1824 that, if the colonies proved obdurate, the mildest form of coercion would be to impose fiscal regulations adverse to their commerce.[1] But the West Indies were now suffering severely from the general depression of trade ;[2] and the Government, far from imposing burdens, meant to ask Parliament to afford them relief. It was impossible, however, to bestow this boon without reference to the amelioration of slavery, and consequently it would be conferred only on those colonies in which an Act had been passed declaring " simply and without qualification " that the Consolidated Order in Council had the

[1] Hansard (1824), x. 1105.
[2] The price of muscovado sugar had fallen from 37s. in 1828 to 22s. 8d. in 1830.—Tooke, ii. 414.

force of law. To permit verbal alterations would be
to revive the " interminable controversy " as to the
sufficiency of colonial Acts ; and Goderich concluded
by warning the Assemblies that, if they continued to
withstand the growing force of public opinion in this
country, they would involve themselves in calamities
" from which it may be beyond the power of any Government to protect them." [1]

The anti-slavery agitation had recently been intensified in a manner which made this warning opportune.
Ever since the meeting of May 15, when it had been
resolved not to insist on the emancipation of children
born after the end of that year,[2] the younger members
of the Society had been dissatisfied with the cautious
policy of their leaders, declaring that nothing decisive
would ever be done in Parliament till means had been
taken to increase the " pressure from without." George,
fourth son of James Stephen and legal adviser of the
Society, was one of this number ; and in 1831, after a
scheme he had devised for rousing the country had been
rejected as " well-meaning but impracticable," it was
taken up by several wealthy Abolitionists, the chief of
whom were James Cropper and Joseph Sturge, a corn
merchant of Birmingham. Both were members of the
Society of Friends, and the former promised £500, and
the latter £250. This led to the formation of the Agency
Committee, so-called because it employed agents—six
of them paid—to lecture and organise, and quite independent of the Anti-Slavery Society, though, in order
to avoid the appearance of schism, it occupied rooms
in the same building in Aldermanbury—an arrangement
not appreciated by the older body, which complained
that it was held responsible for methods and statements
which it did not always approve. Sturge was the life
and soul of the movement, which continued from July
to the late autumn, when it was suspended in deference

[1] *P.P.*, 1831–2, vol. xlvi.   [2] See p. 196.

to the efforts for parliamentary reform ; and so great was his influence in the Midlands that Birmingham as a centre of operations was second only to London.[1]

The general election of 1831 had given a great majority to the Whigs, who had hitherto been in office without being in power ; and the passing of the Reform Bill would weaken, if not destroy, the West Indian party in the House of Commons. If this danger was too remote or too problematical to capture the imagination of the colonists, they could at least see that the agitation which they had thought menacing enough on the other side of the Atlantic was now at their doors. Quite recently nobody in the West Indies would have dared to say a word in favour of emancipation ; but now, in its most extreme form, it was being advocated in the colonial press ; and, as Buxton said in Parliament, the controversy raged with greater violence in Jamaica than in Britain. Nevertheless the obstinacy of the planters, which their best friends as early as 1826 had described as suicidal, was unshaken. Lord Goderich's offer was everywhere repelled ; and St. Christopher, which pleaded poverty, was the only colony which apologised for its rejection. Jamaica declared that any further amelioration in the condition of its slaves " must emanate from ourselves." Barbados and Dominica were bluntly adverse ; Antigua said that " the speculative propositions which have been so authoritatively addressed to it," could not be entertained ; the Bahamas returned " a rude and discourteous message " to their Governor ; Grenada took its stand on British liberties and chartered rights ; Tobago resented " a species of dictation before unheard of " ; and, though the decision of St. Vincent was delayed, the Governor could hold out no hope that it would be favourable.

The slave-owners were never to have another chance

---

[1] Richard, *Memoirs of Sturge*, 1864, pp. 92–9 ; Sir George Stephen, *Anti-Slavery Recollections*, 1854, pp. 120–58.

of conforming to the resolutions of 1823; but their
deplorable situation at this period made it an ungrateful
task to coerce them even for their good. They were
suffering, not only from acute commercial distress, but
from the effects of two recent disasters. On August 11,
1831, a terrific hurricane had swept over several of the
islands. It was bad enough in St. Vincent and St. Lucia,
but worst of all in Barbados. In Bridgetown almost
every house was either destroyed or damaged; the
residence of the Governor, the Custom-house, and two
churches were completely demolished; the houses of
the planters, their sugar-works, their woods and crops
were laid waste; and the total loss there and elsewhere
was estimated at £1,700,000.[1] Jamaica escaped this
scourge; but at the end of the year it was subjected
to a storm, of a different kind indeed, but sufficiently
destructive.

We have seen that the planters of this colony had
recently been engaged in rhetorical demonstrations
which, in view of their environment, were about as safe
as playing with fireworks in a powder magazine. The
resolutions passed at their parochial meetings were
published in the *Jamaica Courant* and enforced by
frenzied appeals signed " Dorcas " or " Umbratus " and
attributed to the Rev. R. W. Bridges. In one of these
the agitators were incited to take possession of the House
of Assembly. In another publicity was given in large
type to a rumour that the British garrison had received
" secret orders to remain neuter or to act against us in
the event of disturbance." And, whilst the *Courant*
was asserting the planter's absolute right of property
in his slave, the *Watchman* was proclaiming the natural
equality of mankind and presenting pictures of slavery
which Goderich described as " most disgusting and
appalling."

---

[1] The storm is vividly described in a letter written from St. Vincent
by John Sterling, and printed in his *Life* by Carlyle. Of Bridgetown,

No pains were taken, and probably none would have availed, to conceal from the slaves a movement in which they were so deeply interested. They were not even excluded from the parochial meetings. Some of them could read, and the *Courant*, to which every planter subscribed, was usually within their reach. But intelligence was more widely diffused by a class of degraded whites whom the negroes called "walking buckras." These were usually discharged sailors or book-keepers who went about begging, and frequently had newspapers which in return for food, rum, or lodging they read to the slaves. The numerous negro servants overheard enough to excite, if not always to enlighten, them in the conversation of their masters. Some of the latter even taunted their slaves with the prospect of freedom, saying that meanwhile they would "sweat them" or "take it out of them." The result was that the same idea which had prevailed with far less reason in Demerara in 1823 now took possession of the slaves in Jamaica—that their "free paper" or charter of emancipation had come out and was being suppressed. The talk of secession as the only means of averting the abolition of slavery confirmed them in this belief and also gave rise to the idea—which was so indiscreetly published by the *Courant*—that they could count on the neutrality, if not on the assistance, of the King's troops. When the free coloured people were admitted to citizenship in 1830, the slaves had thought that something would soon be done for them ; and they are said to have been "elated to the highest pitch of joy" when on November 2, 1831, Beaumont, one of the most prominent members of the Assembly and a man of great independence and courage, brought forward a motion in favour of compulsory manumission. But this motion, and

---

Sterling wrote : "The town is little but a heap of ruins, and the corpses are reckoned by thousands, while throughout the island there are not, I believe, ten estates on which the buildings are standing."

reported, "Nine-tenths of the whole slave population have this morning refused to turn out to work." It appears from the newspapers that on the previous day in the adjoining parish the same demand had been made and refused. The abridgment of holidays may have precipitated a crisis; but it is not mentioned by any of the witnesses who were examined by a committee of the House of Commons; and the Abolitionists were quite out of their reckoning when they sought to prove that the revolt was unpremeditated,[1] that it was welcomed, if not provoked, by the planters as a means of stopping the agitation in Britain, and that the story of a plot was no better founded in 1831 than it had been in 1823.

The issue of the proclamation had been occasioned by two isolated outbreaks before Christmas; and on the 27th there was a widespread commotion. The insurgents were so far faithful to their leader's instructions that they did not offer violence to the planters, but they compelled them to leave their estates. On the same day a property called Kensington was fired by some drunken negroes who had broken into the rum stores; and then, as some of them afterwards said, "the devil got into their heads." They began a regular system of setting fire to the mansion-houses and sugar-works, but not to the plantations, apparently with the idea of preventing the return of their owners; and that night the fugitives at Montego Bay read the fate of their properties in a horizon which "for miles was lighted up with a strong lurid glare." The work of destruction would probably have been arrested at this point if the task of its suppression had not fallen into incompetent hands. Owing to the custom of maintaining a guard during the Christmas holidays, the militia were more or less under

---

[1] *Reporter*, v. 244. A sort of city of refuge was subsequently discovered in the deepest recesses of the woods, consisting of twenty-one houses, "completely ready for occupation."

arms ; but they were all in or near the coast towns,
with the exception of the Western Interior Regiment—
all planters and under a planter-colonel named Gignon.
This officer was retreating on the 26th before the rising
had actually begun, and he fell back from one post to
another on each of the two following days. On the
29th, having been reinforced by a coloured company
of the St. James's Regiment, he made a stand at Mont-
pelier, where Lord Seaford had a large sugar estate.
The newcomers did all the fighting in so far as there
was any, and the rebels were easily repulsed ; but the
coloured men were naturally indignant ; and Gignon,
apparently because he could not get another company to
take their place, retired with his whole force on the 29th
to Montego Bay.[1]

The consequences of this retreat were of course
disastrous. Nearly the whole interior of the county of
Cornwall was lost. For several days not a white person
was to be seen, and the rebels, not only terrorised the
peaceable slaves, but induced many to join them by
representing that the " buckras " had abandoned the
country. On January 1, 1832, Sir Willoughby Cotton,
the British commander, landed at Montego Bay, where
he found the people " in the greatest confusion and
panic " and expecting every night that the town would
be burned. Next day he issued a proclamation offering
pardon to all but the ringleaders, which had an " extraordinary effect " ; and the regular troops soon restored
order, though they found great difficulty in getting at
the rebels through the dense woods and along the precipitous mountain paths. On January 5 Sir Willoughby
reported to the Governor that tranquillity was " fast
returning " and that crowds of negroes were coming in
to avail themselves of the proclamation. The militia
were more active in putting down the remains of the

---

[1] Colonel Gignon was court-martialled ; but, owing to some technical
objection, the trial was discontinued.

from the pulpit and even incited their converts to use the torch as well as the sword. All efforts to incriminate the missionaries failed, though six were arrested and two were tried.[1] We cannot, however, wonder that the discharge of their difficult and delicate task had exposed them to suspicion. Sent out at the expense of religious societies to preach the Gospel, they were protected and encouraged by the British Government with the express object of creating an atmosphere favourable to emancipation; and how could they prepare the slaves for freedom without at the same time making them impatient of their bonds? The Church of England missionary[2] was supposed among the planters to have an aptitude for this work which was wanting in the less educated Dissenter; but the former was favoured mainly because he was less zealous or at all events less active.[3] The negroes had usually to come to him at his chapel, where as a rule he gave only oral instruction, whilst the Wesleyan and the Baptist sought out the negroes in their huts, preached to them on the estates and taught reading wherever it was allowed. We are told that many of the slaves wished to be able to read merely on account of their interest in the movement for abolition; and, when such a spirit was abroad, the missionaries could keep it in check only by inculcating the Christian virtues of resignation and patience. This was not so difficult in such islands as Antigua and St. Christopher where they worked under the patronage of the planters;

[1] A large landed proprietor wrote to Knibb " that religion had nothing to do with the late disturbances, but on the contrary, its absence was a chief cause of them."—Hinton, *Memoir of Knibb*, p. 133.

[2] The Society for the Propagation of the Gospel was in the unfortunate position of being a slave-holder on the two estates belonging to Codrington College in Barbados. It is remarkable that the use of the driving whip was admitted by the Society as late as 1829—six years after its abolition had been recommended by the British Government. —*Reporter*, ii. 420.

[3] Episcopal missionaries, when they did exert themselves, as in the case of Mr. Harte in Barbados, were equally unpopular. See Hinton, p. 136.

and even in Jamaica, where the slave was often flogged
or imprisoned for attending chapel, they were wonderfully successful. In St. Thomas-in-the-East the agitation of the planters had been as violent as elsewhere ;
but this was the only parish in which missionaries,
Church and Nonconformist, had practically full scope ;
and here the slaves continued to work as usual, though
nearly all the overseers and book-keepers were away on
militia duty. The same phenomenon was to be seen
even in the tumultuous north-west, where the planter in
many cases owed the preservation of his property to the
loyalty of Christian slaves. On one estate they mounted
guard every night, saved the trash-house when it had
been fired by the rebels and took several of them
prisoners ; and seven other estates are incidentally
mentioned which were protected in the same way, whilst
on four of them the Baptist head-man, who had acted as
manager, obtained his freedom.[1]

Missionaries as well as slaves were, however, to suffer
for this revolt ; and on January 26, 1832, whilst martial
law was still in force, an association was formed which
called itself the Colonial Church Union because its
principal object was to prevent the dissemination of
doctrines at variance with those of the English and
Scottish Churches. These doctrines were to be dealt
with by eliminating their source ; and Bruce, the dis-
reputable Scotsman who edited the *Courant*, reminded
his readers of John Knox's advice in regard to the monks :
" To get rid of the rooks, you must destroy their nests."
Bruce indeed both headed and circulated a list of names
to be signed by those who would volunteer to destroy
the Dissenting chapels ; and the work was begun at
Falmouth on February 7, when " the brave and intrepid
men of the St. Ann's Regiment," encouraged by two of

---

[1] *Report of the Commons' Select Committee*, 1832. A planter who
was examined by the Committee testified that religious instruction made
the slaves more obedient and raised their market value.

their officers and by several magistrates, distinguished
or rather " ennobled themselves by razing to the earth
that pestilential hole, Knibb's preaching shop." [1]   This
was the Baptist chapel, and thirteen similar places of
worship as well as six Wesleyan were soon demolished.
The chapels were held in trust for the slaves, out of whose
contributions they had been built ; and, if " the brave
and intrepid men " were aware of this, it would no doubt
stimulate their valour.   Some of the rioters were prosecuted ; but the grand juries threw out the bills, and the
Courant said truly that they need not fear punishment
" so long as the jury-box lies within their range."   There
was no rioting at Kingston, where the coloured people
took measures to prevent it ; but elsewhere the missionaries fared little better than their chapels.   They were
mobbed, silenced, or expelled ; the houses and shops of
their coloured friends were wrecked ; and men and even
women were tarred and feathered.   Lord Belmore
proved quite unable to put down the disorder, though
he made himself extremely unpopular by telling the
Assembly that " this fine island can never develop the
abundance of its resources while slavery continues " ;
and nothing effectual was done till after, and indeed
too long after, the arrival as his successor of Lord Mulgrave, afterwards Marquis of Normanby, on July 26.
The new Governor seems to have found it difficult to
believe that persons whose duty it was to suppress disturbances could really have been concerned in them ;
but, once satisfied on this point, he acted with vigour.
Cox, the custos of St. Ann's parish, was forced to resign ;
two militia officers who had canvassed for the Colonial
Church Union amongst their men when actually under
arms were dismissed ; Colonel Hilton, " father of the
Union," having taken part in a meeting to protest against
this step, was also dismissed ; and on January 29, 1833,

---

[1] Beaumont, who defended the missionaries in the Assembly, must
have thought even less of the militia after this exploit.

in terms of a royal proclamation, the Union was suppressed. A few days later, Colonel Brown had the audacity to make a speech to the troops on parade reflecting on the dismissal of his predecessor ; but the Governor disposed of him by reprimanding him at the head of his regiment and depriving him of his commission.[1]

The first of two despatches in which the Governor of Jamaica described the outbreak and suppression of the revolt was dated January 6, 1832 ; and Goderich in acknowledging this communication on March 1 reviewed at length, and in a manner by no means flattering to the planters, the whole chain of causes which had led up to the disaster. He wrote in ignorance of how the Assembly had received his recommendation to adopt the Order in Council ; but he intimated that the Government had no intention of revoking their demand and were indeed of opinion that recent events had made the need for compliance only the more urgent. " The present calamity might prove to be but the precursor of disasters still more lamentable, should it fail to convince the local Legislature that the time for concession has fully come and that the opportunity of conceding with dignity and safety may ere long be irretrievably lost." [2] Eight days after the date of this despatch Lord Belmore reported the Assembly's decision as already stated—that any further amelioration of the slave code " must emanate from ourselves."

The colonists in this their ninth year of prevarication and resistance were, however, to have yet another reprieve ; and for this they were indebted to the political agitation which was coming rapidly to a crisis in England. In the autumn of 1831 the House of Lords had thrown out the Reform Bill ; rioting and general commotion had ensued ; and now in the spring of 1832 the same

---

[1] Bleby, pp. 158–268. Brown lived to repent of his bad opinion of missionaries and to declare in the Assembly that they were " the true friends of the country."—*Ibid.*, p. 268.

[2] *P.P.*, 1831–2, vol. xlvii.

measure was again passing through the Commons. The West Indian magnates were nearly all Anti-Reformers; they knew that the abolition of slavery, which their own conduct or that of their agents had made all but inevitable, could be averted only by the fall of the Government; and Tory statesmen did not hesitate to combine with them in what was virtually a joint campaign for the preservation of property in rotten boroughs and human beings. Vainly did Peel and his friends attempt to deny that they were supporting that very " contumacy " which Canning had sought to overcome. Canning had not required the colonial legislatures to enact *verbatim* an Order in Council; but he had taken what in those early days, when resistance was but three years old, was a hardly less extreme step—he had sent out certain heads of legislation and required the Assemblies to convert them into laws. In 1826, when the resolutions of the Commons were sent up to the Lords, he had said that he could not " deny but that from the spirit which the colonies had already displayed on this subject it was more than probable that the time might arrive when it would be necessary for that House to interfere more directly "; he had foreshadowed fiscal pressure and even direct parliamentary intervention; and he had talked of giving the colonies " one further trial." Yet the present Government was denounced merely for offering to purchase the compliance of the colonies— pandering, as Peel called it, to their avarice. Lord Howick said that Canning " held out a threat to the disobedient; his noble friend [1] a promise of reward to the obedient"; and he pointed out that verbal adoption of the Order was essential, as otherwise it would be impossible to decide whether the reward had been earned.[2]

It was on March 23 that Howick thus defended the Government; but the colonists had a more favourable field of action than a Whig House of Commons; and

---

[1] Lord Althorp.   [2] Hansard (1832), xi. 822-5.

on April 17 a petition was presented to the Lords from a meeting of West Indian proprietors and merchants in which they prayed that the state of their interests should be referred to a Committee. Lord Harewood, who presented the petition, said that he understood the Government was prepared to grant its request ; and, after Lord Suffield had expressed his astonishment at this decision, the reasons for it were explained by Lord Goderich. He had tried to dissuade the planters from asking for the inquiry which in his opinion would serve only to prolong and increase the prevailing unrest ; but their misfortunes had entitled them to consideration ; and he had assented with the less reluctance as the colonial legislatures might thus be brought to see the necessity of adopting the Order in Council. Here the debate might have ended but for the general desire to make a demonstration in support of the colonies and to justify what Howick called " the miserable and tem- porizing policy" of the late Government. Canning's unfortunate word " contumacy " was understood by Lord Ellenborough as by Horton [1] to mean that the colonies should not be coerced so long as their opposition was sane enough to be " founded on reason." Lord Seaford extolled the " superior degree of liberality " shown by the legislature of Jamaica, which had made citizens of the Jews and enfranchised the free coloured people after an agitation of less than seven years, whilst the British Parliament had taken twenty-four years to enfranchise Roman Catholics ; and, in response to his statement that it had at least provided for the religious instruction of the slaves, the Archbishop of Canterbury declared that in fifteen years more churches and places of worship had been built in the West Indies than anywhere else in the same period. The Duke of Wellington remarked that compulsory manumission was the only one of the proposed reforms that had not been adopted in " some

[1] See p. 171.

the question of compensating the planters should be considered after, and not before, emancipation. The alteration he had rejected was consequently proposed as an amendment and was carried by 163 votes to 90 ; but the minority was far larger than he had expected ; and he had the additional satisfaction of having obtained a Committee which was as much calculated to hasten emancipation as that of the Lords to postpone it.[1]

The two Committees sat till the end of the session, when they discontinued, without having concluded, their labours. They both confined themselves to Jamaica, and both attempted no more than a mere compilation of facts. One is not surprised to see that the Lords' Committee found the evidence as to the condition of the slaves " of the most contradictory description," and that they did not venture " to submit to the House any definitive opinion."

One of the last measures of the last unreformed Parliament was to provide for the relief of distress in the West Indies. The poorer sufferers from the hurricane in Barbados, St. Vincent, and St. Lucia had already obtained a gift of £100,000 ; and now a loan of £1,000,000 was to be given in compensation for structural losses due both to the hurricane and the revolt, half of which was to go to Jamaica. As none of the colonies had adopted the Order in Council except the Crown colonies which had done so under compulsion, it was not deemed advisable to benefit the latter by preferential duties but merely to compensate them for the restraints of the Order by a grant of £57,000. We have seen how strongly the Order had been opposed ; and the Government must have been gratified when Marryat, who had headed the opposition in London, admitted that it was working satisfactorily in Trinidad.[2]

The demolition of Baptist chapels in Jamaica was

---

[1] Hansard (1832), xiii. 60, 62, 66, 96 ; *Memoirs of Buxton*, pp. 286–92.
[2] Hansard (1832), xiii. 1173 ; xiv. 1106.

now to have a repercussion in this country which cannot have been foreseen by the Colonial Church Union when it began its activities by destroying " that pestilential hole, Knibb's preaching shop." The Baptist, like the Wesleyan, missionaries were instructed not to meddle with colonial institutions and in particular to respect the relation of master and slave; but it was no longer possible to carry on the work to which these instructions applied; and they naturally concluded that either the bondage or the religious instruction of the negro must cease. In April 1832 Knibb was commissioned by his brethren to put this view of the case before their superiors; and he reached England in June. When the pilot came on board his vessel, he asked him for news and on being told that the Reform Bill had passed said, " Thank God, now I'll have slavery down." The Quakers were the only religious denomination which had yet identified itself with the Abolitionists, and the Baptist leaders were not disposed to abandon their neutrality; but their reluctance was overcome when Knibb told them that he was determined, even at the cost of dismissal, to prosecute his campaign and that, though his wife and children might be reduced to penury, he was prepared to " take them by the hand and walk barefoot through the kingdom." At the annual meeting of the Society on the 21st he presented himself amidst great enthusiasm as " the unflinching and undaunted advocate of immediate emancipation "; and this was the beginning of an agitation which he carried on with great vigour in the principal towns of England, Scotland, and Ireland. Much as the planters detested Knibb, they would have done better in their own interest to tolerate him in Jamaica. As his biographer remarks, " They had flung the firebrand from their hearths and it had fallen on the powder-magazine." [1]

[1] Hinton, *Memoir of William Knibb*, pp. 137–52, 194; Richard, *Memoirs of Joseph Sturge*, 1864, p. 100.

" a measure of authority which was probably never before exercised by so young a man in a position so subordinate." His superiors are said to have submitted to his harangues with " a little good-humoured surprise," though on one occasion he talked to Goderich " for five mortal hours almost without interruption."

In the autumn of 1832 plans of emancipation began to be seriously considered ; and the main difficulty that presented itself was that of liberating the negro without leaving him free to indulge his supposed repugnance to labour. In other words, how was slavery to cease and yet the cultivation of sugar to continue ? Taylor was equal to tackling this or any other problem and was called upon to produce at least a basis of discussion. His scheme was elaborated in a paper of 85 folio printed pages and proved to be an adaptation of the Spanish or *coartado* system of compulsory manumission. The slave was to be started on the road to freedom by purchasing for him Monday and Tuesday ; with the labour of these two days he was to purchase for himself another day, and so on till he had acquired the whole week ; and Taylor calculated that, as the result of this " self-accelerating process of emancipation," he would or might become wholly free in exactly three years and sixteen days. As Howick had no liking for this scheme, it was promptly suppressed, and another, which seems to have been Howick's own idea, was worked out by Stephen. The slaves were to be unconditionally set free and a loan of fifteen millions was to be given as compensation to their owners ; but they were to be kept on the estates by laws against vagrancy, and a tax of 40s. an acre was to be imposed on land used for growing food in order to make it difficult for them to obtain a subsistence without working for wages. Taylor mistrusted the efficacy of this tax and so also did Stephen. Believing that free labour might be substituted for slavery in the new colonies where wages were high, he doubted whether it would be obtained in Jamaica, and feared that, if this plan did not answer, the negroes would relapse into barbarism. Goderich consented to identify himself with the scheme which, however, was opposed by Brougham and satisfied neither the Cabinet nor the West Indians ; and it would appear that as soon as this proposal had been discarded attention was given to the plan of indentured labour which, as we shall see, was actually adopted.

Goderich was thus engaged when his tenure of the Colonial Office was unexpectedly cut short, the reason being that Lord Durham had resigned the Privy Seal owing to his dislike of the Irish Coercion Bill, and that Stanley, the Chief Secretary for Ireland, who was rather too zealous for coercion, had been promised Cabinet rank. It was consequently arranged that Goderich should become Lord Privy Seal in place of Durham and that Stanley should succeed him as Secretary for War and the Colonies ; but Goderich, who had set his heart on being, nominally at least, the Moses of the slaves, was most unwilling to resign till he had led them out of bondage, and only " after a desperate resistance knocked under." As some compensation he was created Earl of Ripon. Howick, the Under-Secretary, resigned on April 2, a few days after his chief. Nobody doubted *his* zeal for emancipation ; and Althorp had once spoken of him to Buxton as " one of yourselves." Stanley had all the energy and determination which were wanting in his predecessor ; but the complaints of the West Indians, who dreaded the influence of Stephen and even of Taylor, would probably in any case have impelled him to assert his independence ; and he lost no time in depriving these subordinates of their " usurped functions " and reducing them to their " original insignificance." [1]

---

[1] Sir Henry Taylor, *Autobiography*, 1885, i. 63, 67, 69, 118, 124, 127–31 ; *Correspondence*, 1888, p. 34 ; Leslie Stephen, *Life of Sir James*

their produce at the price which could be obtained for
it abroad. But he insisted that even if they were right
in their diagnosis it was too late now to think of stopping
the agitation or of keeping it from the knowledge of the
slaves. " The only course left to you is to advance.
The only dangerous course is happily impracticable—
you cannot recede—you cannot stand still." The
question of over-production naturally led him to ask
whether, if slavery could be shown to be destructive
to life, its continuance should be tolerated for the sake
of raising a million more hundredweights of sugar
than this country could consume ; and, taking the somewhat extreme case of British Guiana, he showed that, as
the output of sugar went up, the population went down,
and that, the smaller the number of the slaves, so much
the greater was the number of recorded punishments.
The remainder of this general survey, which occupied
three-quarters of his speech, was given to the question
whether freed slaves could be expected to work for wages ;
and, in reply to those who urged that emancipation ought
to be deferred till the negroes had acquired industrious
habits, he asked, " Do men ever show a disposition to
labour until population presses upon food ; and will
that ever take place so long as the depopulating influence
of slavery prevails ? "

Stanley may have been mistaken in giving so much
more attention to the necessity of emancipation than
to its proposed method, which, though it must have been
already known to most of his audience, was much in
need of explanation. There were no surprises on that
Tuesday evening. The Government scheme had been
communicated to the West Indian leaders on the previous
Thursday ; and the newspapers had published much
fuller accounts [1] than the meagre " outline " now submitted to the House. Slavery as a legal status was to

[1] There is a full account, reprinted from the *Globe*, in the *Scotsman* of
May 15, 1833.

be abolished; and the negroes would thus be released
from all the disabilities imposed upon them as slaves
by the colonial legislatures.   In other words the slave
codes, which ten years of pressure had failed to reform,
would cease to exist ; but, whilst slave children under
six years of age were to be emancipated, their elders
were merely to be " entitled to be registered as
apprenticed labourers and to acquire thereby all rights
and privileges of freedom."   In return for food, clothing
and lodging, but without wages, they were to work for
their former owners three-fourths of the day—seven
and a half out of ten hours ; and for idleness and disobedience they were still to be flogged, though only at
the discretion of magistrates responsible to the Home
Government.   The remaining two and a half hours were
to be at their own disposal.   They might work where
they pleased ; but employment on the plantations was
to be offered to them at a fixed rate of wages.   The rate
was to depend on the price put by the owner on his slave
at the beginning of a twelve years' apprenticeship ; and
during that term the latter was to be credited annually
with a sum equal to a twelfth of his price so that at the
end of the period he would be in a position to purchase
his freedom.   This was ingenious, as the planter could
not put too high a value on his slave without having to
pay so much more in wages.   Slavery—or what was left
of it—would thus be abolished in twelve years, and the
owners would then have received their own estimate of
its value ; but meanwhile they would lose a quarter of
their accustomed unpaid labour and would be hampered
in their exaction of the rest ; and for these disadvan-
tages the Government proposed to give them a loan of
£15,000,000.   Stanley suggested that Parliament might
decide to relieve the slaves by making this a free gift ;
and he concluded by moving the adoption of his proposal in five resolutions.[1]

[1] Hansard (1833), xvii. 1193–1231.

Such was the scheme which the Cabinet had preferred to the plan of immediate emancipation devised by Goderich and Howick; and the latter at once attacked it, though both his father and his mother were said to have done their best to dissuade him.[1] Stanley had spoken for three hours, and Howick managed to speak for two, despite " feelings so painful as hardly to leave me the power of utterance." His main contention was that there could be " no intermediate state between slavery and freedom," that the incentive to industry must be either compulsion or self-interest, and that this scheme impaired the one without substituting the other. Parliament for ten years had been trying to establish a compromise; but in the Crown colonies where Canning's regulated slavery was in force it had been found that the disuse of the whip as a stimulus had resulted only in its more frequent use as a punishment;[2] and, though punishment might be effectual when inflicted at the discretion of an overseer, would it succeed when restricted to a magistrate? If the apprentices could prove that they had been at work for the requisite number of hours, how could he know whether they had been diligent or idle? Nor would the difficulty be avoided by setting task work; for, though the magistrate might be able to determine what was an average day's labour, he could not have the intimate knowledge necessary to allow for differences in physical strength, in the nature of the soil or in weather. And, if coercion failed, there could be no other motive. Stanley had said that the negro would be at least as well off as an agricultural labourer in England who in return for a bare subsistence had contracted to work for some

---

[1] *Greville Memoirs*, ii. 371.

[2] It does not follow, however, that Canning's scheme had been a failure. If slavery had continued, the Order in Council of 1831 would have profoundly modified its character; and, even as it was, there had been an astonishing improvement in the vital statistics of St. Lucia. See Jeremie, p. 92.

particular employer; but the negro in Jamaica raised
his own food, and the supplies he received from his master
—salted herrings, clothing, and medical attendance—were
probably overvalued at 52s. a year.   Thus he would be
working for twopence a day, whilst the hire of a jobber
for the same number of hours was half-a-crown ; and it
was just the low payment of indentured as compared
with free labour which had led to the failure of this
system in New South Wales, wherever emigrants had
taken out Europeans bound to serve for a lower rate of
wages than that current in the colony.   It was true that
the negro was to have two and a half hours daily to himself ; but the wages he earned were not to be his own or
even laid out in some way for his benefit.   They were
to be taken from him as the price of his freedom ; and,
though the planter might have a good claim for compensation against Parliament which had so long upheld
and encouraged slavery, what claim could he have against
the victim of his oppression ?   Howick maintained that
the detailed provisions necessary to give effect to this
scheme exceeded the right of Parliament to legislate
for the colonies ; and he concluded by contrasting the
probable consequences of partial and complete emancipation.   The cultivation of sugar would probably
languish in the former case and might cease altogether
in the latter ; but the negroes would be more likely to
rebel if they got the shadow without the substance of
freedom and would almost certainly do so if the colonial
legislatures should refuse their co-operation.   Rights had
been so long withheld that neither plan might avert a
revolt ; but, if the slaves had to be shot down after
obtaining their freedom, there would at least be " the
consolation of knowing that this necessity had not been
occasioned by a denial of justice." [1]

Several members were as anxious as Howick to be
heard in reply to Stanley's speech ; but Peel urged that

[1] Hansard (1833), xvii. 1231–59.

full time should be allowed for inquiry and deliberation ;
and, in deference to what he called " the unspeakable
importance of this subject," the debate was adjourned
to May 30.[1]

The Government scheme had been submitted to
Parliament without the concurrence of the West Indians,
who indeed had condemned it as neither safe nor satisfactory, and had vainly besought the Minister to postpone his statement. At a meeting on May 27, the
newspaper report of which occupied nine columns, they
did nothing but give vent to their indignation ; and this
was the attitude of their spokesman when the debate
was resumed. Sir Richard Vyvyan began by lamenting
the abolition of the nomination boroughs through which
persons connected with the colonies had obtained seats
in Parliament ; and he quoted an address of the Assembly
of Jamaica to the Governor in which they said that,
as they had always denied the right of the House of
Commons to legislate on their internal concerns, " even
when the West Indies were indirectly represented in
Parliament," much less could they admit it now when
that House consisted wholly of members in whose election
they had no voice. Having thus shown that Jamaica
might exercise a right of interference in Britain which
in respect of her own affairs she denied to Parliament,
Vyvyan next resorted to intimidation, advising the
House to conciliate the colonists, as time and circumstances might offer to them " the temptation of receiving
foreign assistance." He then tried to answer Stanley's
indictment of the colonial legislatures for not responding
to Canning's appeal for the amelioration of slavery, and
showed how incorrigible was the West Indian mind on

[1] Peel's sole contribution to the mitigation of slavery was his insist-
ence on the admission of slave evidence, and he was unfavourable, as
we have seen, to the enforcement of this and the other reforms. As to
emancipation, he thought the schemes of Goderich and Stanley " equally
hazardous," and suggested that a grant might be made to assist the
slaves in purchasing their freedom.—Hansard (1833), xix. 1064.

this question by his mode of justifying the failure to prohibit the separation of families. If the sale of one slave would be enough to discharge a debt, " would it not be hard to compel a party to dispose of a whole family to meet the claim ? " He could not deny that as sugar increased population too often declined—only it must not be assumed " as a matter of course." If the slaves were overworked, so also were the factory operatives at home ; and, whereas the annual cost to the owner of a slave family of six was £21, the weaver in Scotland, with or without a family, was now earning only a shilling a day or £15 a year. These and other arguments were simply a plea for the continuance of slavery ; and yet, whilst asserting that the Government plan for its abolition would not work and could not even be carried into effect, he wished the people of England to know that he and certain delegates from Jamaica " went to the full extent of admitting the principle of emancipation." [1]

In reply to this " extraordinary speech," Stanley said that it was impossible to negotiate with such people as the West Indian Committee who, consenting to emancipation " in the abstract," objected to every proposal made by the Government and put forward none of their own. But there was one part of his scheme to which both proprietors and Abolitionists were equally opposed. The former had urged that the repayment of the loan of fifteen millions by the slaves would be merely nominal, as the wages appropriated to this purpose would be paid by the planter ; and the latter had declared that, if the slave was to be free for a quarter of the day, he ought to enjoy the fruit of his labour. Stanley announced that in deference to this twofold objection the Government had resolved to convert the loan into a gift, but that, in order to stimulate the industry of the negroes, they would be entitled individually

[1] Hansard (1833), xviii. 112–31.

principles to legislation ; and Stanley who had hitherto been able to dispense with Stephen—probably because an outline of the measure had previously been prepared [1] —could no longer do without him. Stephen was a prodigious worker, capable, it is said, of dictating enough to fill ten pages of the *Edinburgh Review* before breakfast ; and on this occasion all his energy was required. The failure of Goderich to deal with emancipation to the satisfaction of his colleagues, the subsequent appointment of Stanley and the supposed necessity of prefacing legislation by resolutions had consumed so much time that the session was now far advanced ; and the consequences might be serious if Parliament should declare its determination to abolish slavery without at the same time carrying it out. Stephen received notice to draw up the Bill on a Saturday morning and completed his task by the middle of Monday ; but the exertion cost him a serious illness, and his amanuensis " used to tell the story as an illustration of his own physical powers." [2]

The Bill was introduced on July 5 and had undergone only one important alteration when it became law—to operate eleven months later—on August 29. Buxton moved that the duration of the apprenticeship should be cut down to the shortest period necessary to secure a supply of free labour for wages ; and, this amendment having been lost by only seven votes, the Government decided to reduce the term for predial or field apprentices from twelve to six years and for non-predial apprentices from seven to four years. The former, unless they had previously been jobbers, were to be attached to the soil. The apprentice could at any time be released by his master and could compel his discharge by purchasing it at a valuation ; but on the other hand—and this was one of the Lords' amendments—the local authorities

---

[1] Just when Stanley took office a plan, very like his, was attributed to the Government and described in the *Standard*.

[2] Leslie Stephen, *Life of Sir James Fitzjames Stephen*, 1895, pp. 32–48.

were empowered to exact compensation for " wilful
absence " by making him work overtime or for any
period less than seven years after the expiry of his in-
dentures. The master was bound to give him all the
allowances now required by law, and, if he grew his own
food, to include time for this in his exaction of forty-
five hours' labour weekly ; but these and many other
details were to be adjusted by the colonial legislatures ;
and the provisions of these bodies might even supersede
the Act, if the Privy Council should deem them " better
adapted to the local circumstances." This was to put
more faith than they deserved in the Assemblies, whose
untrustworthiness Stanley had exposed, and almost to
invite them to a renewal of their ingenuity in thwarting
and perverting the intentions of Parliament.[1] The
Government had at one time thought of separating the
general question of abolition from its details and of introducing two distinct measures, but had been deterred
from that course by the fear that one measure might
pass the Commons and the other " by some means or
other miscarry." The executive power for enforcing
the Act and all subordinate regulations was to be vested
exclusively in Special Magistrates who, to the number
of not more than a hundred, were to be appointed and
paid by the Crown. Each of the colonies was to participate in the compensation fund according to the number
and average value of its slaves, and the fund was to be
distributed by Commissioners who, however, were forbidden to deal with any colony till the provision made
by its legislature for giving effect to the Act had been
confirmed by an Order in Council.[2]

Time was needed to show the effect of this measure
on the slaves ; but one can see at a glance that it was a

[1] Wellington would have exposed the resolutions of 1833 to the
same fate as those of 1823. He suggested that they should be sent out
to the Assemblies with a request to enact them.—Hansard (1833),
xviii. 1191.

[2] 3 & 4 Wm. IV. c. 73 ; Hansard (1833), xix. 1192, 1218, 1239.

better bargain for their owners than they had any right to expect. In 1823 there had been no question of the abolition of slavery but only of its gradual extinction; and the position would in all probability have been unchanged if they had complied with this demand instead of treating it with contumely and contempt. In 1832, after ten years of defiance in the colonies and of exasperation at home, when Buxton had twelve of his "special friends and faithful supporters" to dine with him, he found that their "opinions wavered all the way from the instant abolition of slavery without any compensation to its gradual extinction through the agency and with the cordial concurrence of the planters";[1] and who can doubt that, if the Trinidad Order in Council had been established throughout the West Indies, the existence of slavery, in a form becoming less and less rigorous, might have been indefinitely prolonged? The offer to accept this slow but safe solution had long been kept open; but, owing to the rage of a baffled agitation in this country and its repercussion amongst the slaves, especially as shown in the Jamaica rising, it had at last been closed. Whatever difficulties the planters had now to face were certainly of their own creation;[2] and it was magnanimous in Parliament, and especially the Reformed Parliament, to break their fall by instituting the apprenticeship and to endeavour, not only to satisfy their claim for compensation, but even to purchase their good-will.

[1] *Memoirs*, p. 279.
[2] There could hardly be a greater travesty of the facts than Froude's statement: "They begged that emancipation might be gradual; our impatience to clear our reputation refused to wait."—*The English in the West Indies*, p. 332.

CHAPTER IV

THE APPRENTICESHIP, 1833-1838

STANLEY remained long enough at the Colonial Office to establish, but not to superintend, the system he had devised. A strong Churchman and soon to be a Tory, he resigned this post as he had been removed from his previous one for reasons connected with Ireland ; and in June 1834 he was succeeded by Spring Rice, afterwards Lord Monteagle. Spring Rice retained office when in the following month Lord Grey's Cabinet gave place to that of Lord Melbourne, but was of course displaced when Peel's short-lived Ministry was formed towards the end of the year. Lord Aberdeen administered the colonies till April 1835 when Melbourne returned to power, and his place was taken by Charles Grant who next month was created Lord Glenelg.

It savours of paradox to say that the Act which abolished slavery did not emancipate the slaves ; but this is only another way of saying that what Parliament took away with one hand it partially restored with the other. As a social institution slavery disappeared under what the preamble calls " a general manumission " ; but it came back as a system of industry, the negroes, though they had acquired " all rights and privileges of freedom," having to work as slaves for so many hours a week, and for this purpose being so much the property of their masters that they could be seized and advertised as runaways and were liable to be bought and sold. And this so-called abolition of slavery was to be accomplished under conditions unpleasantly reminiscent of those which

holiness." Saturday was given up to festivity, and for
this the negroes " had provided themselves out of their
own means with new apparel from top to toe and enough
of good fare for every purpose."

The same people who had made their exit as slaves
on Thursday night were to reappear as free labourers
on Monday morning ; and it could not be expected that
the mechanism of this transformation scene would run
without a hitch. The planters had agreed to give a
shilling a day to able-bodied negroes and ninepence to
the less efficient ; but, unfortunately for the acceptable-
ness of these terms, they had paid two shillings for
Saturday labour during the preceding harvest. Hours
as well as wages were disputed, the question being
whether work should begin at sunrise or at dawn, and
whether fodder should be collected during the dinner
interval—and paid for—or at other times ; and, owing to
the love of novelty or the unpopularity of managers,
there was a constant shifting of population from one
estate to another. By the end of August about half
of the effective labourers were at work, and in another
month this proportion had risen to two-thirds ; but a
good many of the remainder were not likely to return.
Hundreds had left the plantations to become fishermen,
bargemen, watersidemen, and porters ; and the last,
who were known by their badges, had increased by
300 per cent. Parents, associating agricultural labour
with slavery, were sending their children of both sexes
into the towns. Adult women had now become the
chief support of the planter ; but he could not depend
even on them. After earning three or four days' wages,
they went about huckstering or attending markets ;
and the men, after the same or less exertion, were content to be idle. When the sugar harvest began, there
was naturally great alarm ; and matters were made worse
by the disunion and nervousness of employers who offered
so many different rates and methods of payment that

the Superintendent of Police could not spare time for
" the collection of the various plans that are in existence." The crop, though smaller than the last, took as
long or longer to bring in and manufacture ; a Labourers'
Contract Act had been passed which the Home Government subsequently disallowed ; and there had been talk
even in the Council of setting an example of regular
industry by bringing over European peasants.

Nevertheless the great experiment had succeeded as
well as could reasonably have been expected. If the
labour problem had presented great difficulties, there
had been no disorder and little or no serious crime. In
the official reports we read that the demeanour of the
negroes had been " in the highest degree creditable,"
and that the planters for the most part had honestly
tried to obtain their co-operation and good-will. As
early as October 30, 1834, the Speaker of the Assembly
said " that, far from desponding, he looked with exulta-
tion at the prospect before them " ; and, when ten
months had elapsed, some prominent men who had
predicted the ruin of the landed interest were then of a
different opinion, and the island as a whole was in a
" progressively healthful state."

Reference has been made to a scheme of emancipation prepared by Lords Goderich and Howick, under
which the freedom of the negro would have been qualified
by a system of paternal supervision. He was to be kept
on the estate by laws against vagrancy ; if he took an
unauthorised holiday, wages were to be withheld for a
longer period than that of his absence ; and there were
to be punishments for drunkenness and for the failure
to provide for infant children. Except as regards
vagrancy, which had already been dealt with, the legislature of Antigua appear to have taken this scheme as
their model when in December 1834 they passed their
Labourers' Contract Act ; and it was " with great surprise and chagrin " that they heard of its disallowance

police force ; but the Act for its maintenance had been
allowed to expire at the end of 1831. The militia was
" worse than can be expressed for want of arms and
accoutrements " ; and there were only 239 regular
soldiers. Finding that his presence would be less
necessary to the freed than to the half-freed, MacGregor
came in haste from Antigua to look after the latter ;
and on August 6, when the apprentices, though quite
orderly, persisted in refusing to work, he proclaimed
martial law and continued it till the 18th—a step which
dismayed the Home Government as the only one of its
kind but seems to have been approved by the missionaries. Happily there were no executions ; but five of
the ringleaders were transported and six were flogged.
After this experience the negroes could have no doubt
that freedom, even as decreed by King and Parliament,
was quite compatible with coercion, and they submitted
with surprising alacrity to their lot. " The apprenticeship system goes on far better than I believe any one
anticipated," wrote Nixon on November 18. With very
few exceptions, the labourers were industrious as well
as quiet. Many planters declared that they got as much
work out of their apprentices as ever they did under
slavery, and not a few went so far as to say that they
got more.

In the other Leeward Islands, where martial law in
St. Christopher is said to have had a salutary effect,
the new order was inaugurated under more or less satisfactory conditions. The Council and Assembly of Nevis
indeed took the very unusual course of associating
themselves with the triumph of " the enlightened and
benevolent in the Mother Country."

Jamaica was the first colony to concur in the parliamentary scheme for the abolition of slavery ; and the
prompt assent of this important legislature was warmly
acknowledged. At the end of November 1833, before
the Bill had actually passed, Lord Mulgrave assured

the Colonial Office that it adopted the principles of the Imperial Act almost *verbatim* ; and the measure was welcomed and confirmed in spite of defects which, though pointed out for amendment, were said to be " not vital." [1] There was a change for the worse in June 1834 when the Assembly declared that they had conformed to the law " against their better judgment and to avert the still greater danger of opposing it," and described it in a Memorial to the King in Council as " showing equal ignorance of our institutions and disregard of our public and private rights." On July 2 a Supplemental Bill was indeed passed, giving effect to all the suggestions of the Home Government, except two which the Marquis of Sligo—who by this time had succeeded Mulgrave—thought impracticable ; but its duration was limited to the last day of 1835. The new Governor had of course to launch and superintend the scheme and devoted himself to the task with remarkable energy and zeal. The first of August passed off to his satisfaction, being observed as a day of thanksgiving, and so well observed that hardly a drunken man was to be seen. In the towns some of the masters gave dinners to their apprentices, and on very many estates steers were killed and distributed in addition to a holiday allowance of rum, sugar and salt fish. Business as well as recreation had to be attended to on Saturday, as the Sunday market had been abolished ; and on Monday morning the apprentices turned out with unexpected alacrity and good humour, except in one or two districts, including the notorious parish of St. Ann, where they refused to work without payment, and still refused, despite military intervention, till " a vast number " had been flogged.

The attitude of the various colonies towards the abolition of slavery was determined to a great extent

[1] Stanley was subsequently much blamed for his precipitation ; but the Act had been read and passed by Stephen, and the question of confirmation was referred to the Cabinet.

by what they were to receive in the allotment of compensation. This depended on " a ratio compounded of the amount of exports and the number of slaves," that is, not on the actual number of the latter, but on their industrial value ; and an advantage was thus given to the new and largely undeveloped colonies over those which had a large negro population and a more or less exhausted soil.[1] In the Memorial which has been already mentioned the Assembly of Jamaica said : " Had we anticipated that the miserable reward of our submission would be, in the chief part, withheld from us to enrich the foreign settlements conquered from the enemy, we would have rejected with indignation the unworthy compromise." Another colony which suffered under this rule was Barbados ; and here the apprenticeship was most grudgingly established. Happily for the slaves, the Governor of Barbados and the other Windward Islands was Lieutenant-General Sir Lionel Smith,[2] who avowed himself " warmly interested in the cause of this much injured people." It was with " extreme disappointment," and only after he had succeeded in removing some of the worst blemishes, that he assented to the local Abolition Act. Still more " highly objectionable " in his opinion was another Act by which the Assembly constituted themselves a commission of police ; and the Council showed their ill-humour by refusing to make the first of August a holiday. Even this deprivation, unknown elsewhere, did not upset the

---

[1] The inequalities in the distribution of labour had been stereotyped by the abolition of the inter-colonial slave trade.

[2] Sir Lionel Smith was the first Governor-General of the Windward Islands and nominally, at least, of British Guiana, Trinidad, and St. Lucia—*nominally*, because the administrators of these colonies corresponded directly with the Colonial Office. Before 1833 the four Windward Islands had all independent Governors, and paid a proportion of their salaries. Smith's salary was defrayed by Parliament. The Assembly of Barbados, far from being grateful to the mother country for " this limited testimony of its benevolence," insinuated that it was designed " to estrange the Governor and the governed."—Schomburgk, *History of Barbados*, 1848, p. 454.

equanimity of the negroes, who went to their usual occupations " with obedience and cheerfulness." Perfect tranquillity was reported on August 26, and it continued after the police force had been dissolved. Lord Aberdeen in disallowing the Act for the establishment of this force described it as placing the Special Magistrate and those through whom he must act under the control of planters, and said he could imagine nothing " so calculated to stimulate the prejudices by which the different classes are separated from each other." The other islands of this group—Grenada, St. Vincent, and Tobago —gave little trouble in this connexion to their Lieutenant-Governors ; and Tobago might have been described as the most satisfactory, if its legislature had not restricted the time for the provision grounds to fourteen days in the year. In this island the negroes, even when they were slaves, had had thirty-five days.

In the Crown colonies, which were all of the unexhausted type, the planters were more pleased with the compensation scheme than they cared to admit. Indeed their satisfaction was marred only by a fear that it might be altered in compliance with representations which were being made by the non-resident proprietors of Barbados and Jamaica. The slaves of the Crown colonies, having recently obtained from their sovereign so great a boon as the Order in Council of 1831, had reason to be disappointed ; and one can sympathise with their complaint that they needed no apprenticeship to a business which they already knew perfectly, and that, if the King meant only to emancipate them at the end of six years, he would have done better to say nothing about it meanwhile and then to set them free at once. There was some commotion in British Guiana and Trinidad ; but the Governor of the former colony, Sir James Carmichael Smyth, commented on the readiness of masters to call that insubordination which any one not in the habit of commanding slaves would hardly have noticed ; and Sir Dudley Hill wrote from St. Lucia that, though everything was tranquil, yet " reports of general insubordination, nay even of rebellion," were pouring in. The quiet, order and industry which followed some transitory excitement in Guiana were indeed remarkable. There *was* to have been a police force with twelve stations and a sergeant and ten men attached to each ; but the duties were assumed without payment by the apprentices themselves. Constables selected from among them, with no other weapon than a short painted staff and distinguished merely by a red scarf worn over the shoulder, had sufficed for four months to maintain order and execute at all hours the orders of the Special Magistrates. " It would be difficult in the annals of the most civilised and best informed countries of Europe," wrote Sir J. C. Smyth on January 22, 1835, " to select stronger proofs of the respect and obedience paid to the laws than are hereby daily afforded by the untaught and uneducated labourers who have so lately been released from the bonds of slavery " ; and, three months later, we find him asserting as " the real truth " that no part of the King's dominions was more law-abiding and tranquil. On July 6 he reported that 4263 more hogsheads of sugar had been produced than were to be expected from the diminution in compulsory labour; but he blamed the masters for exceeding their rights, and declared that the future would depend on " themselves and on the mode in which they may conduct themselves to their apprentices during the six years of probation." Both in Gniana and Trinidad great efforts were made to promote task-work as a means of giving the negro extra time to dispose of for wages. In the latter colony the sugar crop was expected to be as good as that of the previous year ; and there was another expectation even more significant—that corporal punishment " will almost entirely cease." Honduras adopted the apprenticeship in a form suitable to its highly anomalous constitution ;

and the Superintendent wrote on October 22, 1834, "Nothing can work better."

We have seen that securities had been provided by Parliament for the execution of the scheme as well as for its adequate adoption by the colonial legislatures; and here Stanley put a construction on his measure not easily to be reconciled with its spirit. The British Act and all the colonial Acts were to be carried out under the superintendence of persons specially and exclusively appointed for this purpose either by the Crown—in which case they were limited to a hundred and were to have salaries of £300 a year [1]—or by the Governors. The object manifestly was to secure a fairer administration of the law than could be expected from the ordinary Justices of the Peace who were almost invariably planters; but, as far more than a hundred magistrates would obviously be required, those Governors went too far who told the negroes, greatly to their satisfaction, that for offences against their masters they would be punished only by persons sent out by the King. On the other hand, it might have been and was very generally supposed that any one included in the general Commission of the Peace would be disqualified for office. Stanley, however, explained in December 1833 that, though a certain number of persons unconnected with the colonies were to be paid for giving their whole time to such duties, there was nothing to prevent the appointment without stipend of any local magistrate. As the Act had passed nearly a year before it came into force, there was time enough, one would think, for all the "Specials" to be at their posts; but the great majority had not yet arrived; and the Governors, who had to excuse their absence to the negroes, were naturally disappointed and alarmed. In exercising their own right of nomination they availed themselves, with one exception, of Stanley's permission and did not hesitate

[1] Subsequently raised to £450.

for his master eight hours a day for four days in the week and half an hour longer on the fifth day or nine hours a day and only four and a half days a week. A whole Friday afternoon was obviously preferable to several detached hours, especially as the negroes had no means of measuring time and were often purposely deceived. Many planters did not scruple to " crib the negroes' time " ; and we read of one of them breaking an hour-glass which had been given to his gang. It was hardly possible to play such tricks with the nine hours' day which, with the usual intervals for breakfast and dinner, extended roughly from sunrise to sunset ; and this system was really essential to the cultivation of the provision grounds where, as was usually the case, they were several miles distant. As early as May 1834, when the negroes were still slaves, the Governor issued a proclamation in which he assured them that after the first of August they would have a day and a half in the week—Friday afternoon and Saturday—at their disposal. Later, but not till the new system had come into operation, he discovered that the 47th clause of the Jamaica Act empowered the planter to give the four and a half hours when and how he pleased so long as the full total was given for the year. Unfortunately he did not make another discovery much more important— that the Amending Act of July 4, usually called the Act in Aid, had enacted a working day of nine hours except where some other arrangement had been made by mutual consent ; but he had now been converted to the eight hours' system by the planters, who complained that when the negro had a full week-end, he usually spent it in going long distances to see his friends and returned on Monday morning so exhausted that he could not work all day. Accordingly in a proclamation to " the newly made apprentices " he not only told them that they must take their four and a half hours as they were given but said, " I recommend to your masters to settle that you should work eight hours a day each Monday, Tuesday, Wednesday and Thursday and eight and a half hours each Friday." Yet at the same time he issued a circular to the Special Magistrates, desiring them to impress upon managers the importance of conciliating the negroes by giving them half of each Friday or every alternate Friday.

The only result of these contradictory utterances must have been to aggravate the controversy as to this coveted boon by stimulating both the demand and the refusal; and there was little abatement of contention till the sugar harvest began, when most managers, in order to obtain extra time for hire, thought it prudent to concede the nine hours' system. When the crop had been secured and there was no longer the same demand for labour, meetings were held for inducing all planters to concur in refusing the Friday afternoon; and Sligo on August 17, 1835, applied for instructions to the Colonial Office. We learn from his despatch that for reasons of policy he was now strongly in favour of the nine hours' system but still thought the other preferable on economic grounds; and in a circular of the 23rd he gave a finishing blow to the Act in Aid by admitting the undoubted right of the master to apportion his hours. One would suppose that even "Mr. Over-Secretary Stephen" had never heard of this Act; for the Colonial Office replied on October 5 that any attempt to overcome the reluctance of the planters in a matter which the law had expressly reserved for their discretion would probably do more harm than good. "Enough, and in truth more than enough, has already occurred to induce the negro population to draw invidious distinctions between the disposition towards them of the executive government on the one hand and of the local legislature on the other; and, however inevitable may have been the causes which have compelled the Ministers of the Crown or the governors of the island to provoke this unfortunate

so." His apprentices acquitted themselves " in a cheerful and ready way " and worked for wages on Friday and partially even on Saturday. One of the defects mentioned in the Assembly's Report was that there were too few Special Magistrates ; and this fact alone ought to have convinced them that the system could not yet have had a fair trial. We hear of one district in which there was no such magistrate for two months after the first of August.[1]

The eagerness of the Assembly to establish or rather to anticipate the failure of the apprenticeship was due to their anxiety as to the sugar-harvest ; and their apprehensions were shared by the Governor, who wrote on November 3 that he felt the impossibility of taking off the crops under the limits of compulsory labour and that reports reached him from almost all quarters that the negroes were most unwilling to work for hire. Before the end of the year he had become much more sanguine. Matters were " hourly coming into a more hopeful state." In many cases where the negroes had refused to enter into a contract with their masters they had done so at once when its performance was guaranteed by a " Special " ; but the men were more willing than the women who, as they could not be flogged and no tread-mill had yet been erected, were " all over the island the most troublesome." In January 1835 optimism had given place to confidence. The Christmas and New Year holidays had " passed off in a manner to excite astonishment," and the negroes had returned to work " with even more exactitude than formerly." Every post was announcing new arrangements for extra crop work and, wherever the negroes were paid every Saturday in ready money, there would be no difficulty in getting as many as were required. This prediction was fulfilled ; for the Governor was soon able to report that the quality of the sugar was " far superior " to what

[1] P.P., 1835, vol. l. ; 1836, vol. xlviii.

it had been under slavery, and that for every hour of labour more than double the quantity had been produced. These facts had not been easy to elicit, those who had predicted failure being unwilling to admit their mistake. " The first prophecy was blood and destruction on the 1st of August : in this they were wrong. The second, that this scene would take place at Christmas, as it had not taken place in August : in this they were wrong. The third, that the apprentices would not work for wages : in this they were wrong, as I know of no instance where the usual wages were offered and where they were refused.[1] The fourth was that the crop could not be taken off : in this they were wrong, as it has been taken off in many places much earlier than usual." Sligo believed that on the whole the negroes worked well or ill according as they were considerately or harshly treated. In cases known to him proprietors or attorneys had expressed their determination never to pay wages to their former slaves ; and his opinion was that the success of the apprenticeship depended wholly on the whites. " If it fails, on them will rest the entire blame."[2]

We have seen that much the same opinion had been expressed by the Governor of British Guiana ; but in this case Glenelg probably knew better than to accept it as confidential. At all events, in a despatch of December 13, 1835, Sligo informed him, first that " there has sprung up a spirit of mutual confidence which I hope may be nurtured," and then that his statement about the responsibility of the whites had given great offence—which was unfortunate, as the antagonism between the executive and the legislature was now approaching a crisis. It has been mentioned that the

---

[1] Sligo wrote thus in June 1835 ; but on September 28 he reported that the negroes had refused to work for wages on 65 estates, whilst on 193 estates wages had not been offered.

[2] *P.P.*, 1835, vol. 1. ; 1836, vol. xlviii.

remove their suspicion by suggesting in his first address that the free blacks and mulattos, who in 1831 had been legally enfranchised, should be given commissions in their own companies of militia. His main task was to secure to the negroes the boon bestowed upon them by Parliament ; and we learn from a later despatch[1] that he " encountered every odium and insult from the whites in establishing their right to be treated like human beings." Next year, after he had accepted with extreme reluctance and displeasure the Abolition Act and Rural Police Act,[2] the Assembly became so ill-humoured that he had to rebuke them for discourtesy to the King's representative. Unlike the impulsive and talkative Irishman, Lord Sligo, Smith treated his opponents with stern reticence and studied contempt. On one occasion he called a special session in such a manner that the first question debated by the two Houses was why they had been summoned ; and he humiliated the Assembly by communicating with them only through the Council. He intimated that the police must be placed " under the absolute and unfettered authority of the executive," and even forbade the Assembly to adjourn till they had complied with his demand—which was naturally denounced as an " unconstitutional attempt to overawe the House." On June 30 he was present at the opening of a new session ; but, instead of making the usual speech, he said, " Gentlemen, you can proceed to your business ; I have no observations to make, no remarks to trouble you with." The Assembly must have known that they could not long refuse to amend their Abolition Act in the manner required by the British Government ; but in August they gave way completely both on this question and that of the police ; and henceforth their relations with the Governor became more and more cordial. When Smith left Barbados about a year later, his popularity with the negroes had given place to execra-

[1] Smith to Glenelg, December 8, 1835.   [2] See p. 252.

tion ; but the Assembly declared that " for a considerable time " he had possessed their entire confidence and had gained it by " a determined resolution to promote and enforce among our labouring classes that industry on the continuance of which the success of the great measure of emancipation wholly depends " ; and the Governor in his reply said, " It is well known that I am a sincere friend to the negroes, but I solemnly declare my opinion that to insist on industrious habits among them is as essential to their own happiness as it is to your rights." [1]

Smith had thus succeeded in conciliating one class of the community only at the cost of antagonising another ; and the words just quoted will help us to understand how this " sincere friend to the negroes "—and such he always was—had forfeited their esteem. We have seen that before 1834 food had been raised in Barbados under the same compulsion as sugar ; but the allotment system was now introduced, and Smith thought rightly that the negroes would be urged to greater exertion, and consequently would have more leisure for cultivating their grounds, if they worked for their masters by the piece and not by time. In the autumn of 1835 he commissioned three planters to draw up " a scale of work to be performed by effective labourers," which consisted of forty regulations fixing both the amount of any particular kind of work to be done by one person in a day and the number of persons required for any particular job. The British Act provided that the apprentices should not be compelled to do task work; and there could have been no objection in principle to this tariff if it had been offered merely as a model for voluntary contracts ; but Smith sent it to the Special Magistrates with instructions to hang it up in their offices; and it was avowedly intended to prevent " diversity of practice" in their administration of the law. In other

[1] Schomburgk, *History of Barbados*, 1848, pp. 454-74.

words, it was to be used as a standard for punishing idleness. Smith had satisfied himself on rather strange testimony—that of " several very old black overseers " —that there was not a job on the scale which could not be finished before two o'clock in the afternoon ; but he seems to have been grossly deceived ; [1] and in any case, apart from the difficulty of securing that the labourers employed should be really " effective," the scale was subject to qualifications which were sure to be perverted or ignored. Thus three labourers were to weed an acre of young canes or potatoes in one day, " the land not being very grassy " ; four labourers were to cover an acre of young canes with trash, " where the trash has been placed conveniently round the field " ; and one labourer was to carry 230 baskets of manure " at a convenient distance from the heap which has been previously turned." The scale must have been in con- templation for a considerable time before it was an- nounced—but not yet communicated—to the Special Magistrates on October 14 ; and one cannot but surmise that the " determined resolution " of the Governor to enforce industry had contributed to make his peace with the Assembly in August. [2]

Sir Lionel Smith brought with him so good a certifi- cate from the planters of Barbados that he was assured of a good reception from the same class in Jamaica, where he arrived on August 30, 1836. At the opening of the legislature on November 1 he complimented the colony on having been the first to carry out the wishes of Parliament for the abolition of slavery ; and, after referring to the " unfortunate feelings " which had im- peded the completion of that work, he said that he would propose " some suggestions of practical improvement

[1] Sturge and Harvey reported, as the result of their inquiries, that it was " such a scale as the strongest negroes could not work upon for a twelvemonth together."—*The West Indies in 1837*, Appendix, p. xxxii.

[2] *P.P.*, 1836, vol. xlix.

likely to put down complaints and restore confidence and goodwill between proprietors and labourers." This must have been gratifying to his hearers ; but they had less reason to be pleased when he touched on the moral and religious condition of the negroes and said he was " sorry to proclaim that they are in this island in a more deplorably backward state than in any other." As the clergy were much too few for the task of conversion, the object must be " to instil the doctrines of Christianity and not to insist on any particular Church discipline "— in other words, to encourage the Dissenting missionaries. " Banish from your minds the idea that they are your enemies. I will answer with my head for their loyalty and fidelity."

Lord Sligo, in a despatch written just before his departure, had said that he left the administration " in as easy a state as can well be imagined " ; but this was not the opinion of his successor, who thought that he had merely wasted his time in " squabbling " with the planters. How anxious Sir Lionel was to avoid such a conflict was at once made evident. He found on his arrival that the parish of St. Thomas in the Vale was very disturbed, " almost in a state of insurrection " ; and he attributed its condition to resentment of the eight hours' system, " added to a great deal of intemperate zeal and partial justice on the part of the Special Magistrate." Dr. Palmer had been appointed to this district in July, and the planters accused him of fostering insubordination because their labourers, knowing his desire to do them justice, were now demanding the redress of grievances which they had previously endured without hope of relief. The new Governor appointed certain persons, at Palmer's own request, to inquire into his conduct, and removed him on receiving their report, though all they could allege against him was that he had stated " his view of the law in place of conciliating and restoring confidence " and—a still more

extraordinary accusation—had " administered the Abolition Law in the spirit of the English Abolition Act." [1]

But, however little the Governor may have relished
Palmer's " intemperate zeal," he had no sympathy with
the eight hours' system of his accusers. He saw at once
what his predecessor had never been able to grasp—
that it was not only unpopular but illegal ; and before
he had been a fortnight in Jamaica he was doing his
utmost to secure uniformity in the hours of labour.
Great hostility was aroused, and for this he naturally
blamed Sligo who, as we have seen, had first promised
the half-Friday in violation of the Jamaica Abolition
Act and then withdrawn it when that boon had really
been secured by the Act in Aid. The Special Magistrates were unable to carry out their instructions to
enforce the nine hours' system, and the Assemby refused
to interfere, saying that the Act in Aid had been
neutralised in practice by the late Governor's second
proclamation and that to enforce it now would only
give rise to fresh misunderstandings. A year later, the
dissension on this subject had become so acute that the
newspapers reported " a state of open rebellion and other
insane accusations usual to men fretting under the loss
of absolute power." In several parishes meetings of
planters were held to support the eight hours' system,
whilst in others the apprentices had demanded and
taken the half holiday, and Smith had not allowed them
to be punished—a course which may have been unavoidable, but did not accord well with the dismissal
of Palmer for fostering insubordination. Owing to the
great extent of Jamaica and the variety of its climate and
soil, he had not been able to conciliate his opponents by
introducing the uniform scale of labour which was so

---

[1] Sturge and Harvey, Appendix, p. lxxxix. The writers do not
mention one cause of the animosity against Palmer—that he had
married a coloured woman.—Lloyd, *Letters from the West Indies in
1837–8*, p. 164.

popular with the planters of Barbados, though parochial scales were prepared and were said at one time to be "in a course of consolidation."[1] That the hours of labour were diverse was not the fault of the law, which required only to be enforced; but Smith thought the system most defective in other respects, in fact, "the worst of all the late slave colonies"; and in 1837 he brought its deficiencies before the Assembly. He declared that on many estates the apprentices were worse off than they had been as slaves. Mothers of six children, pregnant women and the aged of both sexes were not treated with the former consideration; and amongst the particular grievances he enumerated was the refusal of cooks and water-carriers to the working gangs. Instead of resting during their intermissions of toil, the negroes had to search for fuel and to prepare their food; and they were actually deprived of water, as they were not allowed to fetch it. He also referred to the "constant disappointment" caused by the law of appraisement and said that, in proportion as the indenture of the negroes drew to a close, the sums demanded for their discharge had generally increased. His message to the Assembly was dated November 2; and on the 24th he wrote to Glenelg, "I have no hope left that they will correct the evils I exposed."[2]

It was not the system of labour but its diversity which caused so much trouble in Jamaica; for in British Guiana, the next most important colony, where the conditions were less favourable but uniform, there was little discontent. Here under the Order in Council of 1831 the negroes had worked fifty-four hours a week, and now they were restricted to forty-five. Sir J. Carmichael Smyth was anxious that this relief should not be distributed but given at one time—a boon not only more

---

[1] They were much lighter than the Barbados scale, the negro, for example, having to dig from 70 to 80 cane-holes in stiff soil as compared with 150. [2] *P.P.*, 1837, vol. liii.; 1838, vol. xlix.

valuable in itself but essential to the abolition of the
Sunday market which, though it had long been illegal,
he could not prohibit, as even the missionaries admitted,
till there was another free day. He was also anxious
that the apprentices should grow their own food, as this
would attach them to the estate and prevent them
leaving it when fully emancipated in 1840. There was
an old Dutch law in this colony which required an acre
of provision ground to be allowed for every five slaves ;
but it was obsolete, and the planters, thinking their
rich and unexhausted soil too good for anything but
exportable produce, would not hear of its being revived.
Thus they continued to import food ; [1] and their
labourers, having no allotments to cultivate, were required to work seven and a half hours every week-day.
The Governor had to content himself with minimising
the hardships which he could not remove. Unable to
secure Saturday for the negroes, he sought to increase
as much as possible their daily amount of leisure ; and
this he accomplished by procuring the general adoption
of task-work on a scale so reasonable that with ordinary
diligence they could obtain their release at about three
in the afternoon. Most of them were ready enough to
work longer for wages. On some estates they were
deprived of this advantage by being compelled to " lay-
by " in the middle of the day—a practice which the
Governor publicly denounced as " most annoying and
irritating." In all disputes with their masters he found
that they had this or some other legitimate grievance.
No detail of their treatment escaped him, and one of
his devices to improve it was the annual distribution of
medals to deserving managers and doctors. He was
never tired of extolling " the good conduct, industry
and subordination of the labourers " ; but he believed
that the apprenticeship was working well, not only for

---

[1] We have seen that at one time food had been grown by the gang.
See p. 71.

their masters, as shown by a great rise in the value of land and exports, but for themselves. Indeed he pronounced it to be a " complete and triumphant success " and did not shrink from putting his assertion to the test.

Towards the end of 1836 two members of the Anti-Slavery Society—Dr. Lloyd and Mr. Scoble—arrived in British Guiana. They came without the sanction and even without the knowledge of the Colonial Office which, when informed of their visit, did not regard it with favour ; but the Governor gave them full liberty to inspect official documents, to travel about and converse with the negroes. Scoble had an interview with the Governor, who wrote down in his presence the particulars of every complaint ; and subsequently he was invited to make suggestions. Not one but two inquiries were ordered ; and one cannot read the records of this affair without seeing that the abuses reported and proved were not numerous, and were of a kind which could not wholly have been prevented.[1] In the midst of his toils and anxieties Carmichael Smyth was carried off by fever on March 14, 1838. It was with deep feeling that the Government Secretary announced the death of "the intrepid, the just, the signally successful ruler of this not easily governed colony " ; and Glenelg said in his reply, " There is no public functionary of the colonial empire at the present time whose continued services would have been of higher importance." [2]

It will readily be believed that the progress of events in our West Indian colonies was watched with keen

---

[1] The danger of relying on negro gossip was thus exposed. Scoble described a certain Special Magistrate as being so great a favourite of the planters that they had provided him with a boat and two sailors, and " a friend of mine " had seen the list of subscribers. The truth was that the Governor had given this magistrate a boat to enable him to visit the islands of his district, and the so-called subscription list was an assessment imposed on the plantations to pay the boatmen.

[2] *P.P.*, 1835, vol. l. ; 1836, vol. xlix. ; 1837, vol. liii. ; 1838, vol. xlix. Lloyd published an account of his tour which has been already cited. See p. 270.

T

when one would suppose that they had hardly recovered from their amazement at their good fortune in getting £20,000,000 for that which in itself was not a loss but a gain—a positive improvement of their property [1]—even now at the very outset they were attempting to lay hands, not on trifles, but on the essential features and sacred principles of the abolition law." Sir George Grey had no objection to the proposed Committee—indeed he rather welcomed it as a means of vindicating the apprenticeship; and he pointed out that no fewer than three similar Committees had been appointed in Jamaica.[2]

The Select Committee, of which Lord Howick and O'Connell as well as Buxton were members, met on April 19, 1836, and, confining itself to Jamaica, sat at intervals till August 5. Beaumont, who had lived for thirty years in Jamaica, but had never been a slave-owner, was one of the witnesses; and there were sixteen others, of whom four were experts on colonial law, three had been Special Magistrates, and four were planters. One of the last, the proprietor of two very large estates, had made a signal success of the apprenticeship by going out from England to manage it for himself. The negroes had readily agreed to his proposal that they should work ten hours a day for four days a week, thus securing for themselves the whole of Friday and Saturday, and also that they should forego their allowances in return for increased wages. The Committee were by no means satisfied with the working of the Jamaica Abolition Act, for they suggested various amendments : that the negro should be compensated for injury out of the fine imposed on his master; that his day's work should include the

available as free labourers, this comparison is of little use. We have seen that the scheme of Goderich and the original scheme of Stanley both contemplated merely a *loan*, the assumption being that any loss occasioned by the change of system would be but temporary.

[1] The value of slave property, having depreciated during the agitation, would naturally improve with its settlement.

[2] Hansard (1836), xxxii. 451, 475.

time spent in coming and going ; that the usual allowances and indulgences should be secured to him and the
distribution of his hours of labour throughout the week
regulated ; that the tribunal for appraisement should
be remodelled ; that the solemnisation of marriage
should not be confined to clergymen of the Church of
England ; that the Special Magistrates should have
further legal protection ; and that abuses in workhouses
should be corrected. But they stated in concluding
their report that there was " much reason to look forward
with confident hope to the result of this great experiment," that mutual suspicion and irritation appeared
to be gradually subsiding, and that " nothing could be
more unfortunate than any occurrence which had a
tendency to unsettle the minds of either class with regard
to the fixed determination of the Imperial Parliament
to preserve inviolate both parts of the solemn engagement
by which the services of the Apprenticed Labourer were
secured to his employer for a definite period and under
specified restrictions." [1]

The principal points investigated at this inquiry were
those which have already been discussed—the eight
hours and the nine hours system, the hardships connected with allowances and appraisement, the offer of
work for wages and its acceptance or rejection ; but the
Governors, whose despatches have been our chief
authority in dealing with these matters, depended mainly
on the reports made to them by the Special Magistrates ;
and Beaumont devoted most of his evidence to im-
peaching the reliability of these returns. It was natural
that such an attack should be made ; for the Special
Commission, conferred with the express object of main-

---

[1] *P.P.*, 1836, vol. xv. Buxton would have divided the Committee
on the paragraph approving of the apprenticeship if he had been able to
find a seconder.—*Letter to Lord John Russell*, p. 8. But, writing to
Zachary Macaulay, he said he considered it to have been proved that
the oppression of the apprentices " had gradually but decidedly abated
and that feelings of hostility had much subsided."—*Memoir*, p. 382.

It is a fact very creditable to the Special Magistrates that after the first few months they resorted less and less frequently to corporal punishment ; [1] for the planters still believed in flogging and had not the interest in its disuse which prevailed in Barbados, where the apprentice who was imprisoned had to make up the loss of labour out of his free time. Lord Glenelg expressed his approval of this clause in the Barbados Abolition Act, though it involved two punishments for the same offence, but naturally condemned its application to a negro who had been imprisoned for six months without trial and then acquitted. His master claimed that he should forfeit every Saturday for the next three years ; and this modest proposal was actually referred to the decision of the Secretary of State.

One of the findings of the Committee was that female apprentices were still liable to corporal punishment, not judicially, but as a means of enforcing labour in the parish workhouses. From the evidence of a clerk in the Governor's office it appeared that there were eighteen workhouses in Jamaica for which the local justices were empowered to make regulations, and that in regard to six or seven of them complaints of the practice had been received and investigated. The Assembly had acknowledged its illegality, though only as a reason for not legislating on the subject, and " the fullest confidence " was expressed that steps would be taken to prevent it in future. But it was not so easy to touch the conscience of Jamaica. At this very time Sligo was writing to the Colonial Office : " The extent to which the flogging of

faithfully and conscientiously discharged the duties entrusted to them."
—*History*, p. 308.

[1] In the ten months ending May 1836 corporal punishments had been reduced by two-thirds, punishments of all kinds by about a fourth. —*Edinburgh Review* (1838), lxvi. 516. It was estimated in 1837 by one of the best of the Special Magistrates that the punishment inflicted by them did not amount to " one hundredth part of that formerly inflicted by domestic discipline on the estates."

women has been carried in St. Ann's parish without my
knowledge exceeds far all calculation." The supervisor
of the workhouse had pleaded ignorance, and " I understand that it is not intended to visit him with any
punishment."

Very few members had troubled to attend when the
motion to appoint this Committee was brought forward
on March 22 ; and next year a motion to reappoint it
was adopted without discussion. The Committee of
1837 had proceeded " but a little way " in their labours
when Parliament was dissolved, owing to the death of
William IV on June 20, and consequently they resolved
neither to report the evidence nor to express upon it
any general opinion ; but they had no longer any confidence—much less " the fullest "—that the West Indian
workhouses would be reformed ; for they recommended
an immediate inquiry into their condition and " especially
into the construction and use of the tread-mills which
are employed in them and the nature of the coercion
adopted to ensure labour among the prisoners." A
representative of the Colonial Office had already been
sent out to conduct an investigation ; but nothing
effectual was likely to be done till Parliament had been
roused from its apathy on the subject of the apprenticeship ; and we must now consider how this system was
regarded in the country.

Those zealous Abolitionists whose opinions were
represented by the Agency Committee [1] had entirely
dissociated themselves from the Act of 1833. They
objected both to the apprenticeship and to the giving
of compensation to the planters, which they considered
" an acknowledgment of the right to make merchandise
of the souls and bodies of men " ; and, much as they
condemned these two things severally, they condemned
them still more in conjunction, believing that, if abolition
could be said to involve compensation, it ought at least

[1] See p. 206.

worst days of slavery." A copy of the pamphlet as soon as it appeared was sent out by the Colonial Office to Jamaica. Sir Lionel Smith instituted an inquiry; and on November 2 he reported that "the whole barbarous case" had been fully confirmed.[1]

The substantial volume in which Sturge and Harvey embodied their indictment of the apprenticeship was not issued till January 1838 ; but in the interval they found time for public as well as literary work. A speech in which Sturge described his impressions to a Birmingham audience was published ; and he and his colleagues addressed meetings in various large towns. Birmingham took the lead in calling a meeting of delegates which assembled in London on November 14 and sat for ten days. Buxton was no longer a member of Parliament, having lost his seat for Weymouth at the general election of the previous July. The delegates at one of their meetings were informed by their chairman that a Mr. Foster was at the door with a letter from Buxton. It was only after considerable discussion that they permitted the letter to be brought in and read, and its contents proved to be as unfavourable to their project as they had evidently expected. "I observe," wrote Buxton, "that some of our excellent and zealous friends have expressed an invincible aversion to parliamentary committees." There must, however, be committees of both Houses before Parliament would "dissolve an existing contract of its own making," and the planters might contrive to keep them at work almost to the legal termination of the apprenticeship in 1840 ; but he did not believe that there were a hundred men in either House who would vote for their appointment.[2] This advice, good or bad, had no effect on the delegates, who set up a Central Negro Emancipation Committee and

[1] The pamphlet and relevant documents are in *P.P.*, 1837–8, vol. xlix.

[2] The letter is quoted in Hansard (1838), xlii. 98.

presented a memorial to the Government in which it was said that " the apprenticeship system, like all other modifications of crime, has demonstrated the absolute hopelessness of reconciling right and wrong." It was also said that the legislatures and special magistracy of the colonies had shamefully frustrated the benevolent intentions of the Imperial Act towards the negroes who, after so many millions had been given for their emancipation, were regarded as " the very wards and children of the nation." The news of these proceedings in London had not yet reached the West Indies when Sir Lionel Smith wrote on November 13 that the agitation founded on Sturge's " hasty visit " to Jamaica was causing considerable anxiety among the planters as to whether the apprenticeship would be continued or abolished. The matter had been discussed in the Assembly, and the debate had ended in the " imprudent resolution " to shut out all further discussion from whatever source it emanated.[1]

Sturge was about ten weeks in Jamaica. He had a letter of introduction from Sir George Grey which, however, can hardly have included his companions ; for we have seen that the Colonial Office had never heard of Scoble and Lloyd till informed that they had turned up in British Guiana. Sir Lionel Smith complained that Sturge had been a fortnight in the island without calling upon him. The period was only six days ; but he refused the Governor's invitation to dinner ; he circulated at least one anti-slavery placard—one of a " pile " which was seen at his lodgings ; and his conduct in the case of James Williams was referred to with strong disapprobation in Parliament. He had the story of this boy from his own lips on February 25, almost six weeks before he left Jamaica ; but instead of communicating it to the Governor, who had invited his confidence, he kept it

[1] Richard, *Memoirs of Joseph Sturge*, pp. 163-6 ; *P.P.*, 1837, vol. liii. ; 1837-8, vol. xlix.

undivulged, if not quite unverified, for publication in
England. The alleged facts would have been all the
more convincing had they been officially confirmed;
but they might of course have been disproved, and
apparently he did not care to run this risk, even at the
cost of allowing so very bad a magistrate as Rawlinson
to continue in office. His book may have been a revela-
tion, though a one-sided one, to the uninitiated; but
no reader at all acquainted with the subject can have
been much the wiser. He mentions frankly enough
such humane managers and Special Magistrates as he
came across in his travels; but the indictment of the
apprenticeship which constitutes the second last chapter
takes no account of the only thing that needed to be
ascertained. Most intelligent people must by this time
have been aware that there was no conceivable evasion,
if not violation, of the Abolition Law which was not
being practised somewhere in Jamaica. The only
question was how far the normal working of the
apprenticeship was vitiated by abuses which, if not
uncommon, were far from being general; and Sturge is
of no use to us here, the evils he mentions being always
introduced with some such phrase as " in many cases."
One third of a long appendix is occupied with " Statements of Apprentices "; but this testimony, dubious
enough at best, is drawn from only seven parishes, and
three of these notoriously the worst. The most valuable
parts of the book are those in which Sturge describes as
an eye-witness the workhouse discipline of Jamaica; and
these passages must have been the more effective as
confirming what had already been told by Williams.[1]

There were gaols in Jamaica and there were workhouses or houses of correction. Apprentices who had

---

[1] A study of the apprenticeship in the first half of 1835—when it
was too early to be of much value—had been made from the economic
standpoint by John Innes, who published his impressions in a " Letter
to Lord Glenelg."

been apprehended as suspected runaways or had been sentenced to punishment were always sent to the latter, and whereas the keeper of a gaol might be summarily dismissed, the supervisor of a workhouse could be removed only after trial and conviction. These officials were sometimes prosecuted but never punished. One who had caused the death of a man by repeated floggings was acquitted of murder, though found to have been guilty of cruelty.[1] It was common enough for drivers in workhouses to flog the women prisoners if they would not submit to their desires, and there was no dismissal in a case where this offence was proved. Runaways were advertised for four weeks during which they were worked in the penal gang ; and all women detained on this or any other charge had their hair cut short, which deprived them of protection from the sun and was an indignity they greatly resented, never having been subjected to it as slaves. No Special Magistrate could sentence a female apprentice to flogging, but he could sentence her to the tread-mill, which in practice was much the same thing. Prisoners had usually to undergo this punishment for fifteen minutes twice a day. They were strapped by the wrists to a bar above the machine, and if they failed to " catch the step " were flogged, whilst the cylinder, owing to the sharp edges of the steps, cut their legs as it revolved. " Dancing the treadmill," said Williams, " is very hard work." The prisoners perspired so profusely that it was " just the same as if you throw water on the steps " ; their cries could be heard a mile away ; and, what with the flogging and being " mashed up with the mill," they had to go down to the sea-shore—this was at St. Ann's Bay—to wash

[1] One of the jurymen, who was a Jew and consequently unable to eat the food provided for them, held out against this decision for sixty hours, and might not have given way even then if a bad form of measles had not broken out in his house. The case was that of Jenkins, supervisor of the Hanover workhouse.—Sligo, *Jamaica under the Apprenticeship*, p. 25.

off the blood. Lord Sligo tells us in his pamphlet that the Assembly would never do anything to stop the flogging of women, though the number of cases he discovered and brought to their notice was " perfectly astonishing." There is no reason to suppose that the practice had ceased when Sturge went to Jamaica about six months after Sligo had resigned. He did not indeed see women or even men flogged on the mill in Jamaica, though he did see it in Barbados ; but two supervisors admitted that it was necessary in the case of both sexes " to touch them up " ; and he saw enough of treadmills in use to realise their efficiency, apart from this aggravation, as instruments of torture. Except for one of " English construction," the machines he saw were badly made, and one was so insubstantial that when the prisoners all stepped at once it revolved so rapidly as to throw them all off. Describing a visit to St. Ann's workhouse when " two mixed gangs of men and women " were put on the mill, he says, " We observed this morning that not only was the floor sprinkled and the steps stained, but the very drum of the mill was spotted with blood. If the prisoners cannot keep step they are suffered to hang, battered by the wheel, till the time expires." [1]

The Baptist missionaries of Jamaica addressed a letter to Sturge and his friends in which they were urged to exert their influence to bring about " the total abandonment " of the apprenticeship. It was signed by Knibb, whose view of the system had not always been so unfavourable as it now was. In January 1836 he wrote to a friend, " I bless God for what has been done, but I do not like the apprenticeship system because it is unjust ; yet it is not slavery and it must issue in freedom." But in July 1837 he wrote to Sturge, " Leave no plan untried to get this abominable system down in 1838 " ; and in a subsequent letter he said that, if he were not so

[1] Sligo, pp. 20–27 ; Sturge and Harvey, pp. 204, 206, 244, 291.

deeply in debt, he " would come home and have another hit at the monster." [1]

With the appearance of Sturge's book, the agitation which had been going on for some months in the country made itself felt, under rather strange auspices, in Parliament. It could hardly have been anticipated that Lord Brougham would become the spokesman of a movement which, so far, had been discouraged by Buxton ; for the influence of Brougham, if not his casting vote, had prevailed in the Cabinet against Goderich's emancipation scheme, and it was mainly his opinion as Lord Chancellor that had weighed with his colleagues in accepting, with all its defects, the Jamaica Abolition Act. Nevertheless on January 23, 1838, in presenting a petition of the usual kind from the inhabitants of Birmingham, he denied a report that he had questioned the general truthfulness of the statements made by Sturge and his companions at public meetings. All he had said was that it was an exaggeration to assert that the Abolition Act, instead of bettering, had rendered worse the condition of the negroes. This was mild enough, but a month later he delivered one of what Greville called his " flaming speeches." On this occasion he did not spare either the price paid for the Act or the manner in which it had been infringed. " The twenty millions have been paid in advance on the supposition of a loss being incurred. No loss but a great gain has accrued to the planter. Then he has received our money for nothing ; it is money paid under a mistake in fact, to propagate which he himself contributed." It was even suggested that the planter should be required to refund the money if two years after complete emancipation he should not be able to show losses equal to the sum he had received. Brougham admitted that the abolition of the whip for driving and its use as a punishment only under judicial

[1] Sturge and Harvey, p. 249 ; Hinton, *Memoir of Knibb*, pp. 239, 243, 244.

U

by insisting that the interposition of Parliament could
no longer be delayed. The Duke of Wellington, who
had always tried to excuse the colonial legislatures for
their failure to ameliorate slavery, said on this occasion
that they " had behaved exceedingly ill," and " had
wholly neglected or carefully evaded the taking of the
necessary measures." Nobody in either House of Parliament could speak on this subject with the authority of
Sligo. He welcomed the Bill ; for, far from agreeing
with those who thought that the nation had been " hum-
bugged and bamboozled," he considered that all that
could be alleged against the apprenticeship was the
" want of complete success." [1]

The Bill to amend the Abolition Act included all the
apprentice colonies and became law on April 11. Most
of the evils complained of were dealt with by giving the
Governors a discretionary power to legislate on these
subjects by proclamation, but some were directly
abolished. No female apprentice was to be placed on
the tread-mill or in the " chain or penal gang," or to be
whipped or have her hair cut short ; and no male apprentice was to be whipped after August 15, 1838, except
in the case of offences for which free persons were liable
to be similarly punished. Moreover the Governors were
empowered to make rules for the treatment of apprentice
prisoners. [2]

It is doubtful whether this measure would at any
time have satisfied or even pacified the Abolitionists.
At all events it had no chance of acceptance now, when
introduced so late and apparently in reply to a proposal
of immediate emancipation. Brougham told the Lords
that on March 14, at a meeting in Exeter Hall of which
he was chairman, " the bare attempt to mention the
Government Slavery Bill was met with tremendous, I
will not say dissatisfaction, but abuse and abhorrence."

[1] Hansard (1838), xli. 802-13, 819, 821.
[2] 1 & 2 Vict., c. 19.

He declared that the agitation was the most general, the loudest and most determined he had ever known and referred to " thousands of petitions signed by myriads of persons." [1] The petitioners, in so far as they had any religious designation, were mainly Dissenters ; but a good many were Churchmen, and Blomfield and Phillpotts, the two ablest bishops and the latter himself a slave-owner, had declared for emancipation. Other prominent men who had hitherto held aloof or been hostile were taking the same course, though Brougham may have exaggerated when he described them as rising " night after night and one after another " to declare their conversion. Buxton, who had refused to support the movement in November, believing it to be hopeless, joined it in March. So did Lushington, who had the advantage over his friend of being still in Parliament ; and both were influenced by the example of Sligo. That estimable but somewhat erratic man, almost immediately after he had defended the apprenticeship on March 13, published a letter in which he advocated its abolition and announced his intention to release his own negroes on the first of August. [2]

Brougham had given notice that he would reintroduce his motion after the Easter recess ; but meanwhile it was brought forward on March 29 in the Commons by Sir George Strickland—who had succeeded him in the representation of Yorkshire—and occasioned a two nights' debate. Strickland stated his case in the manner usually adopted by the more zealous Abolitionists, citing all the worst abuses, especially those detailed by Williams, and assuming that they were the common lot of the apprentices ; but his speech was fairness and moderation as compared with that of his seconder, who ventured

---

[1] It was claimed on May 28 that over 3,000 petitions, signed by more than a million persons, had been presented during this session to the House of Commons.

[2] Hansard (1838), xlii. 18, 31, 210, 214.

refusing to protect its negroes from cruelty and oppression and protesting violently when that duty was undertaken by Parliament.

Gladstone was anxious to confute Brougham's assertion that the planters had rather gained than lost by abolition ; but, as the apprenticeship was more akin to slavery than freedom, the question could not profitably be discussed at this stage except in relation to Antigua, where certainly the critics of compensation had a strong case. When Innes visited this island in 1835, he found that the cost of sugar-production under free labour was practically the same as it had been under slavery ; but, two years later, there was said to be a saving, which the Speaker of the Assembly described as " considerable " and others reckoned at from one fifth to one sixth. Here then was a colony which might be said in Brougham's words to have " received our money for nothing " ; [1] but, according to Gladstone, who relied merely on a fall in the value of the exports,[2] it was a loser to the amount of about £22,000 a year. The general effect of emancipation could not, however, be inferred from its working in Antigua, the exceptional situation of which was described with substantial accuracy by Lord Sligo : " A small island, every acre of which is well known ; in which it is said that there exists not a single spring of fresh water and where the provisions are all imported ; where there is no resource but work, with the produce of which the negro goes to market and purchases his daily bread." [3]

Sir George Grey had met Strickland's motion by moving as an amendment the Order of the Day for the

[1] One of the Antigua planters told Gurney in 1840 that the 25,000 dollars he had received as compensation was " a mere present put into his pocket—a gratuity on which he had no reasonable claim."—*A Winter in the West Indies*, p. 56.

[2] We have seen (p. 248, note) that the diminution was soon more than made good.

[3] Innes, *Letter*, p. 64 ; Sturge and Harvey, pp. 48, 70 ; Hansard (1838), xlii. 103, 235.

second reading of Glenelg's Bill; and the amendment was carried by 269 votes to 205.

As Birmingham was the centre of the agitation, it might have been supposed that this resolution would have been introduced by a member connected with that part of the country; and in fact it would have been moved by Sir Eardley Wilmot, member for Warwickshire, had he not been indisposed. Wilmot was too keen an Abolitionist to let this misfortune stand in his way; and on May 22, after presiding at a meeting in Exeter Hall, he revived the motion, partly on the technical plea that it had not been met by a direct negative. Himself a Tory, he was seconded by Villiers, already conspicuous as an opponent of the Corn Laws, who declared that there was a systematic attempt to pervert the Abolition Act and " so far successful as to render the condition of the negro apprentice worse than that of the negro slave." There was a thin House and none of the Ministers took part in the debate; but the motion was carried by a majority of three—96 to 93.[1]

A large majority against emancipation had now been replaced by a very small one in its favour, and, ambiguous as the situation was, neither side was really anxious that it should be cleared up. The Abolitionists did not want to expose their weakness in the House by bringing in a Bill which was sure to be thrown out; and, though the Government could easily have reversed the decision of May 22, they did not wish to take such a step, knowing that it would be unpopular and being no doubt reluctant to appear so directly against emancipation at a time when they were pressing it on the colonial legislatures. Both sides therefore were content, in military parlance, to manœuvre for position. On Thursday the 24th Wilmot was asked by Lord John Russell whether he meant to take any step in furtherance of the resolution he had carried, and replied that he would like in the

[1] Hansard (1838), xliii. 87–123.

first place to know whether the Government proposed to give effect to the resolution or to rescind it. Russell's answer was that, as Strickland's resolution on the same subject had been rejected in a full House, he did not think it necessary to do anything in regard to that of Wilmot, but that, if he liked to bring in a Bill, he might have Monday for the purpose and the Government would then " give it the most strenuous opposition." Wilmot asked for time to consider this not very attractive offer ; and on the following night after a meeting in the afternoon at Exeter Hall, where the Abolitionists at this period seem to have been in almost perpetual session, he announced that he would do nothing to follow up his resolution, his reason being that the Anti-Abolitionists had always objected to the agitation as an obstacle to voluntary manumission and that the resolution as it stood might induce " the slave-owners to do that voluntarily which the Bill would compel them to do." The real reason no doubt was that the loss of a Bill would do more to dishearten the negroes than the resolution to encourage them ; and indeed it had been announced at the meeting that the news of Wilmot's victory was already on its way to the West Indies. Sir George Grey described this as " practising a delusion upon the people which he would not stop to describe." On Monday he called upon the House, not to rescind its resolution of May 22, but to declare its opinion that it was inadvisable to act upon it ; and this occasioned a long debate in which the arguments, so often urged on both sides and now worn almost threadbare, were again put forth. The motion was of course carried, the figures being 250 to 178.[1]

If the House of Commons could be said not to know its own mind on this subject, the planters at least had to make up theirs. The question of universal or partial emancipation was now being considered throughout the West Indies—in some cases it had even been decided ;

[1] Hansard (1838), xliii. 149, 280, 379, 380, 430.

and the merits or demerits of the apprenticeship, which engrossed so much attention at home, were not the determining factor. Whether that system had succeeded or had failed, the Assemblies would still have to deal with a difficulty inherent in the Imperial Abolition Act. In Jamaica some 50,000 non-predial apprentices— about a sixth of the whole number—were entitled to their freedom on the first of August, and their release could not fail to unsettle the remaining five-sixths, especially as the line of demarcation between the two classes was not clear. The Act laid down that all slaves not usually employed in agriculture or in the manufacture of colonial produce, whether attached to the soil or, as in the case of jobbers, unattached, were to be considered as non-predial apprentices. Mechanics as such were obviously in this class ; but what was to become of those employed as coopers, carpenters, masons and smiths on the estates ? In the usual interpretation of the Act they were reckoned as predials, and this classification, though much complained of by the Abolitionists, was not unreasonable ; for the occupation of an estate artisan was ancillary to the manufacture of sugar, and the reason usually assigned for prescribing a shorter term of apprenticeship for the non-predials— that their services were unlimited instead of being restricted to forty-five hours a week—did not apply to him. Indeed in the rules drawn up for the guidance of the Commissioners of Compensation estate artisans were classed under " predials attached." The doubts on this question ought long ago to have been set at rest ; but Glenelg was dilatory and it was not till March 30 that he sent out a despatch intimating the opinion of the English law officers that estate artisans must be considered non-predials. This decision upset a Classification Act in Tobago—and possibly in other colonies—which had been confirmed and proclaimed. In addition to the risk of defying Exeter Hall, the planters had now to reckon with the loss of their mechanics; they had either to give up the apprenticeship or to continue it as amended by the British Parliament; and it is not surprising that the Colonial Office succeeded in inducing all the colonial legislatures, one after another, to agree to general emancipation.

Montserrat had the honour of leading the way. We have seen that in this colony the apprenticeship would have been dispensed with in 1833 if the Council had not thrown out the Bill. In 1836 it would have been abandoned but for one adverse vote in the Assembly; and an Act was passed on January 13, 1838, for general emancipation in the ensuing August. Nevis followed in March; Tortola in April; St. Vincent, Barbados, St. Christopher and Tobago in May; Grenada, the Bahamas and Jamaica in June; Dominica in July. Grenada, which exchanged felicitations with its Lieutenant-Governor, was the most, if not the only, cheerful giver. Elsewhere there was more or less reluctance, qualified to some extent by the success of emancipation in Antigua, where the planters were said to be prosperous and in high spirits. Some colonies declared that their compliance had been forced by the British Amending Act and the new classification of non-predials, and Barbados hinted at the necessity for further compensation; but nowhere were indignation and ill-humour carried to such a height as in Jamaica. As early as March some of the planters were said to be conspiring to bring about a commotion on the first of August amongst those of the apprentices who would then be entitled to their freedom, with a view to coercing them and obtaining a pretext for cutting off some of the missionaries. The statement was made in a joint letter of the Baptist pastors to the secretary of the mission in England; and Knibb wrote, a few days later, that he himself was to be the first victim.[1] There may have been some truth in

[1] Hinton, *Memoir of Knibb*, pp. 246, 248.

this story, wild as it seems ; for on May 17 Sir Lionel
Smith wrote confidentially to Glenelg : " Many there
are in the island who would be delighted to get up an
insurrection for the pleasure of destroying the negroes
and missionaries. They are in fact mad." And amongst
several " silly things " he mentioned a report that the
militia was to assemble of its own accord, for what purpose he did not know—" also that I am to be shot." [1]

At the opening of the legislature on June 5, Sir Lionel
urged the necessity of giving the colony " repose by the
removal of a law which has equally tormented the
labourer and disappointed the planter, a law by which
man constrains man in unnatural servitude." He was
strongly supported by the Council which heartily con-
curred in his " wise and humane recommendation " ;
but the Assembly in their reply expressed a hope that,
if they did resolve to remove an " unnatural servitude,"
they should be left free to discharge their functions without further parliamentary interference. Four days later,
the British Amending Act came into force, and soon afterwards emancipation was granted on the best terms
which the Council could procure. The Assembly drew
up an address to the Queen in which they declared that
in consequence of an Act recently passed by Parliament
—" an Act dangerous in its tendency to the peace and
welfare of the island "—they had been compelled to
relinquish the remaining term of the apprenticeship,
but did not give up their right to an indemnity for their
loss. Much more remarkable was a " Protest " in which
they denounced the Slavery Abolition Amendment Act,
which " placed in the hands of one man the power of
making law and dispensing with law by proclamation,"
as illegal and unconstitutional, and declared that in the
success of their legislation they did not " dread a comparison with the Commons of England." In Jamaica
there were no armed opponents of tithes, no rick-burners,

[1] Quoted by Sir Henry Taylor, *Autobiography*, i. 244.

no strikers trying to raise wages by outrage and murder, no Burke-and-Hare atrocities, no Corn Laws for the benefit of the rich or prisons called workhouses for the poor. The tribunals of Jamaica were never occupied with the obscenities which disgraced the English courts nor did husbands and daughters "resort to them to expose their own shame for a money-price"; and it was not in Jamaica that unfortunate mothers made away with their new-born offspring "in order to avoid the cruel persecution of a hard-hearted and destroying morality." There was a strange combination of strictness and laxity in this allusion to ethics. Marriage being the exception in Jamaica, divorce must necessarily have been almost unknown and illegitimacy easily condoned; and one rather wonders that these Jamaica moralists did not complete the parallel by contrasting the barbarity of British prisons with the humanity of their own.

The news that Jamaica had been captured by the Abolitionists, the greatest if not quite the last of their conquests, reached England on July 16. Speaking the same evening in the Lords on the necessity of immediate emancipation in the Crown colonies, Brougham warmly congratulated the man to whom, most of all, he attributed "the glory of that day"; and he afterwards said to Cobden, "Joseph Sturge won the game off his own bat."[1] This may not have been exaggerated praise; for the Slavery Abolition Amendment Act, which precipitated emancipation in Jamaica, was long overdue when it passed in April, and, but for the agitation started and headed by Sturge and so greatly stimulated by his visit to the West Indies, it might never have been introduced.

We have seen that Jamaica, having much waste land capable of cultivation, was one of the colonies in which emancipation, if not delicately handled, might be

[1] Richard, *Memoirs of Joseph Sturge*, pp. 174, 179, 180.

detrimental to the planter, and that in Goderich's scheme, in order to make it difficult for the negro to maintain himself without working for wages, it had been proposed to put a tax on land used for growing food. It is evident from the Jamaica Emancipation Act that its framers were regardless—they cannot have been unconscious—of this danger. The Act provided that, if any person now an apprentice should refuse to quit his house or allotment after three months' notice, he was to be deemed a trespasser and might be summarily ejected on the order of any two Justices of the Peace. The clause was objectionable in itself as perpetuating a distinction between the late apprentices and other tenants ; and, though aged and infirm apprentices were allowed to retain their houses for ten months, the penalty for violation was only £5 currency and could not be levied by distraint of goods. Glenelg intimated that the Queen's decision on the Act must be deferred till these points had been brought before the Assembly ; and Sir Lionel Smith was sufficiently distrustful of the planters to make a request—which had been anticipated by the Colonial Office—that he should be allowed to retain for a time as many of the Special Magistrates as he thought expedient. He retained practically two-thirds—forty-two out of sixty, and claimed that he had kept only those whom he could depend upon to do justice to the labourers.[1] Their special jurisdiction would of course cease and, in order to distinguish them from the ordinary Justices of the Peace, they were to be called the Queen's Stipendiary Magistrates.

Many of the negroes had recently bought up the remainder of their apprenticeship at a high and even exorbitant price. They now found themselves no better off than those who had paid nothing ; and to this

---

[1] This, I think, settles the controversy as to the judicial character of this body (see p. 277), especially as most of the magistrates who were retained proved themselves firm friends of the negro.

grievance was added the avarice of planters who, highly as they had rated the services of their apprentices, were now trying to engage them at a low rate of wages. The usual terms offered were a shilling currency a day with house and grounds free ; and, when these or worse offers were not accepted, advantage was taken of the Act, at least among the small planters, to issue notices to quit. The negroes were much attached to their dwellings and especially to the gardens in which they had buried their dead ; but they had friends who took care that they should not be intimidated or duped. On July 12 the Governor addressed at Falmouth some 2500 apprentices who had come as delegates from nearly all estates in the parish of Trelawney and from many in that of St. James ; and in the evening there was a meeting at the Baptist chapel. Special Justice Lyon who presided warned the negroes to be cautious in entering into agreements for the breach of which they might be severely punished. A missionary of the Scottish Church, in moving a resolution that they were willing to work for adequate wages, suggested a minimum of 1s. 8d. with house and grounds or 2s. 6d. with rent ; and he was seconded by Knibb, who said that, if there were some small non-resident proprietors who could not afford this remuneration, they ought to come out and manage their own estates. " What right had they to employ attorneys at 200l. or 300l. per annum and drive in their carriages through Regent Street and have their boxes at the Opera ? " He exhorted his hearers not to be frightened at the notices which had been served upon them, telling them that they would find employment elsewhere, and that he had an offer of £10,000 from a friend in England which, if necessary, should be used to buy land on which they could settle.[1] In the same month the Governor intervened in a manner more amiable than discreet.

[1] There is a full report of the meeting in Sir Lionel Smith's despatch of May 3, 1839.

Addressing the apprentices at Morant Bay, he advised
them not to allow their wives to do " heavy field-work " ;
and, according to the planters, this was taken to mean
that the women should not work at all. Sir Lionel
explained that by " heavy field-work " he meant only
holing, and that the civilising of the negroes depended
on the elevation of their women. " I preferred the
dictates of humanity to the interest of short-sighted
planters." [1]

The movement we have traced in these pages had
now attained its object and our task is accomplished ;
but emancipation in Jamaica was the outcome of a
conflict between the Assembly and Parliament which
had begun with the agitation against the slave trade ; [2]
and it may be well to follow this quarrel to its conclusion,
particularly as in doing so we shall see something of the
negroes and their employers in the first days of freedom.

The abolition of the apprenticeship was celebrated
on the first of August, 1838, with far more enthusiasm,
but with no less sobriety and good order, than had
characterised the so-called abolition of slavery on the
first of August, 1834. " I never beheld a more im-
pressive and affecting scene than Spanish Town
exhibited," wrote the Bishop of Jamaica ; not one
instance of intoxication was to be seen either there or at
Kingston ; and the clergy reported " the same correct
behaviour generally throughout the island." Churches
and chapels were crowded, as they had been on the
previous night. Floral arches and transparencies had
in many cases been erected over their doors. Sir Lionel
Smith addressed 7000 negroes and 2000 children who had
walked in procession through the streets, carrying
banners in his honour and in that of Queen Victoria,
Lords Mulgrave, Sligo and Brougham, and Joseph Sturge.

---

[1] *P.P.*, 1839, vol. xxxv. ; Hinton, *Memoir of Knibb*, pp. 286–90.
[2] For a brilliant and entertaining survey of this conflict see the
Edinburgh Review (1839), lxix. 527–45.

They looked radiantly happy, but are said to have moved
" with the solemnity of a funeral " ; and, if this staid
demeanour gave way later, it was only where a missionary
was carried shoulder-high or " our governor, father and
friend " was surrounded and the horses taken out of his
carriage. Similar scenes were enacted in other towns ;
but at Falmouth a harsher note was struck by the
courageous and irrepressible Knibb, whose combative-
ness was far from being characteristic of his class. Con-
ducting a religious service, he paused, amidst breathless
silence, just before midnight, and, pointing to the clock,
said, " The hour is at hand ; the monster is dying " ;
and, as the last stroke sounded, he cried out, " The
monster is dead ; the negro is free." Then there was
a prodigious shout, followed by three cheers for the
Queen. Early next morning a coffin was displayed, and,
after there had been placed in it a chain, whip, iron
collar and other insignia of slavery, it was solemnly
interred. A week or two later, there was a serious
commotion, due to a rumour that Knibb was to be
assassinated, the truth being that some exasperated
whites had resolved to burn him in effigy.[1]

Admirable, however, as was the behaviour of the
negroes on their first day of freedom, it was quite eclipsed
by their patience and forbearance under the vexations
to which they were subsequently exposed. The first
difficulty that arose between them and their employers
was of course that of wages. The planters offered now,
as many of them had offered in advance, 1s. 0½d. currency or 7½d. sterling a day with house and grounds.
This was the rate in Antigua after emancipation in 1834 ;
but we have seen that the planters in that colony were
prejudiced by the fact that they had paid 2s. a day for
extra labour during the preceding harvest, and in Jamaica
from this point of view the situation was much worse.

---

[1] Phillippo, *Jamaica : its Past and Present State*, 1843, pp. 176–84 ;
Hinton, *Memoir of Knibb*, pp. 256–61.

For some time before the end of the apprenticeship the negroes had been paid at the rate of 2s. 6d. to 3s. 4d. a day for their half-Friday and Saturday, and the usual rate for the purchase of freedom had been 2s. 6d., not for every working day, but for every day in the year. Instances occurred in which a sum based on this valuation had actually been paid by a negro to the employer who was now offering him 1s. 0½d. Antigua could have afforded to take risks with its negroes, having no waste land to which they could withdraw; but there was no eviction clause in its Emancipation Act, the labourers being allowed to retain their cottages, not for three, but for twelve months, whereas in Jamaica the offer of low wages was in too many cases accompanied by notices to quit. " Strange infatuation ! " wrote Daughtrey on August 14. " Masters appear to think that they have them more in their power than during the apprenticeship and some have had the folly to vaunt of this in their presence." He mentioned that " not a few of the most valuable people " were already looking out for independent settlements, and added, " Nothing can be more obvious than that the attempt which planters are making to depress the rate of wages below its present fair value must tend to produce ultimately the very opposite effect." The impolicy of threatening eviction was emphasised by another of the Stipendiary Magistrates who referred to " the daily number of faithful labourers who were to be seen carrying in their hands these 'notices to quit' as a reward for a life of toil and suffering " ; and in a Jamaica newspaper of August 23 the threat to eject vast numbers of the negro population on one day was described as " nothing short of absolute insanity."

Probably very few of those who indulged in such menaces had any serious intention of carrying them out, for the number actually ejected seems to have been small ; but more than enough had been done to endanger the future manning of estates. In November Knibb managed to secure ground for the building of a village which was to be called Birmingham ; and this was the first of the negro settlements which in four years had increased to little short of two hundred.[1]

That the negroes would take at least a week's holiday after their emancipation had been anticipated, and the period of their complete idleness did not last much longer. On some estates they accepted the shilling currency a day, on others they did piece-work or gave two days' labour a week ; but contracts at the current rate were discouraged by many of the Stipendiary Magistrates and by the Baptist missionaries, whose leading spirit was styled by his enemies " King Knibb " and the " Dan O'Connell of Jamaica " ; and the planters, having failed to intimidate their labourers, were constrained to improve upon their original offer. Towards the end of August the rate was raised in most of the parishes, first to 1s. 3d., and then permanently to 1s. 8d. The latter rate was in some cases proposed by the Governor himself on behalf of the managers.[2] But the settling of this dispute merely gave rise to another ; for many planters sought to recoup themselves for the increase in wages by a claim—immediate, not prospective—for the payment of rent. The Act abolishing the apprenticeship made no mention of rent nor was the subject referred to during the discussion in the Assembly ; and it had been generally assumed that the three months' tenure of their cottages and grounds was secured to the negroes as compensation for the withdrawal of their allowances and in order to give them time to take off their crops and to make agreements for wages ; but the Attorney-General, when this question was referred to him by the Governor, gave it as his opinion that they were liable for rent from the first of August.

[1] Hinton, *Memoir of Knibb*, p. 299.
[2] Sir Lionel Smith's zeal for a " living wage," great as it was, was overrated by some of the negroes, who believed that he had ordered the

The publication of this opinion on or about the 29th upset the industrial situation just as it was beginning to settle down. Bills for rent charges were soon being served " wholesale " ; and the Governor could do little to counteract the effects of his unfortunate application, though opinions directly opposed to that of the Attorney-General were obtained from the other two members of the Jamaica bar who were not connected with plantation property, and subsequently from the Crown lawyers in England. It was not, however, the demand itself, unexpected though it was, that caused the difficulty but its extravagant amount. In this matter many of the planters confirmed what the Governor had said of them on the eve of emancipation, that they were " in fact mad " ; and one of the Stipendiaries wrote that, if the reports of their conduct had come from only one quarter, Lord Glenelg would have been justified " in doubting the veracity or sanity of the informant." The negro was charged for his hut, which in most cases he had himself built and kept in repair, for his plot of inferior or worn-out land, and for his right to graze stock ; and he had to pay rent, not only for himself, but for every occupant of his cottage. Daughtrey reported that in nine cases out of ten the whole family had to give three days' labour, and to make up the deficiency if any of them had happened to be ill, before the 1s. 8d. a day was paid for Thursday and Friday ; and instances occurred where rent at the rate of £8 13s. 4d. per annum was charged for a hut which was scarcely worth the odd shillings, and £17 6s. 8d. for two acres of land, the annual value of which was not more than £2. Even the negroes who had consented to work for a shilling a day were not exempt ; and the Governor wrote on September 24 that he had many complaints of labourers credited with 5s. a week in wages who were charged 8s. for rent—a demand

police to apprehend and flog any of them who were found working for less than 2s. 6d. a day !

legislate, except so far as necessary to secure the public credit, until the Queen should make known whether they were to recover their right of self-government or were to be treated as a conquered colony. The Governor met this protest with a brief prorogation; and on November 3 he enumerated some of the measures he proposed to recommend, including one for regulating the mutual relations of employer and employed and another for the prevention of squatting. The Assembly replied that they were well aware of the necessity for such laws, but refused to alter their decision; and Sir Lionel then dissolved the House, though he had no hope of the election of " more intelligent members." The result justified his fears; and on December 24, after he had prorogued the new House, he wrote to Lord Glenelg that no Assembly [1] could now be expected which would acknowledge the authority of Queen, Lords and Commons to make laws for the colony.

How this crisis was dealt with at home can only be alluded to in a work which has already exceeded its scope. Behind the trouble which had arisen in Jamaica was the difficulty in all the colonies of a black population eligible, but not yet ready, for the franchise; and the proposal of the Colonial Office, expressed in a long minute which was written by Taylor [2] and adopted by Glenelg, was that Crown colony government should be established throughout the West Indies. The Cabinet rejected this scheme, which certainly could not have been carried; for, when it was proposed merely to suspend the Jamaica Assembly for five years, the Bill was opposed by some who were shocked, and by many who professed to be shocked, at the suppression of a popular legislature, and the Government majority was reduced to five. Melbourne resigned in May 1839, but in four days was again in office; and his new plan, defective enough at best, was so mutilated by the Lords that the Assembly

---

[1] The Council had supported the Governor throughout.
[2] *Autobiographhy*, i. 249.

continued, unchecked and unimproved, till, after the negro revolt of 1865, it voluntarily abdicated its powers.

Meanwhile the course taken by the Assembly to promote " the peace and wellbeing of the colony " was producing its natural result. Seventeen annual Acts for the maintenance of public services had expired at the end of 1838, and industry was disorganised from the want of legislation to enforce contracts and payment of wages. The Assembly had always been accustomed to appoint committees which were not affected by prorogation or dissolution, and on this occasion they had appointed a Committee of Correspondence. The purpose of this body was to procure resolutions and reports in regard to the ruinous effects of emancipation and the evil influence exercised by the Governor, the Stipendiary Magistrates and the Baptist missionaries. The papers were sent to Burge, the agent for Jamaica in London, who communicated them to the Colonial Office, and thence at last they came into the hands of Smith, who called upon his traducers, when they were not anonymous, to justify their assertions and replied vigorously and copiously on behalf of himself and his allies. He always maintained that the prejudice against the Stipendiaries and the Baptists originated in the stand they had made for the negroes before the first of August against " a combination which was to grind them down to gratuitous labour for their old masters," and declared that, if he had been able to keep order without militia and without moving a single soldier or policeman, it was due to the loyalty " which these very teachers, calumniated as they have been, have sedulously inculcated on their flocks." He was unwilling to relinquish his post so long as there was a possibility of its being made effective ; but the defeat of Melbourne's first Bill mitigated his regret when he was recalled in August 1839. " Constituted as the popular branch of the legislature now is, *no governor will be permitted to do justice to the negro population.*" [1]

[1] Letter to Sturge.—*Memoirs*, p. 184.

We have seen that when Sir Lionel Smith entered on his duties in Jamaica he blamed his predecessor for having wasted his time in "squabbling" with the planters, and perhaps, after the policy of conciliation imposed upon him by the Home Government had broken down, he was more relieved than disappointed to find himself in the same position. An old soldier, who had fought in almost every quarter of the globe, he probably believed that obedience to orders was the first duty of a civil as well as a military officer, and he may well have thought in view of his apparent success in Barbados that he would best protect the negro by not antagonising his master ; but it cannot have been a congenial task, and he must have suffered acutely under the misrepresentation to which he was exposed. Barely two years had passed since Joseph Sturge had declined an invitation to his table and had gone home to publish a book in which he was studiously depicted as inimical to the negroes, with the one exception that he had supported them in their refusal to apprentice their free children ; and now the same Joseph Sturge, probably quite unabashed, was sending him a copy of a petition which had been presented by the Birmingham Anti-Slavery Society against his recall. He is said to have left Barbados " amidst the execrations of the crowds of free blacks and apprentices assembled on the beach " ; but this incident must have been effaced from his memory by the grief and consternation which prevailed in Jamaica when it became known that his tenure of office was at an end. The scene of his departure is vividly described by Phillippo, the Baptist missionary of Spanish Town ; and it is impossible to read this affecting narrative without participating in the emotion which the Ex-Governor, overpowered by a demonstration " altogether without a parallel," was unable to restrain.

INDEX